SON OF WAKE ISLAND

A son's tribute to his Father and the Marine and Civilian

DEFENDERS OF WAKE ISLAND

"It was a Heroic short Battle, but a long time spent in Hell"

DAVID PEARSALL

ISBN Paperback: 9798843069186

ISBN Hardcover: 9798843069377

Printed in the United States of America

Published by WritersClique.com

TABLE OF CONTENTS

INTRODUCTION & DEDICATION

It is an honor for me to dedicate this book to the memory of the gallant Defenders of Wake Island

To the 449 soldiers and airmen from the United States Marine Corps.

To the 68 sailors from the United States Navy

To the 6 soldiers from the United States Army

To the 1,150 civilian construction workers from Morrison-Knudsen/CPNAB

To the 45 employees of Pan American Airways

All of them will be named at the end of this book.

I dedicate this book to my Family

To my father Marine John Edward Pearsall and my mother Margorie.

To my wife Carole and her daughter Melissa Gulinson and husband Dr. Mark and their children Chelsea, Jacob and his wife Angelica, Cailey, and Chloe. I will forever be their “Papa Dave”. To Carole’s sons Tom and his wife Annie, and Anthony.

To my son Sam Pearsall and his wife Mary and their children Kamryn, Hazel, and Conner.

To my brother John and his wife Susie and their children; son Christopher and his wife Julie, their children Max, Jack, Cole, and their daughter Sarah Pearsall Lambert and her husband Bob, and their children Maddy and Isaac.

To my sister Carol Brankin and her husband Phil. Their children, daughters, Dr. Catherine Brankin, Amy Hendriks, and her husband Peter, and their children Greyson and Isla. Sons Phillip Brankin and husband John and Tom Brankin and wife Brianna.

I dedicate this book to the Families of the Defenders of Wake Island

To my fellow sons and daughters of Wake Island and all their children.

To the nieces and nephews and all the grandchildren of Wake Island. And to the progeny yet unborn.

May we always remember Wake Island and its Defenders for their heroism in battle, their determination to survive under unbearable conditions, and their desire to go home and build a better America. Welcome and first let me say thank you for starting to read my book. I am writing this not to tell the actual story of the battle of Wake Island. There have been a few previously written that do a great job at that. I shall mention them later. This book is more of a personal story about my marine corps father, a survivor of Wake Island. It is about his life and my life growing up with him and the stories he and his Wake buddies told me and shared with the world. It is also the story of many of the other survivors and tributes from their families. My story is much like the other families. We grew up hearing about Wake Island what they did there and how they survived nearly 4 years in Japanese POW camps.

I had two of the greatest experiences of my life traveling back to Wake Island in 1985 and again in 1988. These reunion trips took the survivors, family members, and media on emotionally charged visits to a place most never thought they would return or see. I took many pictures on these trips. Many are in this book. It is an honor for me to share them with you. Through the years and mostly on the reunion trips, it was amazing for me to meet and talk to almost all of them, both Marines and Civilians. There were special bonds between many of them (and me). It was more than enjoyable to witness these. Being in the travel industry I had the opportunity to plan most of the events for the two reunions.

I would like to thank a few people for their encouragement in writing this book and those who sent me important materials that I used.

First to my wife Carole who has supported me in my efforts of editing and reviewing. She has provided me the sometimes-needed encouragement to finish writing the book, so that many could learn about these brave men.

I would like to thank Seth Randal from Boise, Idaho who is completing his documentary "Workers of Wake." One day in one of our phone calls he said to me "you need to write a book". Ok, friend, here we are. Seth also started the Facebook page "Families of Wake Island Defenders."

To the Families of Wake Island Defenders who submitted tributes to their survivors, I cannot thank you enough. Many brought tears to my eyes.

To Dr. Gregory Urwin, Professor of History at Temple University and most prominent Wake Island historian. Thank you for your assistance and materials.

To Jennifer Castro and Alyson Mazzone curators at the National Museum of the Marine Corps in Quantico, Virginia. Thank you for digitizing my dad's diary and for sending the pictures of his exhibit at the museum.

Thank you to my family and the Families of the Wake Island Defenders for your support and love.

Today, Dec. 7th, 2021, on the 80th anniversary of the beginning of the battle I am writing this dedication. How fitting is this? May we always remember and honor these brave men. Please enjoy my book!

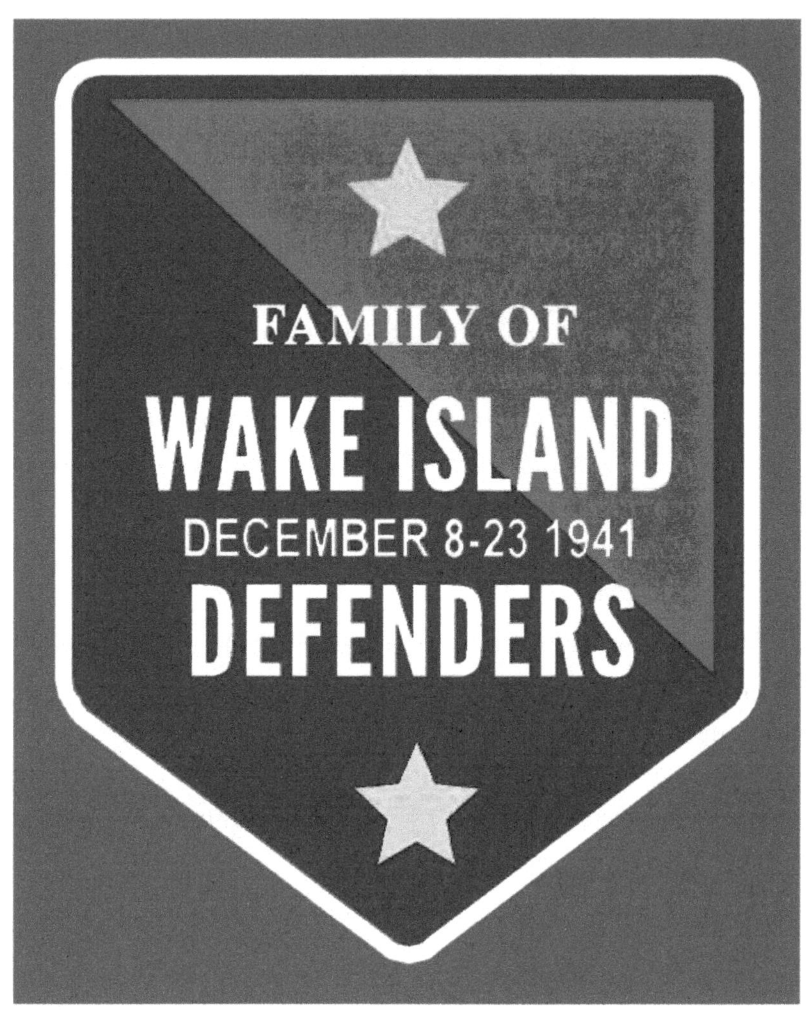
FAMILY OF
WAKE ISLAND
DECEMBER 8-23 1941
DEFENDERS

FORWARD

- BY PATRICK AKI

- LONE SURVIVOR OF THE DEFENDERS OF WAKE ISLAND

Pat Aki is the lone living survivor of the Defenders of Wake Island. He lives in Hawaii. I got to know him a couple of months ago and have spoken with him several times on the phone. He is a remarkable man! It is indeed my honor to have this forward and tribute written by Pat in my book. I want to thank his daughter Natalia and granddaughter Erin for helping Pat prepare this moving tribute.

When David asked me if I would write a short story of my life on Wake Island involving the time before the war, the time during the war, and the time as a prisoner of war, I accepted. I felt that at age 98, and the sole survivor of the 1200 civilian contract workers, I should share my feelings with the dependents of those other employees.

Life Before

My story began in August 1941. At the age of 17, fresh out of high school, I signed up with Contractor, Pacific Naval Air Bases. The only work available for the unskilled was work in the mess hall. However, after only 2 short weeks at the mess hall, Eddie Lee from the waterfront crew got me a job as a deckhand. I enjoyed every bit of time spent there; the work, the pay, the food, living quarters, and coworkers- Everything was great! I would have had no problem staying there for a couple of years.

Life During

The news that Pearl Harbor had been bombed was startling. Who would be so stupid? 4 hours later, a squadron of Japanese bombers bombed the airfield destroying 8 of our 12 fighter planes. We were really at war!

Although scuttlebutt (gossip) was that relief was on its way, nothing came. Hope for relief was dwindling, worsening each day.

The invasion forces attacked in the early morning of December 23; the island's situation was in doubt. The combined efforts of the heroic U.S. Marines and the CPNAB volunteers were simply *hopeless.*

The Right Call: A decision had to be made; was it death or live to fight another day? History revealed the latter was the right call.

My observation: The eyes of the Japanese soldiers, their body language, and their chatter told a story of wonderment. "How did such a small detachment hold off the mighty military of the Japanese?" The superior officers must have questioned, "What will future battles look like? How will we deal with the awakened forces of the Americans?"

POW Life

The Japanese sent all military and most of the civilians off to unknown locations. 300, including myself, were left on the island to finish building the runway. In Oct of 1942, after completing most of the work, 200 of us were shipped to Japan. The remaining 100 CPNAB were left behind. After the war, I learned these 100 were executed in October of 1943.

To me, remaining alive was paramount to returning home. To stay alive, I needed great hope, reliable information, and a strong mindset. These were vital to my survival. I was absolutely certain that we would win the war.

It was like a game to outsmart the enemy. It required humility, no showboating of talents. It also required deception. I maintained strength and energy by deceiving the guards. I acted as though I was working as hard as I could, but in fact, I was not.

It was alright to be sneaky in gathering information. Rather than asking, “Who’s winning the war?” I’d ask, “Where are you winning today?” They proudly answered where, when, and equipment it took to defeat the Americans.

Prison life among the 200 required a strong body and an even stronger mind. We were made to build a hydro-electric dam in a mountainous area of Japan. 25 Prisoners died that first winter. Extremely cold weather, lack of warm clothing, difficult work, and lack of food starvation diet, living in a makeshift shelter with bed bugs and fleas as you are sleeping, companions and little health care, contributed to these deaths.

During the summer of 1945, we could hear American bombers as they routinely bombed mainland Japan. Information from my Japanese source told me they were winning in Okinawa, 600 miles from Japanese mainland. Upon hearing this good news, I knew the end of the war was near. Two atomic bombs, one dropped on Hiroshima and the other on Nagasaki in early August of 1945 hastened the Emperors decision to make the right call of Unconditional Surrender. The war ended August 15, 1945.

The Trek Home

Instructions were to stay put and wait for evacuation. However, LeRoy Meyers (CPNAB) from another camp informed me to go to Kagoshima, the southern tip of Kyushu Island, as American planes were landing there. Myself and four others left the camp and caught a train to Kagoshima where we were greeted by an American Military Policeman. I finally felt safe.

After processing and receiving medical care, another POW and I flew to the Philippines. There we waited several weeks for a ship to Pearl Harbor. No ships were going to Pearl Harbor, all were headed to the West Coast. I and 4 other POWs decided on the trip to the west coast. The ship made an unexpected stop at Pearl Harbor. The captain would not allow us off as we were signed up for the West Coast. However, fellow POW Eddie Lee was able to contact his mother who contacted the governor, who contacted Pearl Harbor base commandant, who contacted the ship's captain ordering the release of the 5 POWs on October 9, 1945. Thank God, home at last!

PS: December 8, the war began is also the day of Immaculate Conception. August 15 marked the end of the war and is also the Assumption of the Blessed Virgin Mary. Both are Catholic Holy Days.

Patrick K Aki 8th of 11 children. Born in 1924

Patrick with his father Henry, shortly after returning to Hawaii from being a POW.

Patrick with fellow POW LeRoy Meyers.

Patrick, Bonnie Gilbert and LeRoy.

Photo taken at the last Wake Island Survivors Reunion in Boise. Idaho.

Receiving an honorary diploma from St. Louis High School in 2021.

A Poem: Wake Island Defense

by Capt. M.A. Terry USMC. Ret.

It's only a dot of coral and sand.
Thousands of miles from any land.
But its Protection was our stand.
Hold at all costs was the command, to the Defenders of Wake Island.

The Japs decided that they must begin.
A conquest of Wake they could win.
An Elite fighting force of handpicked men in planes and ships they would send.
Against the Defenders of Wake Island.

We were young, inexperienced, and untried.
Full of confidence, devotion, and Pride.
A great love of freedom was on our side when we were challenged, many had died.
In defense of Wake Island.

They came each day in the noonday sun.
Leaving death and destruction from the bombing run.
But we fought with every plane and gun.
We had to fight because we couldn't run.
We were the Defenders of Wake Island.

They sent a naval force to take us in.
They began the battle they wouldn't win.
They lost their ships, their planes, and their men.
They would lick their wounds and try again.
Against the Defenders of Wake Island.

Try again, they did, with all they had.
Their losses at Wake Island made them mad.
A few fighting Marines had treated them bad.
History will tell, the outcome was sad.
For the Defenders of Wake Island.

We buried our dead where they fell.
We began a new life akin to Hell.
In many places where we would dwell.
In the dark cold confines of Jap prison cells.
The surviving Defenders of Wake Island.

We had lost our fight but not our pride.
Even though incarcerated we still tried to inflict more wounds
and stem the tide of Japan's claims of success far and wide.
Still the Defenders of Wake Island.

Many dark months would pass us by
In thoughts of our loved ones, we would cry.
From starvation and sickness, more would die.
But a few more fortunate deaths did defy
And remained the Defenders of Wake Island.

At last, came the fall of the rising sun.
They lost the war they had begun
And paid a high price for the deed they'd done.
With the help of God, the war was won
For the Defenders of Wake Island.

The survivors came home and were met by those who loved and praised them.
But there's a feeling of great loss and deep regret for those who gave their all.
We must never forget.
They were Defenders of Wake Island.

There's no Flanders Field where poppies grow.
There's no white crosses row on row.
They rest in a common grave near the ocean's flow,
In the soil where the enemy struck the fatal blow
To the Defenders of Wake Island.

There is no shame in the fact we fell.
And the remaining few still proudly tell
Of the stand, we made on the brink of Hell.
Against such odds, it's said we did quite well
In defending Wake Island.

Time will heal the wounds of war,
And Marines will still fight and die for a way of life in which there's no bar
To the door of freedom that was kept ajar
By the Defenders of Wake Island.

CAPT. M.A. TERRY, USMC. RET.
MAY 20, 1980

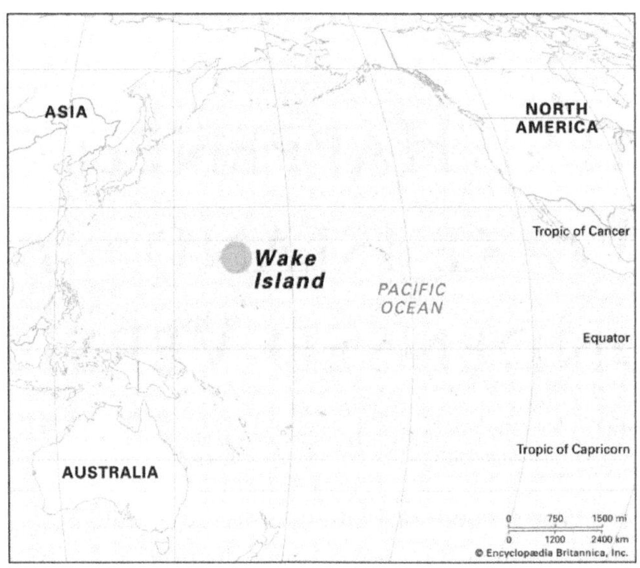

Wake Island is one of the most isolated islands in the world.

2,298 miles (3,698 kilometers) west of Honolulu - 1,991 miles (3,204 kilometers) southeast of Tokyo.

What Happened on Wake Island – A Condensed Version

From Marine Corps History

World War II came fast and hard to the United States across the Pacific Theater. While Pearl Harbor is obviously in the public conscience, there were several other attacks across the Pacific, China, and the Philippines by the Japanese in those first hours of the war. One of these fights would prove to be cathartic to the rapid decline in public morale. The defense of Wake Island from December 8, 1941, to December 23, 1941, stood apart from the others and would take on the element of an "Alamo in the Pacific". It was to become a rallying cry on the home front in the United States and a boon to recruiting for the Marine Corps. It was also unfortunately the loss of a significant opportunity to strike an early blow to the Japanese offensive and their war plans.

For the Japanese Wake was one of their initial objectives for seizure upon the start of the war with the western powers of the United States, Great Britain, and Holland. It was key terrain for them to deny the U.S. lines of communication to the Philippines and was, therefore, a prerequisite to an invasion there. They assembled a strike force 600 miles to the south in the Marshall Islands supported by an important airbase on Roi.

The United States had prepared for a defensive line of fortified islands to maintain its naval Lines of communication across the Pacific Ocean. One of these islands was Wake. Wake is an atoll made up of three islands: Wake, Wilkes, and Peale. It was annexed by the United States in 1899 and initially served as a seaplane refueling base for Pan-Am Clippers starting in 1935. In January 1941, it was decided to turn it into a naval air station. The airfield was commanded by Commander Winfield S. Cunningham, USN. Under his command were two Marine units: 365 Marines and thirteen officers of the First Defense Battalion detachment with three batteries of two five-inch naval guns and three batteries of four three-inch anti-aircraft guns commanded by Major James Devereux, USMC, and Marine fighter squadron VMF211 with twelve Grumman F4F-3 fighter aircraft commanded by Major Paul Putnam for a total of 449 Marines. There were also 68 Navy personnel, a five-man Army communications detachment, seventy Pan American employees, and over 1,100 civilian contractors on the atoll.

Preparation for Invasion

The battle was to start less than five hours after the assault on Pearl Harbor. It was December 8th on Wake due to the International Date Line. At around 0700, words were reached. Major Devereux received word that Hawaii had been subject to a surprise attack. He immediately ordered his unit to prepare for an attack. On Roi, the Japanese sent 36 Mitsubishi G3M2 Type 96 'Nell' bombers at approximately the same time. It would only be five hours before they would reach Wake.

The initial strike inflicted heavy damage. Wake was without radar or sound-ranging equipment and had no warning of the coming attack. All VMF211's fighters had been patrolling in the morning but had to refuel and only four were flying when the attack commenced. Time was not on the Marine's side, had the Japanese been twenty minutes later there would have been eight aloft with two on strip alert. The result was seven out of the twelve fighters destroyed and one damaged but repairable. Worse yet was the loss of 23 out of the 55 aviation personnel and eleven others wounded. The Pan American Airways hotel and seaplane base was destroyed, and ten civilians were killed, as well as two Navy sailors. The air attacks would continue all but two days of the battle. The third raid on the 10th would destroy an explosive bunker with 125 tons of dynamite that caused significant damage to the defense batteries on Wilkes Island.

First Light at the end of the Tunnel

On December 11th, the Japanese moved in with their surface attack. In the darkness just before dawn cruisers and transports with 450 Special Naval Landing Troops (Japanese Marines) maneuvered off Wake to begin the assault. They were led by Admiral Sadamichi Kajioka on his flagship, the Yubari. The Marines spotted the landing force in the light of the moon, but it was not to be romantic for the Japanese. Major Devereux held his fire, ignoring the inaccurate preparatory fires of the enemy until the invasion force was well within range, and then opened fire with all his batteries at once. The Yubari was damaged and forced to withdraw heavily damaged. Battery Lon Wilkes Island, commanded by 2ndLt John A. McAlister, sank the destroyer, Hayate; she was the first Japanese surface craft sunk by U.S. Naval forces in the war. Platoon Sergeant Henry A. Bedell had to reclaim the bearing of his troops when they stopped firing to celebrate and told them, "Knock it off you bastards and get back on the guns! What d'ye think this is, a ball game?"

The battle lasted more than an hour. VMF-211 supported the land-based fires and the combined effort of the defense force sunk two ships, the destroyers Hayate and Kisaragi, by gunfire and bombing respectively. Two more destroyers, Oite and Yayoi were damaged, together with Patrol Boat 33. One transport, Kongo Maru, was bombed and set afire. All three cruisers (Yubari, Tatsuta, and Temyu) received injuries from air or surface attacks.

The setback the Japanese suffered can be attributed to poor planning and reconnaissance. They believed there were 1,000 Marines (there were actually about 400 still on their feet) which tells something of their philosophy of warfare. They thought that their warrior spirit would overcome the fact that they were launching a frontal attack upon an equal force. They never had the chance to see as they also placed all their ships within range of the triangle formed by the batteries (Sears, 38). The only damage the Japanese were able to inflict on the base infrastructure was the destruction of some fuel tanks. The critical loss for the Marines was the damage by flak of Captain Henry Elrod's F4F that resulted in him crash landing at the total loss of the engine on the aircraft. No Americans were killed, only four were wounded and the Japanese suffered at least 700 casualties most of whom would be dead and possibly more. Some of these casualties could have been avoided with better reconnaissance of the battery locations and better preparatory fires while utilizing standoff range before moving in to land the assault force.

The battle that day was a total success; an inferior unit had driven off an attack force and set the stage for a possible showdown when the Japanese would return with a U.S. reinforcement by carrier task forces. Historian Morison wrote: "The eleventh day of December 1941 should always be a proud day in the history of the Corps. Never again, in this Pacific War, did coast defense guns beat off an amphibious landing."

For America, the success of the Marines gave hope to a country only days after the catastrophe at Pearl Harbor. The effect on morale benefited the Marine Corps significantly. It received more attention than ever before; enlistments were stimulated, and the foundation was laid for the Corps' legendary role in the Pacific war.

Many political cartoons portrayed the valiant defense and recruitment and war bonds posters also proclaimed, Remember Wake! It was also reported that when the Marines were asked if they needed anything, their reply was, "Yes, send us more Japs!"

Strategic Blow

The furthest thing from the minds of those on Wake was for more Japanese to come. They were worn tired by the daily attacks and really wanted and needed reinforcement. The next week saw continued aerial bombardment from the Japanese to prepare for their next landing. In Pearl Harbor, Admiral Husband Kimmel, the Commander in Chief Pacific (CINCPAC) implemented a bold plan to relieve them. Its involved three carrier groups. The first group was for direct relief of Wake with reinforcements and radar. The second was to execute a diversionary raid on the Marshall Islands and the last was to cover the relief force.

The Japanese were also planning how to recover from their initial loss. While troop rehearsals were in progress on 15 December, Commander Fourth Fleet urged the insufficiency of his force for the mission, and, in reply, the Commander in Chief, Combined Fleet, now apparently convinced that Wake, by contrast with other central Pacific objectives, constituted a major stumbling block, diverted what, by United States standards, amounted to a carrier task force: two fleet carriers (Soryu and Hiryu, Carrier Division 2); four older heavy cruisers (Aoba, Furutaka, Kako, Kinugasa, Cruiser Division 6); two very new heavy cruisers (Tone and Chikuma, Cruiser Division 8); and a task-force commander, and was also, on 18 December, designated by Commander Fourth Fleet as over-all commander of forces afloat for the projected operation, leaving as before, however, the amphibious force command to Rear Admiral Kajioka.

This would bring about the possibility of the first carrier battle of the war. This also meant that Wake and its Defenders would be subject to dive-bombing from the Japanese carrier aircraft with fighter support.

On December 17th, the first blow to the relief effort occurred. Admiral Kimmel was relieved of command. Admiral Chester W. Nimitz had been designated to replace him but until he arrived, Vice Admiral William S. Pye would have a temporary command.

On December 18th, Admiral Pye was worried about the possibility of fratricide and confusion around Wake, and therefore ordered Task Group 7.2, the Wake submarine patrol, to withdraw from that vicinity and to patrol around Rongelap. This was the first decision Admiral Pye made and to call a support force back days before the island would be reinforced. Left it without any standoff defenses and would prove to be another of the factors in the ability of the Japanese to assault the island. The last of VMF-221's fighters were out of commission by the end of December 22 due to their dogfights with carrier aircraft. The Marines left the squadron then, and less than 20 men joined the defense battalion as infantry. This left the garrison without air or sea support.

Over caution, breakdowns, and fueling problems along with confusion about the enemy's location led to massive delays in the relief force. On December 23, they were still 425 miles northeast of Wake. This would prove the undoing of the Defenders because, at the same time, the next Japanese assault force was ready to land. At 0235, the ships were spotted by the Marines. This time the Japanese force had a landing party of about 1,000 men. They were also smart enough to wait out of range of the shore batteries and provide naval gunfire while the assault force landed. Commander Cunningham informed his headquarters that the enemy had landed. It would only be two hours before he would send another message: "The enemy is on the island. The issue is in doubt." After this, Admiral Pye made up his mind and withdrew the relief force.

Major Devereux had lost communications with many of his units on the three islands as the Japanese had cut the communications lines that they never had an opportunity to bury. This led him to believe that the fight was going much worse than it was. Wilkes Island was in the hands of the Marines after about 37 Marines under Captain Wesley Platt, 2nd Lt John A. McAlister, and Marine Gunner Clarence B. McKinstry had attacked a pocket of 90 Japanese. This was still not enough though as fighting on Wake proper was definitively in the favor of the Japanese. Major Devereux thus consulted with Commander Cunningham and when he found out there was no support of any kind asked for permission to surrender.

Commander Cunningham gave it, and Major Devereux did so and then tour the island to get his men to lay down their arms.

Conclusion

The Defenders of Wake acquitted themselves finely. Overall, they had 122 Americans dead in the battle and 47 wounded. The Japanese lost approximately 800 and had over 300 wounded. The Japanese obviously did not treat their captives gently after such a fight.

Among the factors that led to the loss of the base, the make-up of the detachment from the 1st Defense Battalion sent to defend the atoll was a significant issue. The Marines had no infantry or even light armor assigned to help defend the island if a landing were attempted and no mobility capability either. The minimal air defense provided due to a lack of radar assigned to the battalion also doomed VMF-211 to the destruction of three-quarters of its aircraft on the ground during the initial attack. The Marines valiantly made a stand but with the minimal assets available it could not last indefinitely and the right call was made to surrender.

The fall of Wake Island also closed the door on the U.S. Navy being able to effectively support the Philippines and opened the door to a full-scale Japanese invasion of the archipelago.

The opportunity to make it a significant tactical and strategic victory was lost. When the Japanese were at their most vulnerable to the surface, air, and surface attack while conducting their amphibious assault there was no force available to prosecute the threat. The base had been stripped of its submarine screen days before the critical enemy assault and the recall of the relief force proved to be the decisive point in the battle. After that, there was no hope for victory. The Defenders may have held out two to three days longer, but they could not have indefinitely held out without reinforcement. What could have been a significant strategic victory that may have rivaled or even canceled Midway was rendered a moral victory and propaganda cry. The replacement of Admiral Kimmel before Admiral Nimitz arrived was significant because Admiral Pye was there to just not mess things up any worse than they already were. He was not willing nor had the audacity to attempt the relief and battle needed. When the offensive-minded Admiral Kimmel was removed; it sealed the fate of Wake. With a three to two advantage in carriers, the Navy had a better chance at success than when they would eventually be at Midway, but the chief of naval operations and secretary of the navy were also not foresighted enough to see the opportunity due to the aftermath of Pearl Harbor. They both regarded Wake as a liability, not an asset. Samuel Eliot Morison observed that the failure to relieve Wake resulted from poor seamanship and want of decisive action. The United States would have to wait six months for the victory that would turn the tide in the Pacific.

The first victory in the war for the United States on December 11th was short-lived but was still critical to the morale of the country. At a lone Pacific outpost, a handful of Marines, sailors, and civilians fought a battle that ignited the hopes of a nation and provided a glimpse of light at the end of a very long tunnel to overall victory.

Privates First Class Clifton H. Lewis, LeRoy N. Schneider, and John E. Pearsall of the Wake Island Detachment, 1st Defense Battalion, photographed in 1941 before shipping out from Hawaii. The three buddies survived the sixteen-day siege and then went on to score a moral victory with nearly 96 percent of their fellow Wake Marines by withstanding a hellish three-and-a-half years as Japanese POWs. Image by the Gregory J.W. Urwin Collection.

WAKE ISLAND TIMELINE

- IMPORTANT DATES

Wake Island History

Chronology of significant Wake Island dates and events:

- 2 Oct. 1568 - Wake Island was discovered by Spaniard, Alvaro de Mendana, who named it San Francisco. Two Spanish ships, the "Los Reyes" and "Todos Santos", landed finding neither food nor water.
- 1796 - Captain Samuel Wake of the British trading schooner "Prince William Henry" visited Wake. His name was associated with it thereafter.
- 20 Dec. 1840 - Commodore Wilkes aboard the U.S.S. Vincennes visited Wake Island on a brief scientific survey. A

naturalist, Titan Peale conducted the survey. Wilkes Islet and Peale Islet were named after these gentlemen.

- 4 Mar 1866 - The German Bark, "Libelle" was wrecked on the east shore of Wake Island during a storm while en route from Honolulu to Hong Kong. The survivors spent three weeks on the island. Two lifeboats were launched to Guam. One boat with 22 people aboard, including opera singer Anna Bishop, reached Guam. The other boat with Captain Tobias aboard was lost at sea. The "Libelle's" treasure of $93,943-08 in coins and silver bars buried on Wake by Captain Tobias was recovered by Captain J.H.G. Johnson and his schooner "Ana" based in Guam by the end of June 1866.
- 4 Jul 1898 - Major General Francis Greene from the "Thomas" (part of the Philippine Expeditionary Force) raised the American flag on Wake Island.
- 17 Jan. 1899 - Commander Edward D. Taussig, U.S.N., from the U.S.S. "Bennington" took formal possession of Wake Island for the United States under the authority provided him from Washington DC.
- Dec. 1906 - General J.J. Pershing raised the American flag on Wake Island and left a cache of emergency supplies for possible future shipwreck survivors. Japanese sailors collecting bird feathers usually took what they wanted from such supplies left on Wake Island.
- 23 July 1923 to 5 Aug 1923 - The U.S.S. "Tanager" visited Wake for two weeks with a joint scientific expedition sponsored by Yale University and Bishop Museum in Honolulu. Wilkes and Peale Islets were formally recognized as separate islands.

- 29 Dec. 1934 - Wake Island was placed under the jurisdiction of the U.S. Navy Department by Executive Order No- 6935.
- 5 May 1935 to 29 May 1935 - The "North Haven" arrives at Wake Island to begin offloading construction materials for the Pan American Airlines seaplane base to be built on Wake Island.
- 1935 - The first Pan American Airlines Clipper inaugurating "the China Clipper" service landed on the lagoon.
- 3 Sep 1935 - Wake was surveyed by the crew of U.S.S. "Nitro" lost two long boats in the surf in the process. The "Nitro's" survey was to include Pan American's seaplane base for its military value and for developing areas of cooperation with Pan American Airlines and the Navy.
- Dec. 1937 - A hydroponics garden was started by Pan American Airlines to grow food to be consumed by hotel guests on Wake Island.
- 19 Oct. 1940 - A typhoon struck the island; winds reached 140 mph.
- 9 Jan. 1941 - The first Navy and navy contractor personnel arrived aboard the U.S.S. "William Ward Burrows" to begin fortifying the island and establishing a naval air base.
- 4 Dec. 1941 - Twelve Grumman F4F Wildcats of Marine Fighting Squadron 211 flew into Wake from the U.S.S. Enterprise.
- 8 Dec. 1941 - Feverish attempts to reinforce the island militarily were interrupted by an air raid by the Japanese.
- 9 Dec. to 23 Dec. 1941 - All aircraft, communications, large guns, and above-ground structures are destroyed in sixteen air raids by Japanese planes. Numerous personnel is killed or injured.

- 23 Dec. 1941 - A Japanese land invasion overwhelmed the island forces after 12 hours of brutal, continuous combat. The rescue task force that was on its way to Wake Island is recalled to Pearl Harbor. It took 16 days for the island to fall after the first air raid on 8 Dec. 1941. The Japanese renamed the three islets of Wake Island. Wake Islet became Otori-Shima. Wilkes Islet became Ashi-Shima. Peale Islet became Hani-Shima. Peacock Point became Kubi-Saki.
- 12 Jan. 1942 - Approximately 1221 Wake Island POWs left Wake on the converted Japanese luxury liner, "Nita Maru", a troop transport ship. Five of them were beheaded aboard the vessel en route to Japan.
- 24 Feb. 1942 - The First of several US. aircraft carrier strikes against the Japanese on Wake Island are undertaken.
- May 1942 - Twenty hospitalized Wake Island POWs left Wake aboard the "Asama Marts", one of Japan's finest luxury liners, for Japan.
- 8 July 1943 - A strike by 8 army B24s based at Midway Island hit Wake Island. This is the first attack against the Japanese on Wake Island by land-based aircraft. Others strikes were launched from Kwajalein as well at Midway Island.
- Summer 1943 - The Japanese merchant ship, "Suwa Maru", tried to run the American blockade of Wake Island and took two torpedoes from an American Submarine. The ship's captain grounded the ship on the south shore before it could sink.
- 7 Oct. 1943 - Ninety-eight American POWs who remained behind on Wake Island were executed by order of Japanese Admiral Sakakibara. The executions came at the same time

as a particularly heavy raid against the island that was launched from an aircraft carrier.

- Jan. 1944 to Aug. 1945 - Wake Island is repeatedly bombarded by aerial sorties and naval guns. No land assault against Wake Island is ever conducted by American forces.
- 14 Aug. 1945 - Emperor Hirohito of Japan broadcast his unconditional surrender message to the world.
- 2 Sep 1945 - Japan officially surrenders and WWII ends.
- 4 Sep 1945 - Brigadier General Lawson H. M. Sanderson, USMC, accepts the surrender of Japanese forces on Wake Island from Rear Admiral Sakakibara.
- 20 Oct. 1945 to 15 July 1946 - 400 Seabees from the 85th N.C-B- came to Wake Island to clear the island of the effects of the war and to rebuild its basic facilities of the island.
- 1946 - Pan American Airlines returned to Wake Island to resume its operation here.
- 18 June 1947 - Rear Admiral Sakaibara was hanged on Guam for his part in the deaths of the 98 Wake Island POWs on 7 Oct. 1943.
- 1 July 1947 - The U-S. Navy Department delegates the administration of Wake Island to the CAA although it still was owned by the Navy Department.
- 1949 - The CAA (forerunner of the FAA) built a 7,000 paved runway over the old coral runway.
- June 1950 - The Korean war broke out and Wake Island served as a major refueling stop for aircraft going to that conflict. The aircraft involved in the airlift landed every 20 minutes.
- 15 Oct. 1950 - President Harry S Truman met General Douglas McArthur on Wake Island.

- 16 Sep 1952 - Typhoon Olive struck Wake Island. Fully 85% of the structures on the island were destroyed. Winds reached 180mph. Reconstruction of the facilities on the island was completed in 1953.
- 26 Aug. 1953 - Homer Willis, a CAA employee, imported one hive of honeybees from California to Wake Island. This was the first beehive to be brought to Wake Island.
- 30 Sep 1957 - The Japanese Shinto Shrine (Japanese Memorial) was blessed and dedicated in a ceremony overseen by the Japan Wake Island Friendship Committee. The carved stone from the original Japanese graveyard on the island was mounted on the top of the shrine. This same stone had been relocated to the Terminal area on 29 Dec. 1966 by the CAA. The construction of the shrine was completed on 1 Feb. 1958. Letters written by Japanese soldiers on Wake Island to their loved ones during the war were buried under the shrine. Funds for the shrine were provided by Japan Air Lines Co. Ltd., the Wake Island War Monument Reconstruction Association, and Trans Ocean Air Lines which had a major operation on the island at that time.
- 1957 - Canisters of Chloropicrin (W.W.II vomiting gas) in the water just offshore from the 8" gun on the ocean side of Peale Islet begin leaking. Several personnel is treated at the dispensary. An Army Chemical Warfare team confirms the type of gas. The base of Flipper Point is cut with a bulldozer to make a channel across the foot of Flipper Point to allow the water current in the lagoon to carry water contaminated with the gas out of the nearby recreation area.
- 1959 - The FAA extended the runway to 9,800 feet in length.
- 1960 - Then President Eisenhower stopped at Wake Island.

- 1961 - There was a burst of construction activity on the island in which the "Downtown" area was improved. Some of the facilities that were built were the Bowling Alley, Transient quarters, Dining Hall, and laundry.
- 1962 - The FAA finished construction of the new passenger terminal building. The jurisdiction of the island was transferred from the US. Navy Department to the Department of Interior. The actual administration of the island, however, would be carried out by the current caretaker, the FAA. Then-Vice President Johnson stopped at Wake Island. The Wake Island Code (Federal Aviation Regulations, Part 165) was issued.
- 1963 - A Japanese salvage team came to the island and collected most of the WWII remnants of airplanes, guns, tanks, and landing craft. This "scrap" was shipped to Japan.
- 1964 - Cable telephone service is inaugurated by AT & T after finishing the laying of a transpacific undersea cable to the island.
- 11 Jan. 1965 - A USAF C133 crashed about a half-mile offshore after taking off from runway 10.
- 1966 - The Marine war memorial is completed.
- 16 Sep 1967 - Typhoon SARAH struck Wake Island- Ninety-five percent of the structures on the island were damaged. All the dependents that were on the island were evacuated to Hawaii. Winds reached 104 mph.
- 24 Sep 1968 - A USAF KC135 flying tanker crashed upon making an emergency landing. 11 persons were killed and 23 injured.
- 1970 - Four holes of an island golf course were completed. The current Drifters Reef Bar was completed.

- July 1972 - The FAA turned the administration of the island over to the US. Air Force (MAC) began phasing down its operation here.
- 1 July 1973 - The US. Air Force (MAC) turned the administration of the island over to the USAF 15th Air Base Wing at Hickam AFB in Hawaii.
- 25 Apr. to 2 Aug. 1975 - Operation NEWLIFE, the relocation of almost 100,000 Vietnamese refugees to the mainland US. came to Wake Island. Some 15,000 refugees passed through Wake Island. At one point 8,700 refugees were on the island.
- 21 June 1977 - A US. Navy C130 crashed into the ocean about 1 mile offshore after taking off on runway 10; sixteen persons (all crew members) died.
- 14 Mar 1978 - The ship's bell for the "Dashing Wave" was found on the East Side beach. Dr. Bernd Drechsler of Germany recently researched the history and discovered this ship was built in Hamburg and originally named the "Fetisch". It was later sold to a UK shipping concern and renamed "Dashing Wave". They used it as a Tea Clipper.
- 22 Feb to 8 Mar 1978 - A party of 40 Japanese (including 14 former Wake Island soldiers) exhumed, cremated, and returned to Japan, the skeletons of 954 WWII Japanese soldiers that were buried in the old Japanese graveyard on Wake Island. The remains of 600 more Japanese soldiers could not be likewise removed as the site of their mass grave on Peale Islet could not be located.
- Sep 1979 - A delegation of Kili-Bikini islanders visit the wake to look it over as a possible relocation site for the populations of Kili and Bikini Islands.

- June 1979 - The original Wake Island fighter squadron, VMF 211, came through Wake Island from Japan on their way to the Mainland US. This time they were flying A4 aircraft.
- 15 Mar to 16 Mar 1981 - Typhoon FREDA hit Wake Island with 75 mph winds. A new $7 million seawall was destroyed in about 30 minutes. Only 2,500 feet of useable runway were available after the storm.
- 20 Apr. to 23 Apr. 1981 - A party of 19 Japanese (including 16 former Japanese soldiers who were here during W.W.II) visited Wake Island to pay their respects at the Japan Shinto Shrine for their war dead.
- 1 June 1981 - The American civil POWs from Wake Island finally get awarded military service, rank, appropriate medals, and veterans benefits for defending Wake Island in 1941 and for their hardships in the POW camps.
- 3 Nov. to 4 Nov. 1985 - A group of 167 former American POWs and their wives and children visit Wake Island. This was the first such visit by a group of former Wake Island POWs and their families.
- 24 Nov. 1985 - A Pan American Airlines B747 came through Wake Island to commemorate the 50th anniversary of the inauguration of Pan American China Clipper Service to the orient. Author James A. Michener and Actor John Travolta were among the dignitaries aboard the aircraft.
- 1985 - Wake Island was designated as a "National Historic Landmark" by the Department of Interior's National Park Service.
- 12 Mar 1986 - The Governor of Wake Island, General Counsel of the Air Force the Honorable Eugene R. Sullivan,

proclaimed March 22nd of each year to be "Wake Island Day" on Wake Island.

- 8 Dec. 1991 - Commemoration ceremony for the observance of the 50th anniversary of the attack on Wake Island. The Governor of Wake Island, Air Force General Counsel the Honorable Ann C. Peterson, attended. The US. flag on the pole, in front of the Terminal Building, hung at half-mast for 16 days to commemorate the 16 days that it took for the island to fall.
- 1991 - Wake Island participated in "Desert Storm" as a fueling station for aircraft headed for that conflict. Most of the old FAA housing, the FAA school, and a few other dilapidated buildings were demolished in a $10 million contract.
- 29 Jan. 1992 - A Brilliant Pebbles missile was launched from Wake Island.
- 12 Feb. 1992 - A Brilliant Pebbles missile was launched from Wake Island but fizzled. Back to the drawing board.
- 1 Oct. 1994 - The US. Air Force hands over the administration of the island to the US.

CHAPTER ONE:
MY FATHER – JOHN EDWARD PEARSALL

John Edward Pearsall was born on April 20, 1920, in Virginia, Minnesota. AKA Ed, Eddie, or Swede that he was so affectionately called by his fellow Marines and civilians. His parents were Dr. Robert P. Pearsall and his mother Anna. My grandfather (Doc or Percy) received his medical degree in Chicago (circa) 1910 and shortly after moved to Virginia to begin his medical practice. There he met my grandmother Anna Nelson and they married in 1914. They had 5 children, 3 boys, and 2 girls. My 3-year-old uncle Charles died at age 3 in 1918 of the Spanish flu. In 1918 my grandfather joined the US Army Medical Corps and served on the front lines in France during WWI. He returned as a Major.

The Pearsall family goes back to America to what I am told in the 1720s. The family originated in England. I went back to ancestory.com to the 1850s and found they were farmers. As most of the people at the time were. Some fought in the Civil War.

My grandmother Anna Nelson came to America from Sweden (circa 1890). They settled in Virginia, Minnesota. Many other Swedish immigrants from other Scandinavian counties also settled there. My great grandfather was one of the signers of the original charter of the City of Virginia. I just love the below beautiful photo of my grandmother. She sure has the face of Sweden (circa 1905).

I never knew my grandmother. She died in 1947 before I was born. Some say she died from a broken heart. My grandparents did not know if my dad was alive or dead for over 2 years. This was really very hard on my grandmother. I will tell you more about this later.

It sounds like my dad had a very typical type of upbringing. I guess not knowing what a typical type was then but sounds like it was very normal. I know he loved the outdoors and liked fishing, hunting, and played in numerous sports. One of his great loves was canoeing in the Boundary Waters Canoe Area of Northern Minnesota along the Canadian border. He instilled many of those loves to me while I was growing up.

My father used to joke all the time that he shared a birthday (April 20th) with Hitler. But boastfully would proclaim "I got the last laugh." In later years (me in my late teens) my buddies and I would refer to him as a 420 baby. I don't think he ever figured out what we were referring to. Thank God!

My grandfather was a real character known for his easy-going personality and really caring about his patients. People all over Northern Minnesota had Doc Pearsall stories and all had some form of humor and gratitude for what he had done for them. Seems like he delivered half the population between 1915 and (circa) 1958 when he retired. However, from what I could ascertain my grandfather was a bit hard on my dad. During the depression, most people had little or no money. Many could not pay for his services. So, they would give him animals like pigs, goats, sheep, etc. for payment. Doc really didn't care as money had little value to him. So, he bought a 100-acre farm just outside of Virginia. Here he would locate all these animal payments. They needed to be cared for and my dad was the chosen caretaker. I don't think it set so well with him. It interfered with his personal developing life. Even at that time, my dad was very social. His father (who he always dearly loved) would now cause my dad to make a life-changing decision.

My grandfather Robert P. (Doc) Pearsall

After high school graduation in 1938 and a short stint at the Virginia Junior College, my father ran away from home and joined the Marine Corps. An actual copy of the registration card is below. Date of enlistment – Oct. 31, 1939. Date of discharge - Mar. 5, 1946. He was not age 25, he was 19.

REGISTRATION CARD

SERIAL NUMBER S-239 | 1. NAME (Print) John Edward Pearsall (First) (Middle) (Last) | ORDER NUMBER S-2978B

2. PLACE OF RESIDENCE (Print)
501 6th St. South, Virginia St.Louis Minnesota
(Number and street) (Town, township, village, or city) (County) (State)
[THE PLACE OF RESIDENCE GIVEN ON THE LINE ABOVE WILL DETERMINE LOCAL BOARD JURISDICTION; LINE 2 OF REGISTRATION CERTIFICATE WILL BE IDENTICAL]

3. MAILING ADDRESS
Same ---
[Mailing address if other than place indicated on line 2. If same insert word same]

4. TELEPHONE 1515 (Exchange) (Number) | 5. AGE IN YEARS 25 DATE OF BIRTH April 20, 1920 (Mo.) (Day) (Yr.) | 6. PLACE OF BIRTH Virginia (Town or county) Minnesota (State or country) | 7. OCCUPATION -

8. NAME AND ADDRESS OF PERSON WHO WILL ALWAYS KNOW YOUR ADDRESS
~~R. P. Pearsall, father, same address~~

9. EMPLOYER'S NAME AND ADDRESS
Enlisted Marine Corps Oct. 31, 1939

10. PLACE OF EMPLOYMENT OR BUSINESS
Discharged March 5, 1946
(Number and street or R. F. D. number) (Town) (County) (State)

I AFFIRM THAT I HAVE VERIFIED ABOVE ANSWERS AND THAT THEY ARE TRUE.

D. S. S. Form 1 (Revised 6-9-41) (over) 16—21630 John Edward Pearsall (Registrant's signature)

MY MOM – MARJORIE JANE OGG PEARSALL

My mom was born on March 4, 1919, in Duluth, Minnesota. My grandpa Ogg (Pops) was of Icelandic descent. He owned and operated a grocery store on the central hillside of Duluth for over 40 years, retiring in the early 1960s. He, unfortunately, passed away shortly after retirement. My grandmother (Bomb) as we used to call her, was born Clara Wieland in Duluth (circa) 1894. She was from a very prominent Duluth family (the Wielands) There were 4 Wieland brothers who emigrated from Germany (circa) 1848. They originally settled in Ohio. In 1856, all 4 brothers moved and founded Beaver Bay, Minnesota on the north shore of Lake Superior. This is and was the oldest inhabited community on the north shore. They started several businesses including a tannery and a lumber mill. My great, great grandfather Henry was the oldest of the brothers. My great grandfather Charles was the first white child to be raised on the north shore. The picture below is of Beaver Bay in the early 1860s their Schooner Charley (named after my great grandfather) at the dock. My great, great uncle Christian was an avid surveyor and explorer. He helped in the discovery of iron ore in Northern Minnesota. I have his compass in my living room. If only it could talk. I am guessing it originally came from Germany.

The Wieland family eventually (circa, late 1880s) sold all of their interests in Beaver Bay and moved to Duluth.

In Duluth "Bomb" met "Pops". Married in 1915 they had two daughters, one being my mom. She graduated from Duluth Central High School in 1937 and later graduated from the University of Iowa with a degree in social work. She spent most of the early parts of the war working as a social worker in Detroit. She came back to Duluth in 1944 and shortly after took a position with the St. Louis County Welfare Department in Virginia. It is located about 60 miles north of Duluth on Minnesota's Iron Range. Here approximately 85% of US demand for iron ore comes from. The mining industry on the Iron Range started in the late 1880s and continues to this day. My mom was in Virginia at the end of the war. Little did she know at the time that she was about to meet the love of her life, a returning skinny marine war hero.

The War Years on the Homefront

I know initially, my grandfather was a bit perturbed with my dad for running away and joining the marine corps. He lost his farm caretaker. I don't believe that lasted very long. After boot camp in San Diego, he went back to Virginia on leave. This was just prior to the now the new First Marine Defense Battalion shipping out to Hawaii. Thus, the beginning of the story of the Wake Island Marines.

My grandparents were very active in Virginia. My grandfather with his medical practice and my grandmother with her many civic organizations. Everyone knew and respected both. People have told me that my dad was his mother's favorite. I think at times she felt my grandfather was too hard on my dad.

As the war in Europe and the Pacific loomed, I know they were very worried about their son now stationed on a small island in the middle of the Pacific Ocean. I am sure at the time, hardly anyone knew the name Wake Island or for that matter where it was.

I can imagine their (grandparents) shock and total concern when it was announced on Dec. 7th that the Japanese had attacked Pearl Harbor and a few hours later Wake Island. I can remember my grandfather telling me how he heard of the attack listening to the radio. They used this same radio (it was a short wave) to listen to broadcasts throughout the war. Growing up I would listen to it often. At the time I can remember thinking of the significance of this radio. I remember my grandfather telling the story of listening to a short-wave broadcast coming from the Swiss Red Cross in China naming the Wake Island POWs now in Shanghai. I believe this was (the summer of 1942) one of the first times they knew for sure that my dad was alive.

It would be some time before there was any written communication between them. The first letters from my father arrived in August of 1942. This was a very hard time for my grandmother. I was told she was so worried about her "Eddy" that it made her sick. Some suggest she blamed my grandfather for his now predicament. In sharing stories with my current Wake Family, I am finding very similar comments and stories. They didn't know for many months if their spouses or sons were alive and where they were. I can only imagine what they went through. I think about it often. How many thousands of stories like this were happening around the country? All the way from Europe to across the Pacific, this war was just starting. They were becoming our "Greatest Generation."

This was the last letter sent to my dad from my grandmother just prior to the outbreak of war. Let me say that none of their handwriting is the most legible as I am including several letters exchanged between them. I think this trait has been passed down to the next generation 😊. These letters are proudly displayed at the Marine Corps Museum in Quantico, VA.

December 4, 1941

Dearest Edward.

So glad to hear from you again and thank you so much for the pictures. I have told the Montgomery Ward Co. to check on your radio. It was sent to Pearl Harbor. I hope you get it. For your Christmas gift from Daddy & I, we are sending you a 1 year subscription for Range Facts, a weekly Virginia paper. We are having nice weather no snow. We are all well here and I am always praying that "Jesus never fails" to take good care of you. Heaps of Love from Mother

Not knowing the whereabouts of my dad, my grandparents were desperately worried. They sent these letters on May 1 and 2, 1942.

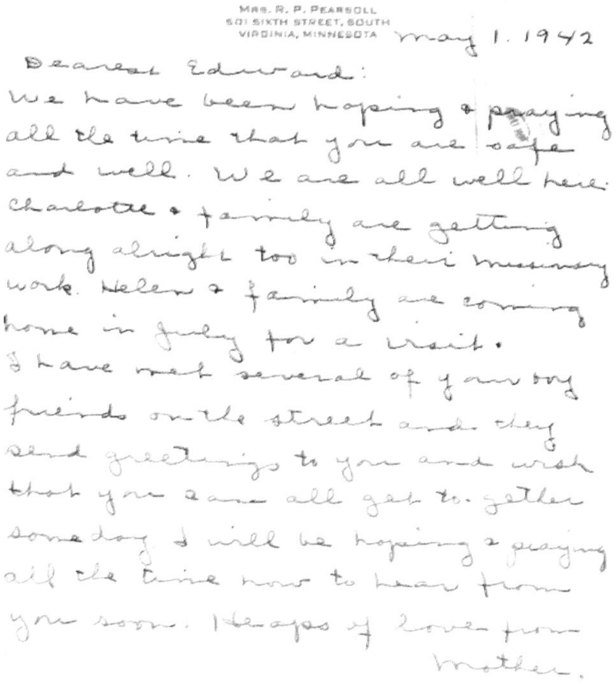

Mrs. R.P. Pearsall

501 Sixth Street, South

Virginia, Minnesota

May 1, 1942

Dearest Edward:

We have been hoping & praying all the time that you are safe and well. We are all well here. Charlotte and family are getting along alright too in their missionary work. Helen and family are coming home in July for a visit. I have met several of your boyfriends on the street and they send greetings to you and wish that you can all get together someday. I will be hoping and praying all the time To hear from you soon. Heaps of love from Mother

My grandfather had terrible handwriting, adding some translations where necessary. His writing was so bad his letters many times passed the Japanese censors without editing.

LENONT-PETERSON CLINIC

Virginia Minnesota

May 2, 1942

Dearest Edward, darling boy: [From Ed's Father, Robert P. Pearsall, M.D.] How our hearts have gave out for you since these days on Wake Island. We as well as the whole city & nation are proud of you.

We have received a citation for you from the President and your commanding officer in Washington.

Your (?) voted several of the Veterans of foreign wars. The first from (?) in this war. We have tried in every possible way we could think of to get in touch with you and this is the first way of possible hope we have had and are trying it. day and night we think of you and pray for you.

We hope God in his mercy will watch over and keep you and someday soon we hope will bring you back to us safe and well. If there is anything we can do to help you in the way of friends, Red Cross packages, etc. let us know.

Try and get word to us if there is any possible way.

(The last sentence was cut off)

They received the following communication from the Marine Corps on May 8, 1942. The Marine Corps had received a communication from the International Red Cross in Geneva, Switzerland. Here they are assuming that my dad is probably a prisoner of war.

276524
AY-280-rb

HEADQUARTERS U.S. MARINE CORPS
WASHINGTON

8 May, 1942.

My dear Dr. Pearsall:

The Department of State has received the following cablegram from the International Red Cross at Geneva, Switzerland, giving the report of conditions observed upon a visit to a Japanese camp for prisoners of war:

"HAVE VISITED CAMP FOR PRISONERS OF WAR ZENTSUJI MARCH 13 ACCOMPANIED BY AID FROM THE INFORMATION BUREAU AND THE JAPANESE RED CROSS STOP LARGE ISLAND OF SHIKOKU IN THE NORTH NEAR INLAND SEA FERTILE PLAIN BETWEEN HILLS COVERED WITH PINES GOOD CLIMATE NO EPIDEMICAL DISEASES STOP MARKET TOWN OF ZENTSUJI WITH 28000 INHABITANTS NEARBY STOP CAMP COVERS SIX ACRES SURROUNDED BY BARBED WIRE AND A WOODEN FENCE TWO ARMY BARRACKS TWO STORIES HIGH WELL VENTILATED 12000 CUBIC METERS IN ALL STOP CAPACITY 500 PRESENT NUMBER 374 STOP ONE ENGLISHMAN FROM SHANGHAI TWO [illegible] FIVE AUSTRALIANS AND THE REST AMERICANS OF WHOM EIGHT ARE FROM [illegible] ISLAND TWENTY FROM WAKE AND THE REST FROM GUAM STOP 46 OFFICERS 10 DOCTORS TWO [illegible] ONE DENTIST STOP BARRACKS RECENTLY DIVIDED INTO ROOMS OF FROM ONE TO FOURTEEN CAMP BEDS EACH HAVING FIVE BLANKETS A PILLOW "UN MANTEAU COUVERTURE" (COUNTERPANE) MATTRESS FOR OFFICERS STOP HEATING BY [illegible] STOVES STOP DAILY RATIONS 300 GRAMS OF BREAD 300 RISE 150 WHEAT PLUS POTATOES SWEET POTATOES GREEN VEGETABLES FISH EGGS ETC TOTAL 2800 CALORIES STOP MEAT SUGARED FOOD AND IN THIS SEASON FRUITS ARE RATHER RARE STOP YOUNG AND ACTIVE PRISONERS ARE LOSING WEIGHT OLD AND THIN PRISONERS GAIN WEIGHT STOP COOKS CHOSEN FROM PRISONERS WORK IN SEPARATE KITCHENS WHICH ARE LARGE AND CLEAN STOP TOBACCO RATION IS 10 CIGARETTES PER ONE TO THREE DAYS ACCORDING TO RANK STOP CANTINE ALMOST FINISHED STOP CLOTHING SUFFICIENT FOR THE MOMENT BUT 150 PAIRS OF SHOES REQUESTED AS SOON AS POSSIBLE DAILY LAUNDERING GOOD HYGIENE LARGE HOT JAPANESE BATH DAILY FOR WORKERS AND WEEKLY FOR OTHERS STOP LATRINES CLEAN AND ISOLATED STOP INFIRMARY IN BARRACKS MILITARY HOSPITAL NEARBY VISITS FROM JAPANESE DOCTORS THREE TIMES A WEEK MONTHLY INSPECTION STOP 15 WOUNDED IN THE INFIRMARY OF WHOM 7 WOUNDED BY BOMBS AND ONE WAS AMPUTATED ABOVE THE KNEE ALL ARE GETTING ALONG WELL NO DEAD STOP AMERICAN DENTIST WANTS TO PRACTICE WE WILL PROCURE INSTRUMENTS FOR HIM STOP PRISONERS WISH BOOKS EQUIPMENT FOR SPORTS AND GAMES PIANO TYPEWRITERS STOP PROTECTING POWER WILL TAKE CHARGE OF THAT STOP RELIGIOUS SERVICES CONDUCTED BY A MINISTER WHO IS ALSO A PRISONER STOP 200 PRISONERS WORK VOLUNTARILY TO CLEAR NEARBY HILL FOR POTATOES SWEET POTATOES WHEAT STOP SATISFIED WITH THIS WORK PAID 50 TO 90 SEN A DAY ACCORDING TO RANK STOP NECESSARY WORK IN CAMP PAID 15 TO 35 A DAY STOP POSSIBILITY OF SAVING 5 TO 7 YEN A MONTH STOP PREPARING TO ORGANIZE PAID WORK IN THE TOWN STOP OFFICERS RECEIVE SAME PAY AS THAT OF CORRESPONDING RANK IN THE JAPANESE ARMY STOP

276524
AY-280-rb

8 May, 1942.

RECOMMENDED TO PROTECTING POWER THE ONLY CIVILIAN INTERNEE 5 WOUNDED AND 5 AGED WITHOUT MEANS STOP 4000 DOLLARS DEPOSITED BY PRISONERS STOP PRINCIPAL NEED IS THAT OF CORRESPONDING WITH FAMILIES LETTERS NOT SENT IN VIEW OF LACK OF COMMUNICATIONS STOP AT BEGINNING OF MARCH OFFICERS AUTHORIZED TO SEND PERSONAL MESSAGES TO THEIR FAMILIES IN AMERICA BY RADIO BUT REMAIN WITHOUT ANY ANSWER STOP PRISONERS WISH TO RECEIVE FINANCIAL ASSISTANCE BY CABLE FROM THEIR FAMILIES THROUGH THE INTERMEDIARY OF THE U. S. NAVY DEPARTMENT OR THE RED CROSS STOP HAVE ALREADY ASKED BY RADIO FOR PACKAGES OF PRESERVES MEAT FRUITS SWEETS AMERICAN TOBACCO STOP NO COMPLAINT ON SUBJECT OF TREATMENT DISCIPLINE AND COOPERATION ARE EXCELLENT STOP COMMANDING OFFICER AND OFFICERS COMPETENT AND FRIENDLY PRISONERS SENSIBLE GENERAL IMPRESSION VERY GOOD STOP"

Realizing your anxiety for news of this nature because your son, Private First Class John E. Pearsall, U. S. Marine Corps, is probably a prisoner of war, this report is furnished with the hope that it will in some measure alleviate your anxiety regarding his welfare.

Again assuring you that any information received regarding your son will be transmitted to you, I am

Sincerely yours,

[illegible]
Lieut. Colonel, U. S. Marine Corps.

Dr. Robert F. Pearsall,
801 South Sixth Street,
Virginia, Minnesota.

2.

Then the first letter was sent to my dad from my grandfather on May 22, 1942.

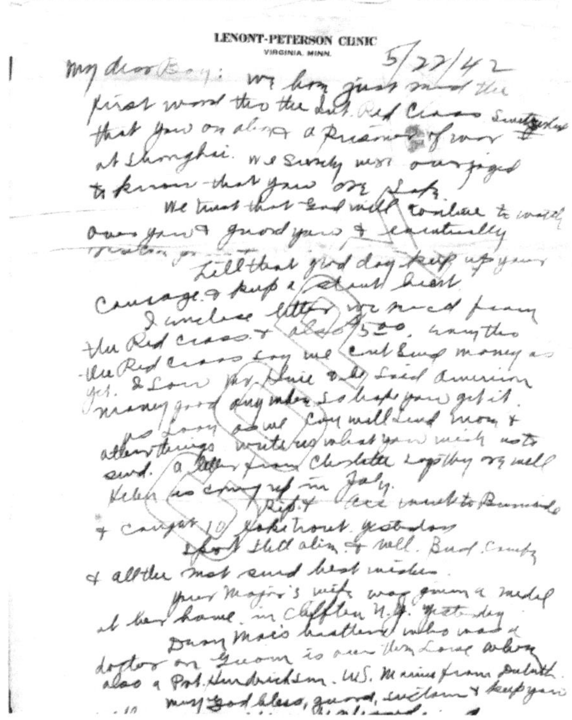

LENONT-PETERSON CLINIC
VIRGINIA, MINN.

5/22/42

LENONT-PETERSON CLINIC

Virginia, Minnesota

May 22, 1942

My dear Boy:

We have just heard through the International Red Cross that you are alive and a prisoner of war in Shanghai. We were overjoyed to know that you are safe. We trust that God will continue to watch over you and guard you and eventually bring you home safe. Keep up your courage and keep up a strong heart.

I enclose the letter we received from the Red Cross and also $5.00, even though the Red Cross said we couldn't send money yet. I heard that American money was Good anywhere so I hope you get it. And then we will send more and other things. Write us about what you wish us to send. Charlotte says they are well, and Helen is coming up in July. Rip and Ace went to Burnside and caught 10 lake trout yesterday. Bud sends best wishes. Your Majors wife was given a medal at her home in Clifton, N.Y. Yesterday Dan Mae's brother who was a doctor in Guam is over there with them and also Russell Hendrickson, U.S. Marine from Duluth. May God bless, guard, and keep you safe.

Affectionately, Dad

You can imagine the same worry and anxiety that all the marine and civilian families were going through. They didn't know if they were alive or dead or as mentioned where they were.

So now after May of 1942 begins the struggle all these familiar were about to endure. I have had many conversations with those family members through the years. They waited in sadness, in prayer, in hope!

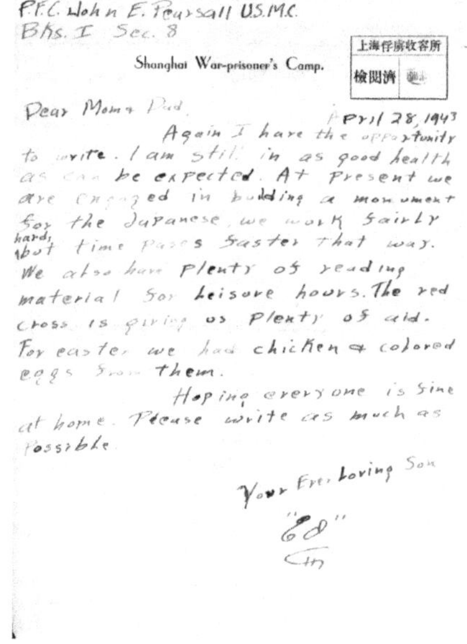

P.F.C. John E. Pearsall U.S.M.C.
Bks. I Sec. 8

Shanghai War-prisoner's Camp.

上海俘虜收容所
檢閲濟

Dear Mom & Dad,

April 28, 1943

Again I have the opportunity to write. I am still in as good health as can be expected. At present we are engaged in building a monument for the Japanese, we work fairly hard, but time passes faster that way. We also have plenty of reading material for leisure hours. The red cross is giving us plenty of aid. For easter we had chicken & colored eggs from them.

Hoping everyone is fine at home. Please write as much as possible.

Your Ever Loving Son
"Ed"

As the years went by, many communications were exchanged. Some of the prisoners' letters were terribly redacted. Many words and sentences were cut out by the Japanese censors. More letters.

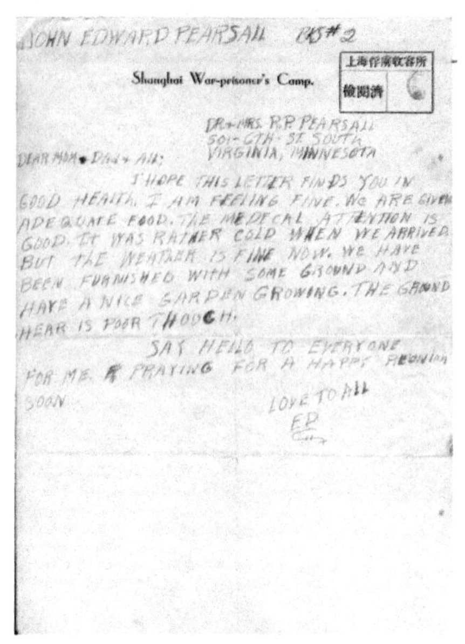

JOHN EDWARD PEARSALL BKS # 2

Shanghai War-prisoner's Camp.

上海俘虜收容所
檢閲濟

DR. + MRS. R.P. PEARSALL
501-6TH ST. SOUTH
VIRGINIA, MINNESOTA

DEAR MOM, DAD + ALL;

I HOPE THIS LETTER FINDS YOU IN GOOD HEALTH. I AM FEELING FINE. WE ARE GIVEN ADEQUATE FOOD. THE MEDICAL ATTENTION IS GOOD. IT WAS RATHER COLD WHEN WE ARRIVED BUT THE WEATHER IS FINE NOW. WE HAVE BEEN FURNISHED WITH SOME GROUND AND HAVE A NICE GARDEN GROWING. THE GROUND HEAR IS POOR THOUGH.

SAY HELLO TO EVERYONE FOR ME. PRAYING FOR A HAPPY REUNION SOON.

LOVE TO ALL
E.P.

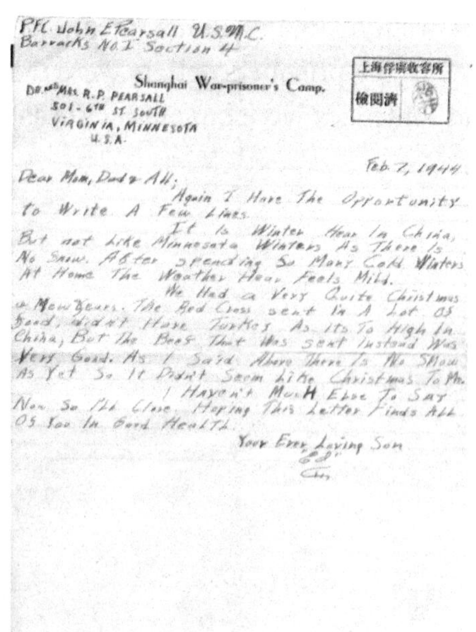

PFC. John E. Pearsall U.S.M.C.
Barracks No. 1 Section 4

Shanghai War-prisoner's Camp.

上海俘虜收容所
檢閲濟

DR. AND MRS. R.P. PEARSALL
501-6TH ST. SOUTH
VIRGINIA, MINNESOTA
U.S.A.

Feb. 7, 1944

Dear Mom, Dad & All;

Again I Have The Opportunity to Write A Few Lines.

It Is Winter Hear In China, But not Like Minnesota Winters As There Is No Snow. After spending So Many Cold Winters At Home The Weather Hear Feels Mild.

We Had a Very Quite Christmas & New Years. The Red Cross sent In A Lot Of Food, didn't Have Turkey As Its To High In China, But The Beef That Was sent Instead Was Very Good. As I Said Above There Is No Snow As Yet So It Didn't Seem Like Christmas To Me.

I Haven't Much Else To Say Now So I'll Close. Hoping This Letter Finds All Of You In Good Health.

Your Ever Loving Son
"Ed"

OCT. 31, 1943

DEAR MOM & DAD,

AGAIN I HAVE THE PRIVILEGE OF WRITING YOU. HOPING YOU RECIEVE THESE FEW LINES. I AM IN AS GOOD HEALTH AS CAN BE EXPECTED.

EVERYDAY IS A DAY CLOSER TO THE TIME WHEN WE ALL CAN HAVE A HAPPY REUNION. UNTIL THAT DAY ARRIVES LIFE IN HERE WILL CONTINUE TO BE MUCH THE SAME.

SOMETIME AGO WE HAD A MOVIE HERE IN CAMP. EVERYONE ENJOYED IT VERY MUCH. WE ARE HOPING FOR MORE IN THE FUTURE.

SAY HELLO TO EVERYONE FOR ME AS I AM UNABLE TO WRITE ALL THAT I WOULD LIKE.

PLEASE WRITE AS MUCH AS POSSIBLE.

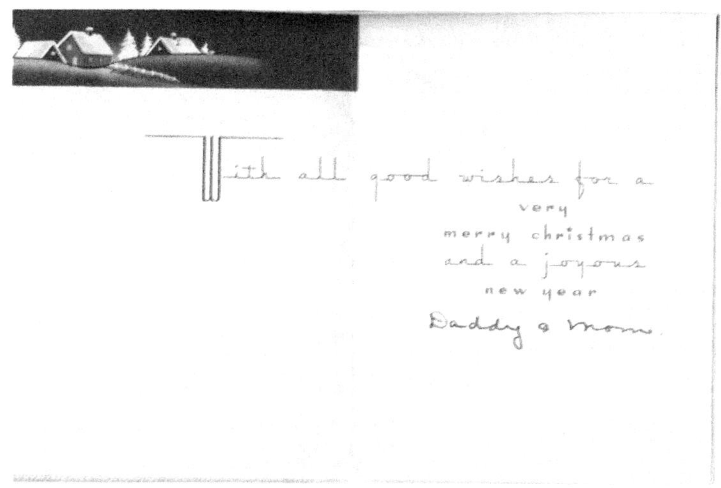

With all good wishes for a very merry christmas and a joyous new year

Daddy & Mom

I haven’t seen these letters for decades as my dad donated them to the Marine Corps Museum back in the mid-1990s. What all the families went through during these times is just hard for me to imagine.

Now I am going to end this chapter with a postcard my dad sent to his parents on Jan. 1, 1945. It will be another 8 months before they are liberated. Every holiday season I read this. Every time it brings tears to my eyes. Just as it did during this holiday season of 2021.

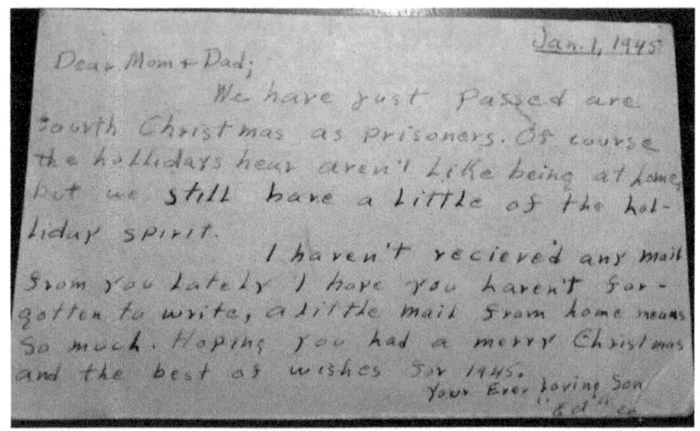

Jan. 1, 1945

Dear Mom + Dad;

We have just passed are fourth Christmas as prisoners. Of course the holidays hear aren't like being at home but we still have a little of the holiday spirit.

I haven't recieved any mail from you lately I hope you haven't forgotten to write, a little mail from home means so much. Hoping you had a merry Christmas and the best of wishes for 1945.

Your Ever loving Son
"Ed"

Thank You!!

And the mothers of the Wake survivors wait to hear what has happened to their husbands and sons. This article appeared in the Virginia, MN newspaper in early 1942. This is my grandmother Anna. The short wave radio is in the background.

ONE OF THE MOTHERS

Typical of the scores of women on the Range, who are waiting to hear what has happened to their sons, husbands, and other relatives, is Mrs. R. P. Pearsall, pictured above, pioneer Virginia resident, wife of Dr. Pearsall, city health officer. They have one son, Edward, 21-years-old, who was stationed at Wake Island, which is reported captured by the Japanese. He has been in the U. S. Marine Corps for two years. While she scans the paper for the latest war news she keeps her ears open for the last radio reports, waiting for news flashes, as millions of other Americans are doing every day. The pictures on the radio are of her son, the one an individual portrait and the other a group picture of the Marine Corps of which he is a member, taken at Wake Island just last month. Mrs. Pearsall had the same experience about 25 years ago when her husband was called into service with the U. S. Army shortly after they had been married. Besides her son in the Marines, Mrs. Pearsall has a daughter in South Africa, married to a missionary, Mrs. James Bissett, the former Charlotte Pearsall.

GROWING UP "THE SON OF WAKE ISLAND"

Finally, he came home! Arrived in October of 1945. Weighed only 85 pounds with every disease you could imagine; dysentery, malaria, beriberi, and malnutrition to name a few. But look at that smile. I can hardly imagine the joy he felt along with his fellow survivors and their families.

Soon after arriving home, my dad was sent to the Great Lakes Naval Hospital in Chicago for treatment. I am not actually sure as to how long he was there, but I know it was until early 1946. He was joined there by many of his fellow POWs. Here he began his long association with the VA (Veterans Administration). This was not always the happiest of relationships. One of the problems that the POWs were facing was the little knowledge doctors had of the diseases that they were now inflicted with. The local medical community also had the same non-familiarity issues. I remember him saying he was sick for months until he met a doctor who had lived in the orient and knew how to diagnose and treat these diseases.

My dad was finally discharged from the Marine Corps on March 6, 1946. Now back in Virginia after several months of treatment, a friend sets him up on a blind date. Well, of course, none other than my mom. I guess it went rather well. My mom had been in Virginia for a short time but had already made friends with several people. Many of those friends she kept for the rest of her life. I guess growing up you really don't ask your parents much about their early romance only to hear them talk about especially amongst their now mutual friends. I know they deeply loved each other. They were married in June of 1947 at the Presbyterian Church in Duluth. They honeymooned at a resort on the edge of my dad's first love (before he met my mom ☺), the Boundary Waters Canoe Area of Northern Minnesota. More about the BWCA later in this book.

Shortly after they were married, they moved to the Twin Cities (Minneapolis/St. Paul) so my dad could attend the University of Minnesota and Dunwoody Institute. He did graduate from Dunwoody with a degree in civil engineering in mid-1949. After graduation, they moved to Duluth where my dad took a job with the Minnesota Department of Transportation.

Their first child was born (my brother John) in June of 1948 while they lived in the Twin Cities. I was born in November of 1949 after they had relocated to Duluth. We all lived there until 1952. Sometime that year they decided to move back to Virginia. My sister Carol was then born in December. The family was complete.

I am guessing that sometime in 1953 my father decided to start a road construction company. He owned and operated this company for the next decade or so. The company-built roads all over Northern Minnesota. Some of my first recollections of life were traveling with my dad to some of the construction sites. He of course had many employees. I remember how these employees respected and loved him. They would do anything for him. I have to say that even though I was very young at the time, I recognized this trait. I wanted to be like that. I wanted people to love and respect me. To this date, I still try to emulate this.

In 1955, my dad's company was awarded a contract to construct a forest road of about 30 miles along the Echo Trail. It stretched just on the outskirts of his beloved Boundary Waters Canoe area. He was all in for this project. He could now spend more time in his North Woods. Unfortunately (as some contracts go), he lost a considerable amount of money.

THE CABIN AT CRANE LAKE

However, there was a big consolation price waiting for him. During his time on the Echo Trail, he learned from the U.S Forest Service (his boss on this project) that they were leasing lake cabin sites in East Bay of Crane Lake. This is one of the border lakes with miles and miles of boat access to numerous lakes along the Minnesota/Canadian border. At a price of $90 per year, he couldn't pass it up. In 1956, we (a whole family project) built a cabin on Crane Lake. It was framed by 2 charming Finnish guys who spoke very broken English but were good carpenters. The only thing my dad would say about the Echo Trail project was he moved a working outhouse to the cabin referred to as "the fifty-thousand-dollar outhouse." It took us years of work to fully complete all the things we wanted to do. This cabin stayed with the family for over 40 years. My dad loved this place. It was his and the family. He could go there, relax, leave his problems in another place, and enjoy the outdoors that he so dearly loved. I early on adopted this love from my father. I became an avid fisherman, hunter, and a 4 seasons outdoorsman. Growing up on Crane Lake played a big part in my life. Almost every weekend in the summer, we would drive the approximate 60 miles to the landing where we stored our boat and then a 3-mile trip by boat across the lake. Our cabin was on the mainland but there were no roads leading to it. It was on the edge of the Boundary Waters Canoe Area Wilderness (BWCA) and the Voyageurs National Park. I must say (considering my extensive travel) that this area is one of the most beautiful in the world. You will see in my dad's diary written while in POW camp in Shanghai that he dreamed of the BWCA and of planning for his next canoe trip. Now he could be there every week and he dearly loved it. Here (on the left) is my dad and his beloved dog "Felix", smoking his pipe at the cabin on Crane Lake. I am guessing the late 1980s. His favorite napping on the couch was accompanied by two of his beloved grandsons, Sam and Chris.

The cabin at Crane Lake would remain my dad's pride and joy almost to the very end. Finally sold it in 1996 just two years prior to his passing.

The Next Career Change

In early 1960, my dad decided to give up on the construction business and call it quits. It had become too hard to compete with larger companies for contacts needed to sustain a profitable business. I know it was very hard and stressful. Even though I was still very young, I could see how it affected him. But he had been in much tougher situations. He was one who could always bounce back and move on. This is one trait I early on so admired. It was a good trait to have seen and learned as I had to use it a few times in my later life.

During the next five years or so he worked as a foreman for a paving company doing road projects all over Northern Minnesota. They paid him well but by no means was it his dream job.

In the late 1960s, he had the opportunity to get to know a consulting engineering company out of Hibbing, Minnesota called Wallace Engineering. He liked them very much and they liked him. He had an engineering degree, and they were looking for people to help expand their business across the Iron Range. It was a great match and to my dad's delight, they hired him as chief project inspector. Most of their work was with municipal governments all along the nearly 100 miles of the Iron Range. It didn't take long for me to realize that indeed this was his dream job. I was so proud of him, and I could see how happy he was. I know his war experiences, especially his long confinement in the POW camps taught him how important it is to be able to get along with people even through difficult situations. He had to deal with contractors, mayors, councilmen, and various groups on the projects he oversaw. I have to say he was good at it. My dad stayed with the Wallace firm until his retirement in the late1980s.

His Honor, The Mayor

I wasn't at all surprised when my dad announced in 1965 that he was going to seek the office of Mayor of Virginia, Minnesota. We were a community at the time of approximately 12,000 residents. Next to Hibbing, the second largest city on the Iron Range and the major business hub. It was a prestigious position. He ran against a well know politician who had been in office for a few years. He did a great job organizing a team to help him get elected. On election night we all waited for the returns to come in. As mentioned earlier, he liked to take naps. So that evening he decided to do just that. About 9:30 pm that November evening, I went into my parent's bedroom, woke my dad, and jubilantly said, "Mr. Mayor it is time to get up." He not only won that election but 5 more the last 3 unopposed. He loved being Mayor and the city loved him. His time as Mayor instilled in me an interest in politics. After his retirement as Mayor, I had the opportunity to serve 8 years on the city council. He was a hard act to follow. His portrait today is in the Council Chambers, City Hall, Virginia, Minnesota.

J. EDWARD PEARSALL

CHAPTER TWO:
MY WAKE ISLAND STORY IN EARLY LIFE

My earliest recollections of Wake Island were probably starting in the mid-1950s. When I think back, those memories were of my dad being sick frequently. Remember all the Wake survivors ended the war in very bad health. These health issues in many cases were lifelong events, both physically and mentally. He made frequent trips to the VA hospital in the Twin Cities. Seemed like he was always fighting with them to receive proper care. He had to fight just to get a 20% disability. They even wanted to take that away from him. I know all the Wake families reading this can attest to this fact. When my dad enlisted in the Marine Corps in 1939, he weighed over 200 pounds at 6'1". At their liberation, he weighed about 85 pounds. So, 10 years after the end of the war he still was suffering effects. I know for a fact that this was common amongst both the marines and civilians.

I can remember a few times hearing my dad screaming in the middle of the night from a bad dream. I can imagine what that dream was about. I know it wasn't about canoeing in the BWCA. Today it's called PTSD. Not much was known about it at that time. Thousands of GIs from the war (and our Wake civilians) suffered greatly with not much care.

One of my next memories of Wake was learning about the company safe he buried on Peale Island just prior to their surrender on Dec. 23. As it became imminent that the island would fall Col. Godbold ordered my dad to bury the safe. It contained about $60,000 in cash and numerous other documents directly related to the First Marine Battalion. My father was the disbursement officer, so he knew exactly what was in it. He sent a letter to Devereux asking him if he might know what happened to it and if it was ever found. He received this letter back from Devereux saying he would check with Godbold.

Letter from James. P.S. Devereux regarding the safe, dated Jan. 24, 1955. At that time Devereux was a member of the U.S. Congress from New Jersey.

SECOND DISTRICT, MARYLAND

COMMITTEE:
ARMED SERVICES

Congress of the United States
House of Representatives
Washington, D. C.

1525 REISTERSTOWN ROAD
PIKESVILLE 8, MARYLAND
PIKESVILLE 7432

January 24, 1955.

Mr. John Edward Peorsall,
1225 South 10th Street,
Virginia, Minnesota.

Dear Mr. Peorsall:

This will acknowledge your letter of recent date relative to the small safe buried on Wake Island.

It was nice hearing from you after all these years, and I shall check with Colonel Godbold, to see what he knows about it.

As soon as I have further information for you, I shall write again.

With kind regards, I remain,

Sincerely yours,

Jas. P. S. Devereux, M. C.

JPSD:c

Letter sent to Colonel Godbold on Feb. 8, 1955

J. Edward Pearsall
1228 S. 10th. St.
Virginia, Minn.

Feb. 8, 1955

Colonel Bryght D. Godbold, USMC
Headquarters, Fleet Marine Force Pacific
C/O Fleet Post Office
San Francisco, California

Dear Colonel Godbold:

I wrote to Devereux regarding safe which we buried on Wake prior to the invasion. His sec'ry missent the enclosed letter to me. I am forwarding same to you.

If you will recall the days prior to the surrender of Wake, we were moving our positions at night. During one of these moves, you instructed me to look after the small safe, which I buried.

Do you recall whether the safe was recovered?

Since leaving the Service in 1946, I returned to school & studied Highway construction. I am at present operating a small construction business. I hope this letter finds you in good health. Kindest rgards,

Cordially,
J. Edward Pearsall
J. Edward Pearsall

It wasn't long after this exchange I remember answering the phone and a man's voice asked, "Is Swede there?" (Swede was my dad's nickname to all the Wake marines). My dad was at work, and I told him he wasn't home. The man said, "tell him General Devereux called about the safe."

Shortly after this call, a tube full of detailed drawings and maps of the island and buildings being constructed by the civilians arrived at our house. In it was a note from Devereux asking, "Swede, would you be so kind to mark on the map and drawings exactly where you buried that safe." I vividly remember my dad's reaction. To use kind words and paraphrase.... "I don't think so!" Ironically all attempts for answers failed.

I was subsequently fascinated with these maps and drawings. I can remember taking out that tube from a closet and rolling them out on the floor. I studied them with great curiosity. Some were marked "classified". At that time I really didn't know what that meant. Although I knew I was hooked. From those days forward there was no doubt in my mind that I was a "Son of Wake Island."

My dad explained to me in addition to the cash there were important papers in the safe, namely a field promotion for him from PFC to Sargent. That would have made a big difference in his retroactive pay given to him after the end of the war. Therefore, it was important for someone else in authority to find a safe other than Devereux. More coming up in this book about the safe.

I have to say that this fascination with maps played a role in my future education path and even my future career in the travel industry.

As I grew older, it seemed that my dad talked more and more about Wake Island. I am sure it had more to do with me being able to understand the significance of what he had experienced. He had frequent phone conversations with his buddies around the country. Also, the monthly delivery of the Wake Island Wigwag, a newsletter keeping the marine survivors updated as to what was going on within their group. I read it religiously each month. So, it gave me a chance to become familiar with them, where they lived, and what was going on in their lives. Every few years the marine survivor's group would hold a reunion. Most of them are in Oklahoma. These were fun times for my dad, and he attended as many as he could.

It was very interesting for me to be around his local buddies and listen to them describe their World War II experiences. There were many veterans on the Iron Range, and they all had great stories. Pearl Harbor, D-Day, Battle of the Bulge, The Bataan Death March, Iwo Jima, German POW camps, and aircrews from all over Europe and the Pacific, just to name a few. All heroes in their own way. Their stories were captivating. I am sure for all the Wake marines and civilians it was a similar situation. It's hard to imagine what some of these guys went through. It is no wonder why they are referred to as the "Greatest Generation".

Growing up in Virginia and Northern Minnesota was a great time in my life. My parents were very loving and participated in my and my siblings' lives. We participated in school activities, sports, and our wonderful church. I know that they were committed to providing a good life for us. Through the years, I had the pleasure to meet and become friends with some of the other sons and daughters of Wake Island. Similar life situations also with them. We were fortunate to have grown up during this time. I look back and relate to present-day life. It is sure a world of difference. Today life offers vast opportunities for our children and grandchildren. This I believe is all well and good. However, in retrospect, my fellow sons and daughters of Wake Island, and the children of the Greatest Generation lived many different lives. Life was much slower then. Our parents had just gone through the "Great Depression" and World War II. They knew life was not just given to you. They instilled in us a family, education, and work ethic to shape our lives. They also taught us a great love for our country. There is nowhere else in the world that provides you the opportunities that America does. I think these days this fact is often not understood. Therefore, their story "the Defenders of Wake Island" should never be forgotten. It is not unlike the stories of other heroic actions of the war, but it is a story of courage under overwhelming odds, so far from home, not knowing what every hour would bring, let alone tomorrow. It is a story of the immense sacrifice of just trying to stay alive not only in battle but in the subsequent years as a POW. It is a story of perseverance, I want to go home, I want to see my parents, family, and friends. I want to go canoeing again in the BWCA. I have seen death more than just one time! I want to live!

MEMORIAL MOMENTS GROWING UP

Indeed, it was a different time growing up. I have so many vivid memories of these times. Not that they were all good but on the other hand most will be fondly remembered for the rest of my life.

For example, our holiday seasons were always very festive around our house. The cutting and decoration of the Christmas tree (usually coming from the farm). My dad's annual Tom and Jerry party at our house. The many holiday meals and specialty cooking like Swedish meatballs. I loved these times as did my parents. After all, he had spent a few holidays under not-so-festive times. Here are my parents (circa, the early 1980s) with my little niece Sarah in the background.

One of the not-so-memorable times occurred when my dad was mayor. I am guessing sometime in 1968. Some of my buddies and I headed over to Mt. Iron, a small community just outside of Virginia. The purpose of this trip was to purchase some beer at a bar that at the time was known for not really enforcing the age 21 requirement. We had made this trip a few times, so it was not a maiden voyage. One of my buddies looked a bit older than most of us. He was the purchaser. We successfully made the transaction and pulled out of town in my dad's station wagon, me behind the wheel. Then flashing red lights from the local police department. We were busted! The policeman said to us after inspecting the back of the vehicle, "You guys get out of town and never come back." We were wearing our Virginia High School letter jackets at that time. When we arrived back in Virginia, the cops were waiting for us. Obviously, they had received a call from the Mt. Iron police with our license plate number. Low and behold, "the son of the mayor." My buddies immediately took off running. The Virginia policeman (who I knew) said, "I am going to follow you home and your dad is waiting for you." Oh boy, I am in big trouble. Sure enough, I pulled into the driveway and there was my dad waiting. He had my sister's twirling baton in his hand and looked angry. Once inside and sitting down my dad unloaded on me, waving the baton in the air, and preparing to smack me. Visions of his beatings received as prisoner went through my mind. I would be far luckier. My mom pleaded, "Don't hit him, don't hit him." Well, a couple of smacks across the legs and it was all over with. I was grounded for a few weeks. In much later years, in recalling this incident, he would smile and shake his head and have a few more puffs on his pipe. By the way, the policeman, again in much later years, told me they enjoyed drinking our beer.

My dad regaled in telling the story of how when we were bad, he would put on his marine corps uniform and spank us. This he would be laughing proclaiming to teach those kids never to join the marine corps.

I think my dad saw a lot of himself in me. My mother in later years, after his passing, confirmed this to me. I really looked at it as a tremendous compliment. He had a great love for adventure and so did I. My dad was a big believer in the Boy Scouts and was one of our leaders for many years. In 1967, I received my Eagle Scout award and traveled to the World Boy Scout Jamboree in Idaho. I was assigned to be a host to a troop from Belgium. I made good friends with a few of these guys. They invited me to come and visit them in Belgium. In 1969, after my freshman year attending Mesabi Community College in Virginia, I decided to do exactly that plan a trip to Europe and visit my Belgium friends and see as much of Europe as time would permit. My dad and mom were very supportive of this idea. So off to Europe, I went for six weeks traveling by myself. The thought did occur to me at the time that I was the same age (19) and as my dad and that we both had just finished our first year of college. Our destinations however were drastically different. He ran off and joined the marine corps, I ran off to Europe. How times had changed. I made memories for a lifetime. He made memories most he wanted to forget. Nonetheless, I felt their pride that I was doing this. I knew my dad was aware of the similar timelines. My upcoming adventure was a world away from what he had hoped was his to be his.

I want to share with you two of the more memorable parts of my trip.

The first was my visit to the Nazi Concentration Camp – Dachau. It is located just outside of Munich in southern Germany. Dachau was the first concentration camp operated by the Nazis between 1933 and 1945. It was their model camp. Here they conducted experiments of various types including the best/easiest ways to exterminate humans. The most being Jews and various political prisoners. Tens of thousands died there. I had studied much about the camp and others such as Auschwitz prior to my departure. I had heard stories from my uncle about the camp. He was part of General Patton's army who liberated the camp in April of 1945. Many horrors happened here. I think many are beyond our comprehension. I did want to see and experience it. I had my traveling bible with me, "Europe on Five Dollars a Day" by Arthur Frommer. There were explicit directions on how to get there from Munich first by train then by bus and a short walk down a road. Here was the entrance to the camp.

This memorial was done just a year prior to my arrival. I was forewarned not to ask for directions to the camp from locals saying they would not be too cooperative. I found this to be very true. I curiously asked a couple of people just to see their reactions. I remember it was on the bus leaving the train station in Dachau when I asked what stop to get off to go to the camp. I knew they understood what I was asking. They either looked away or pretended not to understand. At the end of the war, the U.S. liberating army marched thousands of locals out to the camp to see firsthand what they had done. Keep in mind it had only been 24 years since the end of the war in Germany. For many, this was fresh in their minds. I entered the camp with great anticipation as to what I would see and experience. The first part of the memorial was a building containing artifacts and photos from 1933-1945. Outside were two reconstructed barracks from the original 30+. Down a short road and the most haunting were the crematoriums where the dead bodies were pushed into the ovens. The young man from the north woods was in shock. How could this have happened? How could human beings do this? I noticed a different smell around the place. I can only think it was the smell of death. I will never forget this experience. It became much clearer to me what our parents, men and women alike were fighting so desperately for. Lest we forget!

The second most memorable part of my 1969 trip was to **West Berlin, West Germany.**

The end of WWII in Europe happened on May 7, 1945 (VE Day). After the Potsdam conference, (August 1945) Germany was divided into four occupied zones: Great Britain in the northwest, France in the southwest, the United States in the south, and the Soviet Union in the east. Berlin, the capital city situated in Soviet territory, was also divided into four occupied zones. Traveling to Berlin from West Germany was primarily by 3 (restricted) autobahns and 3 air corridors. Being a history and World War II buff, I wanted to experience Berlin. After leaving Munich, I took a train to Hanover and then flew on Pan American Airways to Berlin. I found the city to be very modern, with lots of new buildings and a very upbeat atmosphere. Again, it had only been 24 years since the end of the war. Much of the city had been destroyed.

One of our next-door neighbors (Connie) in Virginia had a German pen pal. They had exchanged numerous frequent letters dating to the early 1930s. As time went on, she became increasingly enthralled with the Hitler youth movement. When war broke out, the letters to Connie of course stopped. I read all the letters including the one that arrived in late 1945. One of her comments was, "We are now a nation of starving pigs." They continued writing to each other for years. In 1969, Connie told her Berlin pen pal that a friend of hers was coming to Berlin for a visit and asked if he could see her. She agreed to it, and we provided the approximate dates of my arrival. She sent details of her location and I tried to pinpoint it as best as I could (I am a map guy don't forget). On one of the first afternoons in Berlin, I headed out to find her home. I gave a taxi driver her address. He was a bit confused but eventually dropped me off in the general area. If I found the street, I knew I could find the house. I did eventually find the right street but in the process, a police car pulled up and two burly guys got out, picked me up, and threw me up against a tree. I was a bit startled, and I proclaimed, "Me American! They dropped me back down, laughed, and drove away. Only a few houses away I found my destination. Yikes, I thought to myself. It was only halfway there with parts of the house covered with tarps. I tepidly knocked on the door. A frail-looking older woman greeted me as she said, "You must be David". Her English was broken but we were able to communicate. First, I had to tell her about Connie and her family in Virginia. She was delighted with what I told her. She kept apologizing for the condition of her home as she said the invading Russians had inflicted heavy damage and that she never had the money to fix it up. The whole neighborhood looked similar. It was located on the outskirts of the city, so I guess it didn't get much redevelopment priority. She told me stories of the war and what she and her daughter had experienced. Apparently, her husband had been killed in the fighting. His picture was on the wall. It was an interesting visit, especially hearing stories from the German perspective. It was almost like she was apologetic for what had happened. I gave her some gifts and departed, happy to have had this unusual experience.

I had read from my travel bible (Europe on Five Dollars a Day) that you could travel from the American Sector through

"Checkpoint Charlie" into East Berlin. Certainly, sounded like a major adventure to me. One morning, I headed over to the border crossing at "Checkpoint Charlie" and began the very scary process of entering Soviet-occupied East Berlin. I thought about my dad at that time. I knew he would really dig this adventure. To say the least, it really was. The East German border guards were big boys and they looked really mean (and were). To use one of my favorite Minnesota phrases "Uff Dah." Lots of questions and interrogation. Mostly "Why are you going to East Berlin?" After about an hour of this, the gate was raised, and I walked into East Berlin. It was a very uneasy feeling. Where do I go from here? I certainly didn't have any tourist guide books. So, I just started walking around. Down this street, down another. The first thing that really struck me was how different (like night and day) the East was from the West. It was very shocking to see many bombed-out buildings still collapsed on the ground. I stopped and had a beer and brat. It was very noticeable observing people that they didn't look so happy. In retrospect, this was a correct observation. Even on that day, there were attempts to flee and cross over "The Wall." Lucky for me and my good sense of direction, I returned again via Checkpoint Charlie, to West Berlin. This experience, to say the least, was very enlightening. The Allied Powers including the Soviet Union defeated Nazi Germany. Now ironically after the end of the war, adversaries, with two totally different forms of government. This short adventure sure convinced me what form I wanted to live under.

US Army Checkpoint Charlie in 1969 – West Berlin

When I look back at these experiences, it is remarkable that I could have witnessed both Fascism and Communism in less than a week. My dad and the Greatest Generation defeated Fascism, now the same must be done with our newest adversary, Communism. It didn't take me long to come to that conclusion.

The next three years were very busy for our family. My brother and I were in college and my sister was in high school.

My dad loves his job with Wallace Engineering and being Mayor. My mom is the Executive of the local chapter of the American Red Cross. This brings us to 1972. One of the best and most memorable of years. My brother graduated from dental school, myself from college, and my sister attended nursing school to become an RN. On top of it was my parents' 25th wedding anniversary. This marks the year that the 3 of us all head in different directions, careers, interests, and life in general. It was all good. My parents were very happy. I could sense that. It was a good feeling. They had raised us properly, now it was time to go out into the world and do something for ourselves.

I decided that life on your own must start with another "BIG" adventure. My two best buddies (since the 7th grade) and I planned an 8-week European Odyssey. So, Louis (Gigi) Mariucci, Rocci Debreto, and I headed over to Europe right after graduation. It would be a 14-country journey. It included to name a few, pub crawling in London, smoking some weed in Amsterdam, spending Bastille Day in Paris, running with the bulls in Pamplona, Spain, cruising the fjords of Norway in a stolen rowboat (we returned it), and walking with Caesar in Rome. Experiences that we still joyously talk about today. My dad taught me how friendships are so important. He had many! These are my best buddies to this day. Me, Gigi, Rocci at the Hofbräuhaus, Munich Germany in July 1972.

Now begins another chapter in life.

CHAPTER THREE:
OFF TO WAKE ISLAND

(PREPARATIONS OVER THE YEARS)

Times certainly change and for our family it sure did. This transition from growing up to growing older was happening throughout the Boomer Generation. For the Families of the Wake Island Defenders, it was no different.

I was married to my first wife Clarice (Charlie), and we had adopted this beautiful 6-week-old son. I was Firmly ensconced in the travel business.

My brother is married with a son and a daughter and operating a successful dental practice.

My sister is married with 2 sons and 2 daughters and is a very hard-working RN.

This scenario was repeated across the country as we Boomers now had to build our own lives. It was done with great appreciation for what our parents from "the Greatest Generation" had given us and what they had sacrificed to get us to this point.

When I look back at these years, I have to say, that they were the best in my parent's life. No more career pressures for my dad, he had his dream job. My mom loved being head of the local Red Cross office. They now had 7 beautiful grandchildren. They had their cabin at Crane Lake. And now they began to travel. Being in the travel business I was able to help them with great deals. They loved traveling to Hawaii every winter. It was there that I believe my dad had a reckoning with his feelings towards the Japanese. Growing up nothing with the label "made in Japan" was allowed in our house. We never questioned this and from our perspective we certainly understood. While in Hawaii my father met many Japanese tourists. Being with my parents a few times in Hawaii it was interesting to see him try to communicate with some of them with the limited Japanese that he could still remember. I recall one time coming down an elevator with my dad at a hotel on Waikiki Beach. There were 3 very cute Japanese girls riding with us. My dad eagerly tried to strike up a conversation, again using his limited Japanese language skills. The doors opened and we all exited with the girls giggling saying, "You know all the bad words." We all laughed hysterically. However, I think he learned a lesson from this encounter. POW camp Japanese and the real practiced language are a bit different.

I noticed a real transformation in my dad's attitude toward Japan. I believe he could now separate his enemy, his captors, and his beatings from present-day Japan. This certainly could be the case of time healing old wounds. In my dad's case, it was more about his firm belief in "The Golden Rule."

The Golden Rule is the principle of treating others as one wants to be treated. It is a maxim that is found in most religions and cultures.

He from these days forward took great pride and with a bit of humility would proclaim. "I do forgive them." I know it wasn't easy for him to say but it was with his firm convictions. I think all of us in the family were so proud of him.

With this new freedom, I noticed that he now wanted to talk more about his experiences publicly without anger toward his captors. He talked about his time on Wake Island and as a POW to many groups. These would include school groups, different veteran groups, and civic organizations. He became good at it and his audiences (of all ages) were enthralled with his stories. I was so proud of him.

A Dream Idea Emerges

I can't remember exactly when, but I know for sure it was in the early 1980s. My dad and I started discussing how great it would be to return someday to Wake Island. Oh yes, in the back of his mind it was the safe he buried and what had happened to it. For myself that was the real first recollection, I had of Wake Island. Let's go treasure hunting dad!!

Our discussions and dream would continue for a couple of years. In the meantime, I had relocated to Orange County, California, and had a new wholesale travel business. I had ideas about how this dream could really happen. You just don't travel to Wake Island. Commercial stopover Pacific air traffic ended long ago. Now in control of the US Air Force with a primary mission of supporting transpacific military air flights. Basically, no one goes to Wake Island unless involved with this military support function.

How could we ever make this dream become a reality? I told my dad, "Talk to your Wake buddies and see if there is an interest in going back." He was in good communication with several including actual visits with his buddies in Minnesota and in California. In the summer of 1984, the marine Survivors of Wake Island group held a reunion in Des Moines, Iowa. My dad was fully prepared to pop the question. How many of you would like to return to Wake Island and would the group sanction such a trip? The resounding response was, "Hell Yes! Semper Fi. My dad told them his son had an idea how they could pull this off."

My dad gleefully passed on the positive response to me in California. We laid out some areas of responsibility. First, the survivor's group will make an initial request to the Pentagon for approval to travel to the Island as a group. I will handle all travel items including flight transportation to Wake and all planned activities in Hawaii prior to the actual flight to Wake Island.

My dad had a very good friend in the US House of Representatives, from Minnesota's 8th Congressional District. His name was Jim Oberstar. He reached out to him for assistance. Jim and my dad were close friends. Jim provided the group with the needed Pentagon contacts and what the group will need to send requesting permission. Official documents were drafted and submitted with plans.

One of the biggest challenges we faced was how would we get an aircraft of considerable size to transport the group from Honolulu to Wake Island, over 2,000 miles. It was very clear from the beginning that the Air Force was not capable or interested in providing us with such an aircraft.

I knew from the beginning that this was not going to be an issue. This was of the reasons that I had so confidently given comfort to my dad that we could pull this off. You see I had a year-long relationship with the charter department at Hawaiian Airlines in Honolulu. They operated a couple of 250-passenger DC-8 aircraft that had a long-distance capability. It had the perfect passenger configuration that the group needed. Early in 1985, I was working with Hawaiian Airlines on a flight they operated once a month for the United Nations between Honolulu and the Fiji Islands. They flew empty between Honolulu and

Fiji. The aircraft then picked up members of the Fijian peacekeeping forces headed to the Middle East. This rotation took one week. The aircraft then headed from Fiji (empty again) back to Honolulu. I had a contract with Hawaiian Airlines for my passengers from the West Coast to Hawaii. They approached me and asked if I would be interested in buying and filling those empty seats to/from Fiji. I then put some packages together combining hotels in Fiji and a very low air cost.

Early in the relationship, I asked them if they would be interested in chartering one of the DC-8s for a 3-day flight rotation from Honolulu to Wake Island. I received an immediate positive response along with costs. We then provided the Pentagon with a copy of our contract. It didn't take long, and my dad received a permission letter from the Pentagon giving us the ok and asking for dates. By then it was late spring of 1985. Now the major logistics challenges were ahead. The first being when Wake could accommodate 250 guests. It's not like there is a massive hotel on the island. The last one was blown up in the first Japanese air raid on Dec. 8, 1941.

The Dream Becomes Reality

The Pentagon told me here is the name of the commander, Maj. James Westmoreland, and his phone number. Give him a call to arrange dates. I was kind of amazed, just dial the area code and number and you can reach him. So, I did just that. Maj. Westmoreland, I found him to be a really nice guy and very excited to welcome our group. I also had to coordinate dates with Hawaiian Airlines to availability of the aircraft. Finally, we settled on Oct. 29 - Nov. 6, 1985.

I made corresponding plans for our pre and post stays in Hawaii. I couldn't believe this was happening. We were really going to Wake Island. Now we had to get the word out to the survivors. Another exciting thought emerged.

I talked with several of the marine survivors, and all agreed that let's invite the Civilian Defenders of Wake Island. They had never held a reunion together. They all would be very excited to see each other after 40 years. I know there was a great mutual admiration between them. I contacted the Civilian Survivors group in Boise and immediately received a very positive response. The word goes out! The below notices (actual copies) were sent to both the marine and civilian groups. My travel company started taking reservations. We had 800 numbers and they loved it.

DEFENDERS OF WAKE ISLAND
DECEMBER 8 – 23, 1941

ARMY MARINES CIVILIANS NAVY

WAKE ISLAND

DEFENDERS

OF

WAKE ISLAND

REUNION

October 29 - November 6, 1985

HONOLULU, HAWAII / WAKE ISLAND

40th ANNIVERSARY OF LIBERATION

THIS SPECIAL EXPERIENCE INCLUDES:

* Roundtrip airfare from your home city
* Seven nights hotel accommodations at the Pacific Beach Hotel - Waikiki
* One night Wake Island
* Airfare to Wake Island via Hawaiian Air Charter Flight (DC-8 jet aircraft)
* Welcome flower lei greeting
* Welcome cocktail party with hot and cold pupus
* Special joint banquet with Wake Island civilians
* Farewell dinner
* Picnic lunch on Nanikuli Beach
* Honolulu City tour with visit to the Punch Bowl Cemetery, Wake Island Memorial and the Arizona
* All transfers and taxes
* Baggage handling
* Hospitality and tour desk for optional tours and activities registration of all reunion participants

POST TOUR - OUTER ISLAND PROGRAMS

For those wishing additional time in Hawaii, special programs can be arranged to Maui, Kaui or the big island of Hawaii. Please inquire for complete details.

PRICES

WEST COAST		DENVER AND ALL CITIES EAST	
$1,059	per person double occupancy	$1,179	per person double occupancy
Single Supplement add $300.00		Single Supplement add $300.00	
Triple reduction - $100.00		Triple reduction - $100.00	

* Some cities may differ according to airfares
* Prices may vary as to your departure city and are subject to change

DEFENDERS OF WAKE ISLAND

REUNION

OCTOBER 29 - NOVEMBER 6, 1985

ALOHA!

TUESDAY, OCTOBER 29

All day arrivals, Honolulu International Airport.

7:30 PM - 8:30 PM	Welcome Cocktail Party Hot and Cold Pupus, PAPIO ROOM, 3rd Floor

WEDNESDAY, OCTOBER 30

8:00 AM	Breakfast Briefing and Optional Tours AHI BALLROOM, 3rd Floor
	Joint Banquet for Defenders and Survivors of Wake Island GRAND BALLROOM MAKAI - 5th Floor
6:00 PM	No Host Cocktails and Reception
7:30 PM	Banquet, followed by short program. Music to be provided by the Marine Corps Band.

THURSDAY, OCTOBER 31

8:30 AM	Bus Departs Hotel Lobby for the Punchbowl Cemetary.
8:45 AM - 9:30 AM	Ceremony at Punchbowl
10:00 AM	Arrive at the Arizona Memorial. Ceremony and Visit.
1:00 PM - 3:00 PM	Short City Tour with a stop for Lunch.
--to be announced--	Cocktail Party with Civilian Group - time and place to be announced.

FRIDAY, NOVEMBER 1

1:00 PM	Depart Hotel Lobby for Nanakuli Beach. Lunch at Nanakuli.
4:30 PM	Depart Nanakuli for the Bowfin Submarine at Pearl Harbor. Cocktail Party, Pupus and visit of the Sub.
7:00 PM	Arrive back at the Hotel.

SATURDAY, NOVEMBER 2

6:30 AM	Bus Departs Hotel Lobby for Airport.
8:00 AM	Flight Departs for Wake Island.
	Activities on Wake Island.

<u>SUNDAY, NOVEMBER 3</u>

2:00 PM	Depart Wake Island for Honolulu.
9:30 PM	Arrive Honolulu.

<u>MONDAY, NOVEMBER 4</u>

Day at Leisure for Optional Tours.

<u>TUESDAY, NOVEMBER 5</u>

6:00 PM	Cocktails
7:00 PM	Farewell Dinner MAHIMAHI ROOM, 3rd Floor

<u>WEDNESDAY, NOVEMBER 6</u>

Individual Departures for Home.

Pick-up Times Will Be Announced.

MAHALO!

Waikiki Beachcomber Hotel Welcome

We started taking reservations in early June of 1985. My staff enjoyed talking to both the marines and civilians. They all wanted to tell a short story as to who they were and where they were from. Many wanted to talk to me directly. I wanted to talk to as many as I could to get to know them a little before the trip. Every day it just amazed me that this trip was really going to happen. The enthusiasm was just overwhelming. From all over the country they called. We helped many arrange transportation from hometown to/from Honolulu. I know for some the decision to join the reunion trip was a challenge. These being health, financial, and for a few not wanting to experience the horrors of war again. It would be too difficult for them. This was very understandable to me.

I was honored one day at home to receive a phone call from General Devereux. We had a very cordial conversation as he recalled mostly his memories of my father. At the time he had not decided to attend or not. He called again, still undecided but very curious as to who was going. I thoroughly enjoyed our conversations. Finally, in September, Mrs. Devereux called to say her husband's health was not good and would not be attending. General Devereux passed away in 1988. My father and his marine buddies often spoke of Devereux. Early on I could detect a bit of animosity towards him. This seemed to fade as time went on as they eventually realized that his toughness and discipline on them especially in their POW camps helped them survive the horrific ordeals they faced. His full name was James J.P.S Devereux. Laughing, the marines would say the J.P.S. stood for "just plain shit." I don't believe there was much contact after the war between Devereux and the enlisted marines (Unless he was looking for the safe ☺). I know that wasn't the total case between him and his officers. This was confirmed to me after speaking to some of them on this Wake reunion trip and at the last organized reunion in 1995 in San Diego. More on this reunion later. One of the first books I can remember reading was, “The Story of Wake Island”. Devereux wrote this book in 1947. It is still in print and a good read. This book was on a bookshelf in our living room. My dad would often show it to friends or visitors to our home. I can only guess that I first read the book in the early 1960s. It did have a great effect on me as I now was now able to put into context the stories my dad had previously told me. It was indeed, “not just another war story.”

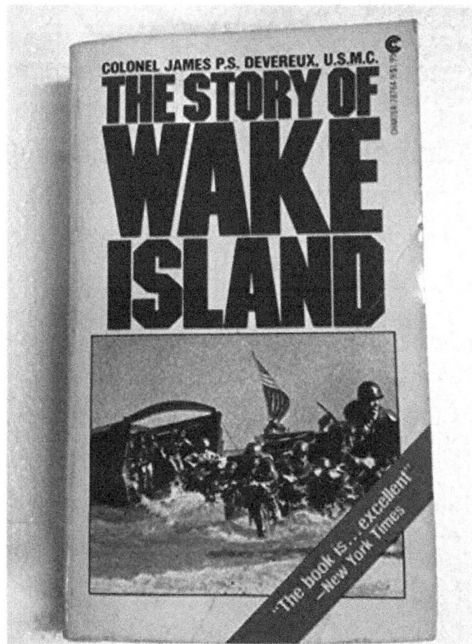

I was disappointed that Devereux could not attend but the momentum and excitement for this trip continued to build. We were getting an equally good response from both the marines and civilians. In addition, 26 officers and enlisted men from the current VMA 211 (The Wake Island Avengers) Marine Corps

Fighter Squadron decided to join us. They were then stationed at MCAS, El Toro, CA. Currently, VMA 211 is flying F-35B stealth fighters and is stationed in Yuma, AZ.

Finally, in early October of 1985, we had a full flight of approximately 250 passengers. Of these, about 140 were actual "Defenders of Wake Island" made up of marines, civilians, army, and a Pan Am employee.

The Letter

I could feel the enthusiasm in the group in the days prior to our departure. Many called me just to share their excitement and disbelief that they were headed back to Wake. I reveled in every minute of it. My dad was really excited! He was in Minnesota; I was in California. Even considering the distance I could feel his excitement. For weeks he would call me every day, "Is everything ok, any problems?" One day he announced that he had contacted the White House by letter and asked if President Reagan would send a welcoming supportive letter. He waited and waited, but no letter. He became a bit discouraged thinking it might not arrive. Then the day before my mom and dad were to leave to join us in California, the letter arrived "special delivery from the White House." He called me and proudly announced it arrived. And to top off the delight of receiving the letter from the President another letter arrived from General Kelly, the Commandant of the Marine Corps. To say the least my father was "stoked". Our trip, never thought possible in the past, was about to begin.

THE WHITE HOUSE

WASHINGTON

October 21, 1985

I am honored to send warm greetings to the Wake Island Defenders as you gather for your 40th anniversary reunion.

In December, 1941, Americans held their breath as a heroic band of Marines and civilian workers defended Wake Island against overwhelming enemy force. More than forty years later, forty years after the final victory, we continue to be inspired by your magnificent valor and moved by the sufferings you endured. There are no words to express the magnitude of your sacrifice for America and for the cause of freedom. But I do want you to know that all Americans are grateful and that we shall never forget what you and your departed comrades did and how much we owe you.

Nancy joins me in sending best wishes. God bless you.

Ronald Reagan

A MESSAGE FROM THE COMMANDANT OF THE MARINE CORPS

On behalf of all Marines, it is an extreme pleasure to extend greetings to the Wake Island Defenders as you commemorate the 40th Anniversary of your release from captivity.

Forty years ago, an elite group of Marines was released from captivity by the Japanese. Four years earlier, all of America learned of the courage of the Marines defending Wake Island against a superior enemy force. Through your valiant stand on that tiny island, Americans were filled with an intense fighting spirit which was to become the deciding factor in the Allied victory in the Pacific. As they did almost 44 years ago, Americans and Marines commend each and every one of you for your courage and love of freedom.

As you once again walk upon the sands of Wake Island and recall those 14 days of intense fighting, please accept my heartfelt best wishes for a memorable anniversary.

P. X. KELLEY
General, U.S. Marine Corps

Defense Installations on Wake Island – 8-23 December 1941

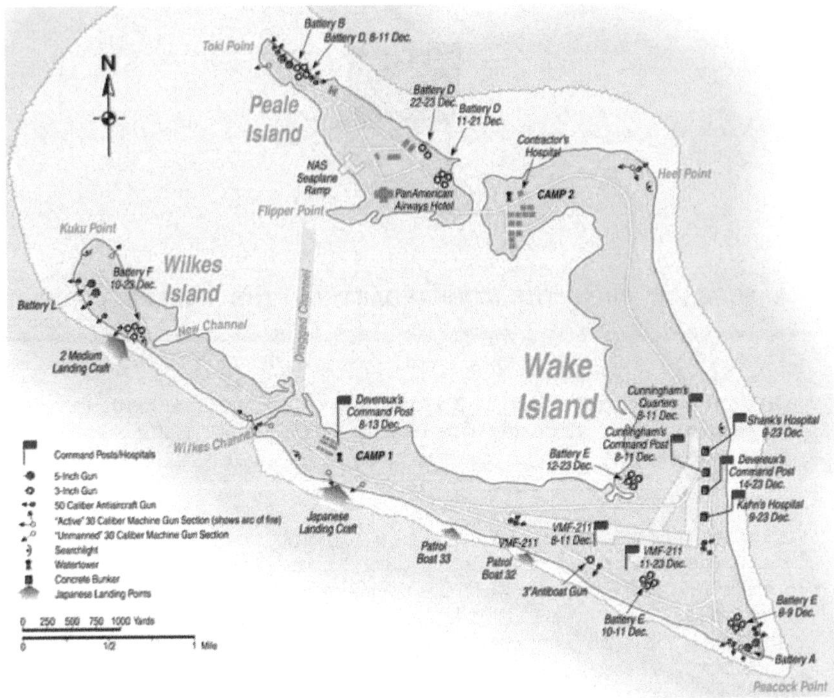

The Historic Reunion Trip Begins

After months of planning and anticipation, we were off to Honolulu and the first 3 days of the reunion. Keep in mind that this was the first official get-together between the marines and civilians. I could feel the excitement between the survivors. Almost all marines and civilians had not seen each other for 40 years or more. This trip was the 40th anniversary of their liberation from their POW camps. I was very curious to witness the initial reactions between them and how many would remember each other. During the preceding months, I had talked to so many of them. I was so looking forward to finally meeting. I know my dad and his marine buddies felt the same way. As the survivors and their families began to arrive at the Waikiki Beachcomber, the hotel lobby became a buzz with shouts of welcome, laughter, and lots of hugs. I knew from that point on this was going to be all that my dad and I had expected and hoped for. For me, it was going to be a trip and experience of a lifetime. For the survivors, it was reacquainting with past friends, and comrades in arms, sharing experiences they had on Wake and in their captivity. I also knew that some of their memories would be difficult, and emotions would surface. I was so right about that. In the meantime, in that hotel lobby (and soon moving to the bar) my emotions surged reveling at what I was witnessing.

As you saw on a previous page, we had lots of activities planned. The first was a reception that first night at the hotel followed the next evening with a dinner and program. A few great speeches and music by the Marine Corps Band. Lots of hoots and hollers. It reminded me of a high school pre-game pep rally. At the time most of these guys were 64 to 75 years of age. I was so impressed with their ability to, as we younger guys would say, "PARTY." This atmosphere would continue throughout the trip. It was certainly ok with me ☺.

One of the most emotional days of the whole reunion trip was on Thursday, the second full day. At least 5 tour buses picked up the whole group early in the morning and headed to The Punchbowl National Memorial Cemetery of the Pacific. Followed by a visit to Pearl Harbor and the U.S Arizona Memorial.

The day was very special. Survivors came to honor their fellow marines and civilians who died on Wake Island. The Wake Island grave at the punchbowl contains the names of 178 Americans killed on Wake Island. Including 47 military and 131 civilians. According to Bonnie Gilbert's blog post from bonniegilbert.com, the Wake Island grave site at the Punchbowl was dedicated on October 21, 1953.

Punchbowl Grave Dedication

J. T. Hunt, father of Sgt Quince A. Hunt, USMC, at the grave site with Gen. J. W. O'Daniel, Admiral S. S. Murray, Gen. F. A. Hart standing. 10/21/1953

A flower wreath was placed on the gravesite by the marines and civilians. I could see the emotions rising in their eyes and expressions on their faces as they stood there staring at the names on the grave. It was a very solemn moment for all of us survivors, and families alike. Then, but very quietly, came the voices of the survivors, each individually……. I remember (name), I remember (name), I remember (name). This went on for quite a few minutes. I could see that this moment was very hard on the civilian survivors. The Wake 98 massacre was one of the worst atrocities of World War II. Now they were reliving those memories. The marines too commented on their fallen comrades. Most of them had been together since June of 1939 boot camp in San Diego. They knew each other very well and stories started to emerge as they honored them. It was a beautiful way to begin this historic reunion trip. Leaving the gravesite there seemed to be a bit of hesitation on the part of the survivors. It was like they wanted to stay for a while and be with all the 178 friends, buddies, and yes even brothers. I looked at them, I could feel their emotions, I could see their tears. It was very quiet as the group reboarded our busses headed to Pearl Harbor and the USS Arizona Memorial.

Laying a wreath on the Wake Island grave.

Survivors, families, and VMA-211 paying tribute to their fallen comrades

My father kneeling at the gravesite

The Wake 98

From: American War Memorials Overseas

Three weeks after the fall of Wake, a transport ship (Nita Maru) came to take all but 360 contractors to camps in Japan and China. The remaining POWs were put to work. The Japanese did not observe the Geneva Convention restriction on using POW labor for war-related projects, and the workers toiled on various military projects. On the last day of September in 1942, all but 98 prisoners were loaded aboard a freighter and sent to Yokohama. The remaining POWs were to continue their work on construction projects.

The Headquarters Company commander, Lieutenant Commander Tachibana, was ordered by Admiral Sakaibara to move the prisoners from their compound to an antitank ditch on the northern tip of Wake Island. There, in the waning afternoon light of October 7, 1943, Lieutenant Torahi Ito of Headquarters Company, had the Americans lined up and seated along the ditch facing the sea. They were blindfolded with their hands and feet bound. Three platoons of Tachibana's company mowed them down with gun and rifle fire. The Americans then were dumped unceremoniously into the ditch and covered with coral sand. The following day, a report from an enlisted man that saw one of the prisoners escape during the confusion of the massacre prompted the disinterment of the bodies. The corpses were dug up and counted, then hastily reburied.

The sailor had been correct: one American was missing. That man, whose identity has not been discovered, was re-captured and was beheaded personally by Admiral Sakaibara three weeks later. During the time of his escape, near where the massacre occurred, stands a large coral rock that this American contractor had carved the date of the massacre along with "98 US PW."

This is what the POW Rock looked like in November of 1985.

Sakakibara and his subordinate, Lieutenant Commander Tachibana, were later sentenced to death for this and other war crimes. The remains of the murdered civilians were exhumed and reburied at the National Memorial Cemetery of the Pacific in section G.

We have families of the Wake 98 on our "Families of Wake Island Defenders" Facebook page. It is so nice to have them in our group and to hear their stories. It was very difficult for them after the war. These men had gone to Wake to earn a living for themselves and their families. Now they were gone, and it was very hard to cope with the loss of the family breadwinner. It is hard to imagine the grief they felt after not knowing for so many years if their loved one was alive or dead. It was a very similar situation for the marine and civilian families back at home.

The USS Arizona Memorial

Not much was said during the bus trip to Pearl Harbor. All the survivors were in deep thought. I can only imagine what was going through their heads. I held my mother's hand as she could not successfully hold back some tears. I think at this moment I felt closer to my parents than I ever had. Today as I am writing this, I am looking for tissues. This visit to the gravesite was the most emotional time for the survivors during the whole trip.

We now arrived at the Pearl Harbor Visitor Center. Here you board the shuttle boats operated by the US Navy to the USS Arizona Memorial. Accompanying us was Daniel Martinez who was to become Chief Staff Historian of the Memorial. He joined us at the Punchbowl and later traveled to Wake with us. It was very nice of him to give the group such personal attention. I could tell he was enjoying himself.

Some of the survivors outside the Pearl Harbor Visitor Center.

Now at the memorial stands marine Robert (Big Mo) Curry. The name of his brother (Bill) is etched on the memorial. He is forever entombed here with over 1,100 of his fellow Navy men killed on Dec. 7th, 1941. Many of the marines remember Bill well as he had invited them to watch movies onboard the ship. They were shown on the massive gun turrets. "Big Mo" didn't know about his brother's fate until after the war. Another emotional moment for all. My dad and 'Big Mo' had a special bond. They were more than brothers. They first met at boot camp in San Diego in 1939. It was like they were inseparable from boot camp to Hawaii to Wake Island and then all those years spent in hell. My dad loved "Big Mo". I did too! I had the honor of speaking at his funeral in 1996 in his hometown of Hemet, CA. Their story is one of undying friendship. I think Swede and "Big Mo" are smiling today upstairs as "Mo's" daughter Roberta and I remain very close personal friends.

The following day we spent visiting some of the marine's hangouts before they were shipped off to Wake Island. As back then a good amount of beer was consumed. That night back at the hotel I could notice the mood changing from all the fun we were having in Hawaii to the seriousness of the next stop of our historic journey and that being Wake Island itself. On the faces of the survivors and in their conversations, you could feel their anticipation of what they were about to experience. At this moment I felt great pride and joy for all these men. What they thought most likely would never happen was about to become reality. The stories were flowing of their ordeal of originally getting to Wake, the work they did there, and finally what they did on those fateful days of 8-23 Dec. 1941. That night the bond between the marines and the civilians was again cemented in history. I can say that for those of us attending family members our joy in what we were witnessing was almost overwhelming. Indeed, excitement was in the air. The conversations went on into the night. I know not many in the entire group slept well before our early morning departure for the airport.

But now the survivors, their families, 26 marines from VMA-211, some media reporters, and some other dignitaries are on the Island. This historic reunion on Wake Island was about to begin.

THE FLIGHT TO WAKE ISLAND

It was a beautiful morning, Saturday, Nov. 2, 1985. The weather fit the mood for all of us. Clear skies, calm winds, and that soothing Hawaiian atmosphere. The marines and civilians loved Hawaii. You could notice that during our 3-day stay there. Our buses pulled away at 6:30 am from our hotel on Waikiki Beach. It had been a marvelous stay in Hawaii. More on that later. But now our group of 200 Marines, Civilians, and family members (like myself) were headed to Honolulu International Airport for our 4 ½ hour flight to Wake Island. The island is located just over 2,000 miles west of Honolulu. We were also joined by 20 officers and enlisted men from the then-current Marine Corps Fighter Squadron VMA-211. Home-based at MCAS, El Toro, California. The Hawaiian Airlines DC-8 charter flight holding 250 passengers was totally full. As we pulled away from the gate, I felt like we were about to begin a surreal experience. Indeed, it was. Our time spent in Honolulu was very festive and that mood continued onto our flight to Wake. I could see and feel the excitement, especially on the faces of the survivors. There was also some apprehension and nervousness. How would they feel? Would the memories of battle be too hard for some to handle? I thought about this. I was preparing myself for what possibly lay ahead.

As we gained cruising altitude and everyone got settled in the atmosphere on the plane, became one of excitement, joy, and almost to the point of celebratory. From our stay in Honolulu, I knew these guys could still party. Believe me when I say that from one who has much experience in that area. The drinks started flowing and the stories kept getting more boisterous. I had heard a few of them before but wow, these were really getting mind-boggling. I would soon see where and how these stories took place. Maybe somewhat embellished but nevertheless first-hand accounts of gallant heroism. This would continue for the next few days on Wake. More to be told in later chapters.

The Hawaiian Air pilots kept us informed on our flight progress and said they would inform us when about a half-hour out. The flight attendant crew was delightful. Our captain invited a few of the veterans to visit the cockpit. I was also asked to step in. This of course was a new experience for all of us. Hawaiian Air even brought along a mechanic. A little difficult to try to fix something 2,000 + miles from home base in Honolulu. Here is marine Chick Bamford in the jump seat and mechanic behind him and a view of our pilots.

We then started descending from 35,000 feet. Our captain informed us we would circle the island a couple of times at approx. 1,000 feet offering great picture opportunities. And then suddenly off in the distance, you could see a land formation. As we got closer the first noticeable thing was the emerald green and aqua-blue waters of the inner lagoon. The mood on the plane suddenly changed. A deafening hush fell over the plane as our veterans and family strained to catch a glimpse of Wake through the porthole windows. There was no talking, but the expressions on each weathered sunlit face told countless stories of their Wake Island experience. We were forever fortunate to experience these stories firsthand. Suddenly there it was off in the distance.

The view from the cockpit of our Hawaiian Airlines charter DC-8.

Upon landing, we were met by a welcoming group of Air Force and civilian personnel. You could see they were very excited to welcome us and were very curious to see the veterans.

The door of the plane opened, and one wife said, "Wow it's hot." Her marine husband replied, "YEAH, and the Japs tried to make it a lot hotter," watching the expressions on the faces of the veterans as they deplaned was priceless. Again, it was another surreal moment.

Our group was then escorted into the terminal building. We all roamed around cameras clicking and purses unsnapping. Soon, the Wake Island gift shop was depleted.

All of us would enter the terminal building to be given a briefing as to the planned schedule for the next 2 days, in addition to explaining the group's accommodation assignments. The terminal store and museum were discovered, and as mentioned earlier, the shelves were depleted quickly. It was here, in the terminal small museum, that I first noticed the survivor's emotions started to be shown. Most of the items in the museum were related to their previous stay on the Island. They stood and looked, some adding comments as to what was being displayed and they knew what and where they had last seen them or even used them. I too was fascinated.

These are two murals on the walls of the terminal building. VMA-211 Grumman F4 Wildcats. Pre-December 8, Pan Am Clipper at their dock on Peale Island.

Now it was off to our accommodations. Accommodating 250 people at any time on Wake Island is challenging. The Air Force commander was prepared and all of us soon would be settling into our accommodations. My mom, dad, and I were led to our rooms by a Philippine porter. This group had been on Wake for years. They performed various jobs on the island including taking care of the dining hall and quarters for mostly transiting flight crews. I guess we were considered VIPs as my dad and I had planned this whole reunion trip. Our porter took us to a building that had a few bedrooms. He said, "you have very special rooms". With a big smile on his face, he said you are sleeping in the same bed as President Truman slept in when he met General Douglas MacArthur on Wake Island on Oct. 15, 1950. Across the hall, my Parents were settling into the room occupied by General MacArthur. I was extremely impressed, to say the least.

It had been a very busy day. Everything had gone perfectly. I lay there in bed. The ever-present sound of crashing waves could be heard in the distance. My thoughts turned to these men that we were so honoring with our presence. What would tomorrow bring? What stories would we hear? I was prepared to experience all I could. My lifetime as a "Son of Wake Island" was about to become reality.

The Marines and Civilians Have Returned to Wake Island

So much was about to happen, so many stories were about to be told, so many emotions were going to be displayed, and so many friendships were about to be made and renewed. Accommodating 250 people on Wake at one time is not an easy task. The Air Force and the civilian contractors did an excellent job organizing all housing units for the group. Some stayed in military housing used by transiting flight crews, and some stayed in housing used by Vietnamese refugees being processed into the United States from April to August of 1975. These tin-shaped units were more like barracks and rather primitive. They were also used in the return reunion trip in 1988 where most of us stayed, including myself and my dad. As previously mentioned, my mom, dad, and I on this trip had “the deluxe accommodations”. We had no idea until after arriving at Wake where we would be staying. However, Air Force Commander Westmoreland, prior to our arrival, had assured us, that everyone would be housed appropriately. This was certainly the case.

After discovering the award-winning mess hall, the whole group converged on The Drifters Reef Bar. All who have been on Wake know the Drifters Reef. A legend in its time! A great beach in front.

Early conversations included how the survivors originally arrived on Wake Island. Many marines and civilians (including my father) came on the USS Regulus that departed Honolulu on August 8th, 1941. From what I could tell there were nearly a thousand men on that sailing. I've seen all the manifests including the one below.

Page 4

LIST OF NONENLISTED PASSENGERS OF U. S. S. REGULUS (AK14)

at date of sailing from Honolulu, T.H. **for** Wake Island

Date August 8, 1941.

NAMES	RANK, TITLE, ETC.	DESTINATION
BRENISTKI, William	Pvt USMC	Wake Island
HAGGARD, Fred D.	PFC USMC	Wake Island
HARRISON, Charles L.	PFC USMC	Wake Island
HYZER, Morris F.	PFC USMC	Wake Island
JOHNSON, Thomas W.	PFC USMC	Wake Island
JOHNSTON, Lillard L., Jr.	PFC USMC	Wake Island
JONES, Otis T.	PFC USMC	Wake Island
NETTSCHER, Leonard G.	PFC USMC	Wake Island
MILLER, Hershal L.	PFC USMC	Wake Island
PEARSALL, John E.	PFC USMC	Wake Island
REED, Dick L.	PFC USMC	Wake Island
ROZYCKI, Stanley J.	PFC USMC	Wake Island
SIMON, Adolph	PFC USMC	Wake Island
TAYLOR, Rudolph J.	PFC USMC	Wake Island
VERGA, Vincent H.	PFC USMC	Wake Island
WEBSTER, Guy P.	PFC USMC	Wake Island
CALANCHINI, Arthur J.	Pvt USMC	Wake Island
COVERT, Phillip C.	Pvt USMC	Wake Island
DODGE, Bernard A.	Pvt USMC	Wake Island
FINLEY, Lloyd B.	Pvt USMC	Wake Island
HICKS, Albert, Jr.	PvtUSMC	Wake Island
JOHNSON, Solon L.	Pvt USMC	Wake Island
JACKSON, Sammy C.	Pvt USMC	Wake Island
KROPTAVICH, James S.	Pvt USMC	Wake Island
MELTON, Kenneth L.	Pvt USMC	Wake Island
MILBOURN, Ival D.	Pvt USMC	Wake Island
PICKETT, Ralph H.	Pvt USMC	Wake Island
RAMSEY, Lewman F.	Pvt USMC	Wake Island
SCHNEIDER, LeRoy M.	Pvt USMC	Wake Island
SHORES, Robert	Pvt USMC	Wake Island
SMITH, Gordon L.	Pvt USMC	Wake Island
WALLACE, Verne L.	Pvt USMC	Wake Island
WINSLOW, Robert E.	Pvt USMC	Wake Island
WISKOCHIL, Robert J.	Pvt USMC	Wake Island
WYRICK, Marion L.	Pvt USMC	Wake Island

[illegible]

For the survivors to get reacquainted, and for the rest of us to explore the Island will have to wait until the morning. In the meantime, The Drifters Reef will have a night that it's never had before or will ever have again. Here, on that unforgettable night, the stories of battle would be told with great enthusiasm. It was remarkable how they could remember in detail what they did and where they were. I sat with Commander Westmoreland for a while. He jokingly explained to me that he had two comfort gauges that he relied on. 1. How much water was in the storage tanks? (No fresh water on the Island). 2. How much beer and booze were in the warehouse. I could tell that #2 was greatly being depleted. ☺

I still look back at this night with amazement. It was like a surreal moment for not only the survivors but for all of us. We were here on Wake Island.

I walked back to our building thinking to myself I am really going to sleep in a bed once occupied by a President of the United States and my parents in one occupied by one of the greatest Generals of WWII. Then I stopped and paused for a moment. I looked up into the sky and there were a million brilliant stars all around. Crawling into a historic bed, looking forward to the next day, I could only think of what emotions were going to be displayed.

My father was an admirer of Harry Truman. He always said he owed his life to him. The POWs generally felt that they would have been used by the Japanese as guinea pigs in an Allied invasion of mainland Japan. The dropping of two atomic bombs ended that possibility.

You know how sometimes a certain song plays in your head. Well, this one kicked in.

Do you remember "A peaceful easy feeling" by the Eagles?

Cause I get a peaceful easy feelin'
And I know you won't let me down
'Cause I'm already standin'
I'm already standin'
Yes, I'm already standin'
On the ground

It was indeed a peaceful easy feeling. Yes, I was standing on the ground that was heroically defended by these men. And oh yes, "the stars were all around". It was a magnificent display. No light pollution on Wake Island. How did I get here? What happened in my life to lead me to this point? I discovered it that night in my dreams.

Dawn on Wake Island

"Where America's Day Really Begins"

On December 8, 1941, most of the marines and civilians were halfway through eggs and hotcakes when 39 bombers streaked from under a darkening storm cloud to begin what would become one of the most famous battles in Marine Corps history. This was the topic of conversation that morning at breakfast. This time they were able to finish.

Now all of us were about to begin a day we had been looking forward to for over a year. We were allowed to go about the Island at our own pace and listen to the survivors reminisce about those fateful days. The Air Force had a few buses and some pickups ready to shuttle us around Wake, Peale, and Wilkes Islands.

But first a flag-raising ceremony. Almost the entire group attended.

Left to right – Pearsall, unknown, Bamford

I was honored to raise the Marine Corp Flag.
Standing next to a 3-inch gun they once manned.

Left to right – Pearsall, Schaefer, Curry, Slezak, Holmes

Now with the transportation support, all of us were allowed to roam the island at our own pace. It took some time to get orientated and decide where to go first. The families, like myself, just hopped on the buses or the back of a pickup truck and headed out with the survivors. We were as anxious to hear their stories as they were to tell them. But first a wreath-laying ceremony at the Marine Corps Memorial next to the terminal building. Just after the flag-raising and now this special ceremony. A fitting way to start this historic day. Another very special and emotional moment that all of us were to experience so many times during our stay.

This is one of my favorite pictures that I have of my parents and me. As we approached the memorial, I could see tears in my mom's eyes. I know that she was thinking of all the things that went on during those 14 days of American history so long ago. She touched the memorial and hugged my dad. I too couldn't stop the tears. I hugged them both. Indeed, one of the most special moments of my life. I will never forget it.

Between the 12th of December to the 22nd, the Japanese bombed every day. The marines with much help from the civilians moved their positions each night.

An Account Of VMA-211

Japanese aircraft began aerial attacks on the Wake Island base on December 8, destroying eight of the VMA-211 squadron's 12 Grumman F4F-3 Wildcats on the ground. Two more aerial attacks followed, and on December 11th, the garrison, with the support of the four remaining Wildcats, repelled the first Japanese landing attempt on Wake Island.

On December 12, Elrod single-handedly attacked a flight of 22 Japanese planes and shot down two, earning him the nickname "Hammerin Hank" among his fellow Marines. He executed several low-altitude bombings and strafing runs on enemy ships. During one of these attacks, he became the first American to sink a Japanese warship from a fighter aircraft, dropping the bombs on the destroyer Kisaragi's stern, causing depth charges to explode, and sending the ship to the bottom of the Pacific.

The remaining Marine aircraft were soon destroyed in repeated attacks and when there was nothing left to fly, Elrod organized troops into a beach defense unit which repulsed repeated Japanese attacks as the invasion of Wake Island intensified.

In Devereux's book "The Story of Wake Island", he tells of Captain Elrod's last moments of life through an eyewitness account from Major Putman, who had been in the defensive battle with Elrod. As Major Devereux arrived at the battle's location, Major Putnam said, "Jimmy, I'm sorry, poor Hank is dead." The book continued, "Elrod had been a fury. Men remember how one enemy charge almost overwhelmed them and how Hank Elrod stood upright, blasting with a Tommy gun, and broke the charge. Japanese fell close enough for him to touch. They remember he was standing up to throw a grenade when a Japanese soldier shot him. The enemy had crawled in among the Japanese dead scattered thickly around the position and waited there for his chance. Somebody killed the Japanese soldier, but Elrod never knew it. He died instantly. Now he lay there, defiant and with his eyes open, the grenade still tightly clutched in his hand."

Elrod, Henry Talmage

Rank and organization: Captain, U.S. Marine Corps. Born: 27 September 1905, Rebecca, Georgia. Entered service at Ashburn, Georgia.

Citation:

For conspicuous gallantry and intrepidity at the risk of his life above and beyond the call of duty while attached to Marine Fighting Squadron 211, during action against enemy Japanese land, surface, and aerial units at Wake Island, 8 to 23 December 1941. Engaging vastly superior forces of enemy bombers and warships on 9 and 12 December, Capt. Elrod shot down 2 of a flight of 22 hostile planes, and executing repeated bombing and strafing runs at extremely low altitude and close range, succeeded in inflicting deadly damage upon a large Japanese vessel, thereby sinking the first major warship to be destroyed by small caliber bombs delivered from a fighter-type aircraft. When his plane was disabled by hostile fire and no other ships were operative, Capt. Elrod assumed command of 1 flank of the line set up in defiance of the enemy landing and, conducting a brilliant defense, enabled his men to hold their positions and repulse intense hostile fusillades to provide covering fire for unarmed ammunition carriers. Capturing an automatic weapon during 1 enemy rush in force, he gave his own firearm to 1 of his men and fought vigorously against the Japanese. Responsible in a large measure for the strength of his sector's gallant resistance, on 23 December, Capt. Elrod led his men with bold aggressiveness until he fell, mortally wounded. His superb skill as a pilot, daring leadership, and unswerving devotion to duty distinguished him among the defenders of Wake Island, and his valiant conduct reflects the highest credit upon himself and the U.S. Naval Service. He gallantly gave his life for his country.

By December 22, Lieutenant Kinney and his mechanics patched up another Wildcat, giving the squadron two fighters for what proved to be its last hurrah. At 10 a.m., Captain Herbert C. Freuler and Lieutenant Carl R. Davidson took off to meet the regular midday raid, and 33 B5N Kate bombers along with six Zero fighters arrived on schedule. Freuler and Davidson dove into the Japanese formation despite the desperate odds. Davidson was shot down and killed, but Freuler managed to down two Japanese planes before enemy fire irreparably damaged his Wildcat. He barely made it back to Wake and crash-landed on the beach. Unknown to him, however, Freuler had exacted some revenge—a Kate bomber he shot down in flames carried Noboru Kanai, the bombardier credited with dropping the fatal bomb on the USS Arizona during the attack on Pearl Harbor.

Japanese G3M1 and G3M2 Type 96 (Nell) bombers in the Pacific before the airstrikes on Wake Island that destroyed more than half of VMF-211's aircraft on December 8, 1941. (Photo: National Archives Photo 80-G-179013)

Grumman F4F Wildcat from VMF-211 destroyed on the ground by Japanese air strikes in December 1941. (Photo: Navy Archives)

211-F-11

THE DEFENSE OF WAKE

OFFICIAL REPORTS indicate that probably no military force in American history, not even the defenders of the Alamo, ever fought against greater odds nor with greater effect in view of those odds. The reports show that during the 14 days of Wake's siege not fewer than 200 Japanese planes bombed and machine-gunned the tiny isle's defenders. This figure does not include those in the final attack, whereof the number is unknown. But as many as 50 bombers, some four-motored seaplanes, attacked the island in a single raid. During the closing days of the siege the defenders had only two and finally one plane. These were patched together between flights. Nevertheless, marine flyers, plus anti-aircraft batteries, managed to bring down at least 12 enemy planes. After the first surprise attack the enemy acquired a healthy respect for this defense combination and gave up low altitude strafing and bombing for high level attack. Even so, until the garrison was overwhelmed by a landing force, the marines, flyers and anti-aircraft batteries continued to give a good account of themselves.

"The first attack on the eighth was made by between 20 and 30 twin-engined bombers, apparently of medium class. These were land planes and possibly from Japan's mandate islands south of Wake. They carried light bombs and were armed with incendiary cannon and machine guns. Four of the 12 Marine planes based on the island were in the air when the enemy appeared in a low glide out of a cloud bank. The other eight planes were being serviced. The enemy went for these at once. Seven were total losses from bomb hits and fire and only the remnants of the eighth salvagable. The landing field was damaged, but remained usable. Also, enemy bombs failed to find Marine stores and aviation gasoline. The gasoline supply of the Pan-American Airways' base was ignited. Casualties in the first raid were heavy. Some 25 persons were killed and more than that number wounded.

"Raid number two followed the next day at almost the same hour. About 20 bombers attacked, these including incendiaries in their bomb loads. Raid number three came before the day was over—this was the ninth of December at Wake Island. Due to vigorous plane and anti-aircraft defenses, damage was less severe than on December 8.

"The third day of the battle, December 12, brought the fourth air raid and the first surface attack.

"As dawn broke, enemy warships started pumping shells onto the flat, virtually shelterless atoll. There is practically not a natural cover against bombardment on Wake. Except for man-made construction, its surface is bare and inhospitable. As the enemy warships opened fire, their aircraft came over in waves. Nevertheless Wake's guns replied with such good effect to this doublle attack

http://www.loc.gov/resource/rbpe.002038ja

that a light cruiser and destroyer were sunk. The defenders also had the satisfaction of chalking up a total of six enemy pllanes destroyed to and including this third day of the battle.

"The effectiveness of the Wake shore batteries, demonstrated by the sinking of two warships, evidently impressed the enemy, for although on that day two transports with escort cruisers and destroyers were sighted, they made no effort to land troops. They held off beyond the range of shore batteries. The purpose of this delay soon was evident. Eighteen planes, making the fifth raid of the battle, appeared from the southwest. As in this day's earlier action, the enemy was badly worsted. Although his bombs did no damage beyond further pulverizing beaches, two of his planes were shot down. Terse official dispatches made no mention of the garrison's feelings, but the results of the blows exchanged December 10 must have been encouraging. And after almost constant action for three days the Marines still had three planes. They lost only one out of the four with which they started the battle, eight having been destroyed on the ground, out of the original force of 12.

"December 11 was another bright day in the defense of Wake. Toward dawn a four-engined enemy seaplane attacked. Marine flyers were ready for it and promptly shot it down. Meanwhile, the convoy reappeared and defending flyers attacked this, severely damaging one of its vessels. A submarine, which was discovered, was attacked with bombs and sunk.

"The enemy did not appear at Wake December 12.

"In early morning of December 13, attacking by moonlight, large four-engined bombers came over the island. They were held off sufficiently by anti-aircraft fire to prevent damage although bombs dropped.

"December 14 was not so heartening. Nearly 50 enemy medium bombers came over in a succession of waves, the heaviest onslaught of the battle. Anti-aircraft and planes brought down three and damaged several others. But of the Marines' three planes, one was destroyed on the ground and another washed out, landing in damaged condition although the pilot escaped.

"The Japanese used incendiary bullets and bombs in this raid and caused heavy damage. By pattern bombing they were able to cover much of the island areas with such large numbers of planes. When the raid was over the Marine defenders had one plane left in service.

"How the Marines were able to patch up another plane in the space of a few hours on the blacked out island with wrecked facilities may never be known. But when daylight of the 15th came the Marines again had two planes.

---

http://www.loc.gov/resource/rbpe.002038ja

"During the night the ninth raid was made but no serious damage was done.

"On the 16th more than 25 bombers raided the island and again in the early evening of the 17th. By now practically every installation on the island was heavily damaged. The storehouse with spare parts and other material was gone, burned to the ground. The machine shop and blacksmith shop were wiped out. Frames of some of the buildings were standing but the roofs and walls were badly damaged.

"On December 18 a heavy force of bombers, apparently medium class two-engined craft which had carried out most of the raids, again attacked. They dropped heavy bombs which caused severe damage to buildings left standing.

"Next day there was no raid, but on the 20th large numbers of dive bombers, apparently operating from a carrier, attacked.

"On the 21st the enemy withheld his hand, then came back on the 22nd for the kill. Both land based and carrier operated planes attacked in large force—how large was never reported.

"Among the carrier planes were modern fighters. Nevertheless, against these overwhelming odds, Wake's two planes went up to give battle. Several enemy planes were shot down, but one of the Wake pilots was lost and the second forced down, wounded. Wake had no further air defenses and the enemy closed in rapidly from the sea after that. The island was shelled heavily and continuously, a barrage being laid down, behind which the enemy began a landing attempt.

"Early the morning of December 22 Wake reported in the next to its last dispatch that the enemy was on the island. Then for the first time did the courageous garrison admit the battle was lost, and even then in as gallant a bit of understatement as a brave man ever wrote.

"'The issue is in doubt,' the dispatch related. That was the end. The last report said the enemy had gained a foot-hold and that more ships and a transport were moving in. Even in this final phase the Wake batteries blasted away with great effect. The last phrase of the last dispatch was the statement that two of the enemy destroyers had been disabled. In all, the Wake garrison shot down at least a dozen enemy planes and took a toll of at least five enemy warships—three destroyers, a cruiser and a submarine." LC

Gift The Windsor Press Feb. 16, 1943.

LC

http://www.loc.gov/resource/rbpe.002038ja

The Surrender

On Dec. 23, Wake the Island surrendered to overwhelming Japanese forces. The marines and civilians were all rounded up and bound together with communication wire near the airfield. The next few days before Christmas were hell! Here in 1985, two buddies are sitting on the exact spot. It was very emotional for me when I took this picture. At that time 44 years prior, Robert (Big Mo) Curry said to my dad "John Edward, take a look at that sun, it's the last time you're going to see it." A machine gun was mounted on the back of a truck ready to execute all of them. Suddenly a rain squall hit, and they covered the machine gun with a tarp. Then a Japanese officer came running down the road and called off the execution. It would not look good for them to have killed over a thousand civilians.

It was remarkable how quickly "Big Mo" and my dad found this spot where their lives came so close to ending. It was the first of his two brushes with death that were to happen over the next few weeks. The other was on the Hell Ship – Nita Maru a few weeks later on the way to their first POW camp in China. That story coming up.

Off to Explore Wake Island, Wilkes Island, and Peale Island.

Prior to this reunion trip, I made personal friends with Col. Art Poindexter. We found that we lived very close to each other in Huntington Beach, CA. He invited me to his house for a visit. Immediately it was discovered that we both had a fondness for Manhattans. He also liked cigars, so naturally, I did partake. Art was a Second Lieutenant at the time of the battle. He retired from the marine corps in 1962. Art said to me, before departing, that I should accompany him out to Wilkes where he led a vicious counterattack against the invading Japanese. So, Art and I, and 3-4 of his troops headed out to Wilkes. Art said to me on the way, "I think of these guys often, of "Red" Terry, "Big Jones" Wright, Terry Polinski, Charlie Holmes, Q.T. Wade, "Peep site" Hassig, and of gunner Gregg and Gunner McKinstry and all the rest." He looked at me and said, "These were gallant marines and civilians." He said continuing, "They laid down their lives and set an example that would reflect the fighting spirit of the Corps throughout the war." It didn't take Art long after arriving on Wilkes to know exactly where they met the Japanese onslaught. "They came in two barges, with many soldiers." Art took off his shoes and waded out into the water. He vigorously demonstrated how that night they did the same thing and lopped hand grenades into the approaching barges. Explosion after explosion and dead Japanese soldiers everywhere. His machine gun platoon finished the rest of them off. Looking back, it was indeed a very graphic account of what happened that night of 22 December. It would be a scene of heroism that would play out, again and again, and into the morning of 23 Dec. When dawn broke that morning, Poindexter said "we had them on the run from our attack. At least we thought we had. We didn't realize how many there were until after the surrender was announced. They came out of the brush to our flank by the hundreds and formed up into platoons. We were stunned by how many there were. It was then we knew the decision to surrender was a sound one."

Here is another account of Poindexter's action on the night of 21 Dec:

Although four machine guns were firing at the barges, tracer ricochets made it apparent that the .30-caliber bullets were not penetrating. A moment later, both barges backed off and attempted to nose in again, as if seeking a break in the reef. Not meeting with success, and still being peppered by machine-gun fire, the Japanese made still another attempt to reach shore, but at no time-probably because of the Marines' fire--did they commence debarkation.

Taking advantage of this momentary stalemate, Lieutenant Poindexter formed two teams of grenadiers to move down to the water's edge and lob hand grenades at or into the barges. One team consisted of himself and Boatswain's Mate First Class James E. Barnes, USN, while the other consisted of Mess Sgt. Gerald Carr, and a civilian, R.R. Rutledge, who had served as an Army officer in France during the previous war. While the machine guns suspended fire, the grenadiers attacked, meeting with partial success when Boatswain's Mate Barnes was able to place at least one grenade inside a barge just as the enemy debarkation commenced, inflicting heavy casualties.

I remained friends with Art for many years after. He also went with us on the 1988 reunion trip. Art also served in the Korean War. He passed away in Jan. 2000 at the age of 82. He is buried at Arlington National Cemetery.

On the way back to Wake, we stopped at the POW Rock. We met up with a few other survivors. I could see the emotions in their eyes as they stood quietly and stared at the rock. Now knowing the full story of what happened, their comments were of sadness and almost disbelief that one of their own was able to have carved those words onto the rock. Marine "Chick" Bamford sits on the rock.

I must tell the story of Robert "Chick" Bamford. From Texarkana, Arkansas. At age 16, he lied about his age and joined the marine corps. In 1939, he went to boot camp in San Diego with most of the other guys from the 1st Defense Battalion. Shortly after arriving on Wake in October of 1941, they discovered he was only 16. This did not sit too well with Devereux. So, he made him his "Orderly". Wherever Devereux went Chick was not far behind. When Chick arrived back to Texarkana in October of 1945, he had a chest full of medals, a war hero, but still not old enough to buy a legal drink or to vote. Chick was, to say the least, a real character. I think of him often as I do all my dad's close marine buddies.

Marines George Robinson, Robert (Chick) Bamford, Mike Economou

Mike Economou looking at a Japanese bunker, most likely built by the civilians kept on Wake after the surrender.

I immediately found it amazing that there were so many ruins left over from the war. Unfortunately, much of it crumbling and in bad shape. Nonetheless, you could tell that something significant had happened here. Terrible typhoons and climate conditions have taken a toll on the Island. Another amazing thing to me was how the survivors, both the marines and civilians, were able to acclimate themselves very quickly. They knew and remembered what they did and where they were. It was a constant mass of storytelling. All of us were thrilled listening to their stories. Some of them we had heard before 😊. Fortunate for us we were there with them, where it happened.

Devereux's command center on Wake Island.

Pearsall, Curry, Bamford, (civilian) Generator (nickname) at the Singapore gun on Peale Island. The Japanese brought this gun to Wake from captured Singapore after the surrender.

Looking back to the beginning of the reunion trip, it was remarkable to see how the marines and civilians recognized each other so quickly. Many years had passed, and the two groups always held separate reunions. At the banquet on the first night of the reunion in Honolulu, my dad recognized one of the civilians and shouted out "Generator" (I can't remember his real name). Generator replied "Swede", and hugs were exchanged. Turns out "Generator" helped my dad operate and fix one of the 3-inch guns on Peale Island. They both were familiar with them. At night they would move positions, so the Japanese bombers didn't know where they were from the previous day's bombing runs. Eventually, the raids exacted a toll on the working generators used to fire and aim the gun. They both would try to repair them as best as they could. As their story goes the generators finally became non-operational due to bombing damage. We were out on Peale Island that day with a group of marines and civilians accompanied by a couple of reporters and a TV crew. My dad and Generator were telling their story with great enthusiasm. One of the reporters asked, "Well then, how did you finally aim that gun without any power?" Dad and Generator laughed and said, "right down the barrel."

There has been much said and discussed about the involvement of the civilians in defending the Island. I can say unequivocally that the civilians played an effective heroic role in all aspects of the defense. I never heard of any marine (ever) dispute this fact. On the other hand, you only heard tremendous amounts of praise coming from marine officers and enlisted. I know this to be a fact as I heard it myself. The civilians laid down their lives just as the marines. Many later would be recognized for their bravery. Many would not survive the battle or their ordeals in POW camps. I was so proud that this was happening.

One of the first things brought up and discussed while on Wake was there is no memorial to the civilians. Marine – yes, Japanese – yes, civilians – no. Fittingly so, the civilian group decided to start their own temporary memorial until a proper one could be built and sent to the Island. The two photos below are the exact beginnings of that memorial. It also marked the first discussions about returning to Wake to dedicate the new permanent memorial after it arrives. This then became a dream, and a mission, for the civilians. Guess what? Some dreams come true and this one did in a big way 😊! More to be told! Next chapter.

Walking the beaches of Wake explaining what happened on Dec. 8th, 1941

My dad found the spot where they were held after the surrender.

At the Singapore gun on Peale Island – Pearsall, Bamford

Left to right – Jim Bamford (brother), Chick Bamford, George Robinson, Mile Economou

Standing next to a 3-inch gun that they manned on Peale Island

Curry, Poindexter, Pearsall

A 3-inch antiaircraft gun on Wake belonging to the USMC 1st Marine Defense Battalion (also operated by the occupying Japanese garrison).

1st DEFENSE BN.

WAKE ISLAND

W

Below is a copy of the first Presidential Unit Citation issued during World War II.

THE WHITE HOUSE
WASHINGTON

5 January 1942

Citation by

THE PRESIDENT OF THE UNITED STATES

of

The Wake detachment of the 1st Defense Battalion, U. S. Marine Corps, under command of Major James P. S. Devereux, U. S. Marines

and

Marine Fighting Squadron 211 of Marine Aircraft Group 21, under command of Major Paul A. Putnam, U. S. Marines

"The courageous conduct of the officers and men of these units, who defended Wake Island against an overwhelming superiority of enemy air, sea, and land attacks from December 8 to 22, 1941, has been noted with admiration by their fellow countrymen and the civilized world, and will not be forgotten so long as gallantry and heroism are respected and honored. These units are commended for their devotion to duty and splendid conduct at their battle stations under most adverse conditions. With limited defensive means against attacks in great force, they manned their shore installations and flew their aircraft so well that five enemy warships were either sunk or severely damaged, many hostile planes shot down, and an unknown number of land troops destroyed."

Franklin D Roosevelt

The marines and civilians loved the Pan Am Clippers. It was really their only access to the outside world. They loved watching clippers land in the lagoon and offload passengers at the hotel. Many of the Pan Am employees were killed when the hotel was destroyed in the first bombing raid on December 8. The PAA Clipper story is below.

Pan Am's founder, Juan Trippe, discovered Wake Island on a map he came upon in the New York Public Library while looking for a navigable route for his growing airline to traverse the Pacific. Wake, comprised of three islands in a hairpin shape, was deserted, with no vegetation and no fresh water, surrounded by a reef, with no coves or harbors, just a central lagoon rife with coral, useless to anyone.

But it was halfway between Midway and Guam, well suited to the range of his new trans-ocean flying boats, and for a short period of about ten years, Wake would prove to be one of the most strategically important places in the world. Pan Am was there first.

And so, in 1935, Pan Am erected a modular 48-room hotel there for transiting passengers, and four tall radio antennas for the new long-range radio direction-finding navigation system devised by Pan Am's communications engineer Hugo Leuteritz that allowed the flying boats to find this tiny island in the middle of nowhere. A crew of mainly Columbia University students blasted away the coral in the lagoon, allowing for the flying boats to land inside, and soon after Trippe obtained landing rights from the U.S. Government. Pan Am's first survey flight arrived that summer, paving the way for the Clippers to make their transpacific runs that continued to Guam, Manila, and eventually Hong Kong.

From my friend John Luetich, Director of Curation and Historian at the Pan Am Museum in New York City. The story of the Pan Am Clippers is fascinating.

PAN AMERICAN AIR WAYS 9

Pan American Clipper Presses On Into Unknown Pacific

From Aboard the Airliner a Colorful Description Is Relayed of That Pioneer Flight From Midway Island Across the Never-Before-Flown Stretch to Lonely Wake Island

By R. O. D. SULLIVAN
Captain, Pan American Clipper

WAKE ISLAND.—With the arrival of the *Pan American Clipper* here this afternoon 5,200 miles of the "aerial bridge" across the Pacific has been flown, studied, and charted. Ahead, for future engineering flights, only three thousand miles remain to be explored. Regular air service across the ocean from America to the Orient is now but a short step away.

In all of the twenty thousand miles of flying over the Pacific, accomplished on exacting scheduled by the *Pan American Clipper*, the last twelve hundred and fifty mile stretch just completed has been the most interesting to all of us—and the fastest.

On the crossing to Hawaii, winds more favorable than on our previous flights advanced our normal speed and crossing was accomplished in seventeen hours and twenty-two minutes. That it was a new "record" for this distance was an entirely unconscious result. The speed at which we fly is governed by severe regulations and explicit flight orders. Transport flying is never confused with racing on our transport operations and no Pan American pilot expects to set a speed record on any course he flies. The wind, if it is particularly favorable, may do it.

The flights between Honolulu and Midway were easily accomplished within a few minutes of the schedule set either way, with a normal cruising speed of 150 miles an hour. Our latest project, the first to be flown over this section of the Pacific Ocean, was aided by good weather. Our speed per hour averaged 155 miles for the eight hours we were en route from Midway.

On today's flight we got a graphic impression of the true vastness of the Pacific. All our previous crossings between the mainland and Hawaii have been flown at night. Flying well above the clouds, usually, for training in celestial and radio compass navigation, we seldom glimpsed the sea below. On the flights between Honolulu and Midway the seascape is much like our Caribbean route over the lower West Indies with little islands, rocks and reefs, scattered the entire length.

Crimson fire flooded the glassy surface of the ocean as we took off from the shelter of the Midway base at dawn this morning. Beyond Kure Island, however, scarcely forty miles from Midway, we saw nothing but water. No land, no rocks, no ships. Only an occasional school of porpoises or dolphins interrupted the unbroken expanse of glittering sea that stretched, endless, to our circular horizon. Hour after hour that horizon remained unchanged. We all experienced a distinct sensation.

In an hour we crossed the international date line, changing our time from today to tomorrow. We alternated watches every hour according to our flight routine. Our radio bearings arriving every thirty minutes from both ends of our route and our hourly "fixes" determined by celestial navigation, proved otherwise; but as far as we aboard the "Clipper" were concerned, we had the distinct sensation of being in suspended animation in the center of that ocean vastness for six hours.

Then clouds broke the spell as they rushed by. Real tropic clouds, new, rising higher and higher, like towering battlements of some fairy giant's snow world, like sheer walls across our course, that dissolved into rainbow-shot silver mist as the "Clipper" flashed through. Coming out of these misty baths the sun, sparkling on tiny drops of water, turned the great wing into a brilliantly glittering strip of jewels. Then, we picked up a tiny dark streak in the water far ahead. Finally a miniature contour appeared, then a tiny dot of color—a flag. Wake Island lay dead ahead at 1 o'clock P. M. (8 P. M., E. S. T.)

From 9,000 feet we could easily make out the contour of the atoll. Wake Island, a "V" of dark-matted brush, enclosing a white apron of sand. Wilkes Island, a thousand yards long and half as wide. Peale, slightly longer, but higher. The rising tide was washing over the coral reef at the open end of the U-shaped atoll, spilling into the big blue and green lagoon.

A large strip, for which the mid-ocean jungle had been hacked away, and the sand showing through, glittered in the bright sunlight, making a fine landmark. As we came closer we could make out the buildings, red roofs, windmills, the radio towers—finally a group of tiny figures near the landing float, bobbing up and down, waving. Two circles of the base, in salute to these hardy pioneers who had isolated themselves, thousands of miles from civilization, to prepare for our coming, and then the "Clipper" settled into the marked channel—eight hours, three minutes from Midway—to the first landing in Wake Island's history.

Tractor-Winch At Pier Building On Peale Island

"Most Heroic Task"—Ferrying the Launch Across the Reef

The First Street in Peaville—Wake Island Group

Hand-Carving a Channel Through Granite-Like Coral

"Tunnel" Through Iron-Wood Jungle

Storage Yards On P.A.A. R.R.

Unloading Float "Number One" On Wake

Below the Pan Am China Clipper sits off the pier (in the lagoon) next to the hotel on Peale Island. Below is the entire Pan Am complex on Peale Island.

On the old Pan Am Ramp – Myself, Chick Bamford, Tom Robinson (son)

What was left of the Pan Am Clipper Pier

THE SEARCH FOR THE SAFE

My dad proudly arrives on Wake Island equipped with a metal detector. Indeed, this was a serious mission. So now late morning, after roaming around the Island and finding the most memorable locations he announces, "It is time to find the safe!" Over the bridge to Peale Island, we go. We had a good size group including many marines from VMA-211. My dad has been waiting for this moment since he buried it on Dec. 23, 1941.

We searched through all the old building foundations looking for the exact spot. "This is it," my dad said. "I can remember these steps and this wall. It's got to be here." Beneath a twisted tree lay four steps leading up to the edge of a crumbling foundation. What once was a large building now is recognized only by leaning walls and concrete posts jutting from the rough coral terrain. These foundations were built by the civilians (many probably meant to be barracks). "I can remember that I buried it about five-feet down he said hopefully. With all the storms that have hit the Island over the last 44 years, I could expect it to be buried 12 feet down or so." With shovels, we dug and dug, not making much progress because of the hard coral rock. The second photo is marine Capt. T.M. Yates. VMA-211 flight officer.

My dad stopped digging and with a great smile on his face says, "Wait, I remember seeing a backhoe back on Wake." His construction background has paid off. We flagged down Commander Westmoreland and asked if someone could bring the backhoe out to Peale. He immediately said, "Well, hell yes." It was quite the sight-seeing that backhoe rumbling through the thick brush on Peale headed to what we hoped to be a history-making moment. The job got much easier, but the disappointment came sooner as well. At the bottom of the 10-foot pit, some Japanese beer and sake bottles were found, vintage World War II. My dad said, "Oh well, I guess I didn't really expect it to be here. The Japanese probably had a big laugh when they stumbled upon it during the war. They probably got drunk and threw the bottles into the pit and thought to themselves, if the Americans ever come back all they will find are these bottles." I still have one of those beer bottles we found. On the bottle "Nippon Brewery." I said, "Come on dad, let's go back to Wake and the Drifters Reef, the safe is not here. OR IS IT??" 😊

NIGHT TWO AT DRIFTERS REEF

Another very memorable evening was underway. The excitement of what everyone had seen and done that day was overwhelming. The families and guests were enthralled with the stories the survivors told. One observation I made was the closeness and cohesiveness that this group displayed to each other. This applied to both marines and civilians. I had felt this in the past and it was certainly on display during this whole trip. The bonds of friendship were forged by destiny. It had been 45 years since their liberation. Yet their memories seemed surprisingly fresh. No greater display of friendship I ever witnessed. A lesson I have learned from my father and these gallant men.

One of the conversations I picked up on was about the Wake Island Relief Operation that was hastily put together in Hawaii on December 14th, 1941. It was designed to resupply the island. However, the operation was recalled, and the task force headed by the aircraft carrier Enterprise returned to Pearl Harbor. After some discussion and initial statements of disappointment that the task force never arrived the survivor's consensus was that it was a good decision as the risks involved were too great. A short account is below.

The situation on Wake had become untenable as time grew on and as more and more forces were massed against it. The naval strategists at Pearl Harbor decided to send out a relief force to resupply Wake with aircraft, ammunition, and men.

The relief operation was assembled on December 14th and dispatched on the 16th. It comprised vessels under the overall command of Rear Admiral Frank J. Fletcher. Given the indecisiveness which ruled in Pearl Harbor and the attitude of the task force commander to play very safe, the progress of the relief task force in the final crucial days was slow, determined by the low speed of the oiler, and was even more delayed because of refueling operations. In the end, the Task Force, only 425 miles and within plane launching distance, was recalled.

As the evening progressed, the conversation turned to the inevitable, and that was their days as POWs. It was like suddenly there was a noticeable mood change in the bar. We have discussed their days in captivity in another chapter but in this case, hearing it directly from so many of them seemed even more fitting. By far the most comments made were about boarding the Nita Maru and the hellish days spent en route to their first POW camps. The boisterous nature of the evening changed as many started recalling their time "spent in hell". Woosung, Kiangwan, Fukuoka, Zentsuji, Sasebo, Soto Dam, Hakodate. Some were pleasant stories of friends and buddies, others of starvation, beatings, sickness, and just trying to survive. You could tell that these conversations brought back some very unpleasant memories. There was a lot of head shaking and statements like "how the hell did we survive?" For the families, like myself, it was a bit painful to hear these stories, many very graphic. We could only think how tough and resilient these guys were.

On a more cheerful note, I kidded Commander Westmoreland about the greatly diminished amount of liquor reserves. He assured me all was ok.

The Last Morning On Wake Island

It was hard to believe, waking up in the morning, that our brief stay on Wake was about to end. Breakfast was a little quieter as all of us were consumed in thoughts of what we had just experienced. A couple of hours before our flight back to Honolulu, the entire group gathered at the Marine Corps Memorial on Peacock Point for a final ceremony. The monument is a concrete obelisk topped with the marine corps emblem. It now became the pivot point of emotion for the group. Members of the reunion group, marines, civilians, and others offered their thoughts to the audience.

"We are proud to be the Wake Island Avengers," said Captain Thomas Yates, an A-4 Skyhawk pilot with VMA-211. "You men leave us a legacy to bear to the Marine Corps and the world. It is your image that we carry on. We are truly proud."

With tears and laughter, hugs and friendly punches, the return to Wake Island ended in a mixed, but pleasant unison. The plane took its time circling the Island one last time. Again, the survivors were glued to the windows. They did not speak, no one did. Their hearts freshly recalled their destiny that seemed to have happened only yesterday.

CHAPTER FOUR:
BACK TO WAKE IN 88

THE STORY OF THE CIVILIAN WORKERS OF WAKE MEMORIAL

On the plane back to Honolulu, I had several discussions with the civilian group about planning another reunion trip back to Wake to specifically dedicate a proper memorial to the civilian construction workers. It was certainly a worthwhile project to undertake. In a very small symbolic way, the group had already begun their memorial. I left it at that. Let us keep in touch and try to make this happen.

For the next year or so, I had occasional conversations with Chal Loveland. He was the head of the civilian survivor's group. He explained that they were trying to raise funds to construct the memorial. Late in 1987, Chal told me that Mrs. Morrison had agreed to fund the construction of the memorial and shipping costs. This was certainly welcome news as now planning for the trip could begin. The major item pending was the date. The biggest factors were:

1. When would the memorial be finished and shipped?
2. Proper lead time is needed to make sure enough people sign up and pay to join the reunion.
3. Pentagon approval is needed.
4. When could Wake again accommodate 250 guests at one time?
5. Finally, the availability of the Hawaiian Airlines aircraft.

One date was set, but one or so of the above factors did not work out. I talked with Mrs. Morrison a couple of times, and she assured me the memorial would be ready when we could set the new dates. Finally, all the pieces came together, and the date was set for June of 1988. This was a big relief on my part. From this point on, the planning became much easier. No major activities were planned in Hawaii prior to the flight to Wake. We wanted to keep the cost down so more could afford to go. Especially considering the main goal of this trip was to get to Wake and dedicate the memorial. It was very interesting to see who was signing up. Many of the civilians and marines who were on the "85" trip decided to go again. Just to name a few, my dad, Big Mo Curry, Chick Bamford, Art Poindexter, Charlie Holmes, and many civilians like Bill Taylor. It would be so good to see them again, plus the new attendees. Of course, during that 2 ½ years span, Poindexter and I shared a few more Manhattans and numerous stories in Huntington Beach.

We had a couple of nice days in Hawaii prior to our departure. After boarding the Hawaiian Air DC-8, we found the exact same flight crew that had been with us in "85". They were absolutely thrilled to accompany us again. Same pilots and same flight attendants. Seniority has advantages. Another wonderful 4 ½-hour flight with similar excitement. This trip had very few scheduled activities except for the memorial dedication. Most of us stayed in the tin huts used by the Vietnamese refugees in 1975. I had to laugh at some of the comments the survivors made about these buildings. "Primitive, but a hell of a lot better than what they had in 1941."

The Air Force again had arranged transportation to take us wherever we wanted to go. Arriving mid-day, it didn't take long for everyone to head out exploring the island. For those of us there in '85", we knew what we had missed or wanted to revisit. I am guessing 2/3 of us were "85" attendees. A few more civilians on this trip. This was their trip, and I wanted to be very special for them. The significant contribution of the Wake Island civilians had been overlooked for too long. They had laid down their lives for their country and equally suffered in POW camps. The construction, delivery, and dedication of the monument was a very important endeavor undertaken by the Workers of Wake community. I was ecstatic to be a part of it. The marines offered tremendous support. This was an enjoyable trip for me. Gone were the pressures of making sure all went on time and as planned.

The first night, and a prior foregone conclusion, after dinner, everyone headed for the Drifters Reef. I make a note here that the support contract has changed since we were last there. In "85," there were Filipino workers staffing many of the non-military functions. Now the support staff was from Thailand. In any case, both did a superb job taking care of us.

The scene that night at Drifters Reef was only a bit more subdued than 2 ½ years ago. Again, story after story at what they had done defending Wake Island during those 14 days in December of 1941. I just could never tire of listening to them.

Back at the airport earlier that day, I noticed a couple of Hawaiian Airlines flight attendants carrying fishing poles. That certainly perked my interest, especially being an old North Woods fishing guide in my younger years. Subsequently, during the day, I asked one of the staff where to fish. He suggested off the bridge between Wake Island and Peale Island. Well, that particular structure was in front of the Drifters Reef. There were five flight attendants with us, four ladies and one guy. Sitting at the bar with them, I suggested we head out to the bridge and do some fishing. One of the Thai workers went and got us some bait. All stocked up, including a couple of cases of beer, we headed to the bridge. It didn't take long, and the action started. We did catch a lot of fish and, not surprisingly, had a good hangover. I believe we finally called it quits between 2-3 am. We weren't alone, people were still leaving Drifters Reef ☺.

The next day the civilians scheduled the dedication for mid-afternoon. Swimming in the lagoon was on my list. I found a snorkel mask and fins on the beach. I've been fortunate to have snorkeled in some incredible places. Swimming out into the lagoon, it became immediately evident that this was on the top of the list. A plethora of different varieties and sizes of fish. My dad told many stories of swimming and fishing in the lagoon. He was so right. The coral formations were striking. There were also some small sharks that I kept an eye on. I noticed shell casings on the bottom. I dove down and picked up a few, some still unexploded. Later I showed them to Charlie Holmes. He was one of the marine ordinance officers. "I guess," he said, "the Japanese must have had an anti-aircraft battery on the point."

Later in the morning, an Air Force officer asked me if I wanted to go ocean fishing off Wilkes Island. That was an easy decision. Most of the cargo coming by ship to Wake is offloaded onto barges and then brought to a small dock on Wilkes. They use these barges at times as fishing vessels. Off we went with a couple of other guys. As we trolled up and down the shoreline, I could only think how this was the view the Japanese landing forces saw as they approached the Island on 22-23 December 1941. This was certainly not a fishing experience I had experienced before. We did catch a few huge barracuda that fought like hell just like our survivors did some 47 years prior. The Thai workers were delighted to receive them.

Now it was time to head over to the site of the new memorial and its dedication. I was delighted that this was finally happening. It is located near the Marine Memorial and the terminal building on Peacock Point. I noticed it earlier, covered by a tarp, waiting for this moment. All of us gathered there for the big moment of this reunion trip. The tarp was removed, a prayer was said, a wreath was laid. The dedication speeches were given. On behalf of the marines – Charlie Holmes. For the civilians – Chal Loveland and Congressman Ron Packard of California (son of Wake civilian). The pictures below do very well in describing the scene.

HARRY MORRISON

IN MEMORIAM

THIS MOMENT IS DEDICATED TO THE CIVILIAN CONSTRUCTION MEN WHO PARTICIPATED IN THE DEFENSE OF WAKE ISLAND DURING THE JAPANESE INVASION DECEMBER 8-23, 1941, AND PLACED HERE BY THOSE MEN STILL LIVING KNOWN AS THE CIVILIAN SURVIVORS OF WAKE ISLAND.

THEY CAME FROM THE FOUR CORNERS OF OUR NATION FROM ALL WALKS OF LIFE AND WITH VARIED SKILLS UNDER THE DIRECTION OF HARRY MORRISON. THE PACIFIC NAVAL AIR BASE CONTRACTORS WERE BUILDING A BASE FOR THE DEFENSE OF THE PACIFIC WHEN THE JAPANESE ATTACKED. THEIR WORK WAS THE FORERUNNER OF THE FORMATION OF THE CONSTRUCTION BATTALION. THE SEABEES USING THEIR EQUIPMENT AND THE MEAGER SUPPLY OF WEAPONS AVAILABLE TO THEM ALONG WITH STRONG WILLS, FAITH IN GOD, AND ALLEGIANCE TO THEIR CHRISTIAN NATION. THESE MEN FOUGHT ALONGSIDE THE UNDERMANNED MARINES. MANY TO THEIR DEATH. THEY RESISTED THE ENEMY FOR 16 DAYS, A PROUD PART OF AMERICAN HISTORY. ON DECEMBER 23 AGAINST OVERWHELMING ODDS THE GARRISON WAS FORCED TO SURRENDER.

WITH THE EXCEPTION OF 98 MEN HELD ON WAKE AND EXECUTED BY THE ENEMY WITHOUT CAUSE IN OCTOBER 1945, THOSE SURVIVING THE CONFLICT WERE SHIPPED TO PRISON CAMPS WHERE MANY PERISHED.

NEARLY 40 YEARS LATER THE UNITED STATES GOVERNMENT GRANTED MILITARY RECOGNITION TO THESE CIVILIANS FOR THEIR HEROIC ENDEAVOR

A group of Wake civilians in front of the terminal building

Left – marine – Charlie Holmes

Right – Congressman Ron Packard, California – son of Wake civilian

This could have been the scene from a Japanese landing barge on Dec. 22-23, 1941, headed for Wilkes Island and the waiting marines. Many of them did not survive.

That evening was a final return trip to the Drifters Reef. The mood that evening seemed much more subdued than our previous evenings spent there. The survivors seemed much more relaxed and content. The purpose of their journey was complete. They had proudly dedicated their memorial.

The Hawaiian Airlines crew was back on the bridge fishing. Not for me tonight as I had a more important duty. In the back of my mind, I knew for many, it would be the last time I would see them. My duty was to talk to as many as possible. I wanted to hear their stories for one last time. As any good politician would do, I worked the crowd. One (amongst many) I vividly remember was talking to civilian Bill Taylor. His was a fascinating story worthy of a Hollywood movie. In early 1945 during the transfer of the marines and civilians from Shanghai to Japan, Bill and a couple of others escaped from the train boxcar between Shanghai and Peking. I know for sure one of the guys broke a leg jumping from the train and was recaptured. However, Bill made it across China and over to the Chinese Communists lines. Here he met Mao Zedong or better known as Chairman Mao. From there, he was flown over what they called "The Hump" to India and eventually back to the US. Bill wrote a book in 2007 to share his story of escape. It is called "Rescued By Mao" and is available on amazon.

My dad and his accompanying buddies continued to have the time of their lives, enjoying every last minute on Wake. They knew it would be their last. As I mentioned before, the comradery between the military and civilian Defenders of Wake Island was now officially and forever cemented in history. I was so proud to have been a part of it.

We departed Wake the next morning. It was very similar to the departure two years prior. Most headed to the terminal gift shop for last-minute items. After take-off, the plane again circled the Island. It was noticeably quiet. Some had tears but shortly turned to smiles. For the survivors, it was a time of reflection, a feeling of accomplishment and pride. I felt a bit sad, knowing that, for most, I would not see them again. These guys had been a huge part of my life for the past four years. It was one of the most memorable and remarkable parts of my life. I wanted to give something to them. I wanted to make my dad proud. I can now only look back with a feeling of great success. I will never forget them for as long as I live.

CHAPTER FIVE:
THE HELL SHIP – NITA MARU

The Nita Maru September 27, 1946

John Edward Pearsall

"On December 23, 1941, Wake Island was surrendered to the Japanese with the Marines, Civilian Workers, and other service personnel. For one month from this date, we were held prisoner on the Island. We were enclosed in an improvised stockade.

On January 12, we sighted a large liner, which anchored off the Island. The civilians spread the rumor that it was a Portuguese ship and that it had come to eradicate them. But these rumors were unconfirmed when we read the Page of Orders given to each Prisoner. The next morning, we were aroused by the Japanese to prepare to embark. We were taken by motor launch two miles in rough waters to the ship.

I read the name on the ship, Nita Maru, and remembered reading that this ship had been a Luxury Liner traveling between California and Japan. By hand motions, we were ordered to climb aboard.

As I climbed aboard the Jacobs ladder and over the rail, a Japanese soldier using his rifle as a baseball bat and me as the ball sent me into a hold. It was the start of a 14-day discomfort, bearing punishments and starvation. Our diet was of gruel served twice daily and one dipper of water with each meal. Some days we were given a small fish. On the first day, we threw away the heads, bones, and insides. The second time we had fish, not a head was thrown away.

We were forced to lie on the deck of the hold, and we could only get up at mealtime and when nature called. I went 20 days without a bowel movement. The Marine and Naval officers were confined in a large room above our hold, being a little handier to the Japanese guards. They were beaten more often.

One day some Japanese guards came down into the hold and started poking different men and ordering them to get up. I was poked, but because I was so severely beaten, I could not get up. They took the man lying next to me. None of them returned. We did not know until after the war what happened to them.

We were taken from Shanghai down the river to Woo Sung. We disembarked, and I had never seen a ghastlier-looking group. During the next four years of imprisonment, we would hear rumors of the Nita Maru sinking. At our lowest morale, it was always a morale booster to hear that some ill had befallen the bat-swinging crew of the ship.

On September 16, 1945, we were liberated, and one of our first questions was, "Have you heard what happened to the Nita?" Sometime later, we learned that the Nita Maru had been sunk by an American submarine in 1943 off the China coast. To us, victory was complete."

Beatings on the "Hell Ship" – Nita Maru

Each prisoner was given these orders before embarking on the ship.

Commander of the Prisoner Escort
Navy of the Great Japanese Empire

REGULATIONS FOR PRISONERS

1. The prisoners disobeying the following orders will be punished with immediate death:

a. Those disobeying orders and instructions.
b. Those showing a motion of antagonism and raising a sign of opposition.
c. Those disordering the regulations by individualism, egoism, thinking only about yourself, rushing for your own goods.
d. Those talking without permission and raising loud voices.
e. Those walking and moving without order.
f. Those carrying unnecessary baggage in embarking.
g. those resisting mutually.
h. Those touching the boat's materials, wires, electric lights, tools, switches, etc.
i. Those climbing ladder without order.
j. Those showing action of running away from the room or boat.
k. Those trying to take more meal than given to them.
l. Those using more than two blankets.

2. Since the boat is not well equipped and inside being narrow, food being scarce and poor you'll feel uncomfortable during the short time on the boat. Those losing patients and disobeying the regulation will be heavily punished for the reason of not being ....?

3. Be sure to finish your "Nature's Call", evacuate the bowels and urine before embarking.

4. Meals will be given twice a day. One plate only to one prisoner. The prisoners called by the guard will give out the meal quick as possible and honestly. The remaining prisoners will stay in their places quietly and wait for your plate. Those moving from their places reaching for your plate without order will be heavily punished. Same orders will be applied in handling plates after meal.

5. Toilet will be fixed at the four corners of the room. The buckets and cans will be placed. When filled up a guard will appoint a prisoner. The prisoner called will take the buckets to the center of the room. The buckets will be pulled up by the derrick and be thrown away. Toilet papers will be given. Everyone must cooperate to make the room sanitary. Those being careless will be punished.

6. Navy of the Great Japanese Empire will not try to punish you all with death. Those obeying all the rules and regulations, and believing the action and purpose of the Japanese Navy, cooperating with Japan in constructing the "New order of the Great Asia" which lead to the world's peace will be well treated.

The End

Two War Atrocity Trials Under Way in Yokohama

Sailors Accused of Beheading Wake Survivors

YOKOHAMA, JAPAN — (AP) —Two war atrocity trials were under way in Yokohama today, with five Japanese sailors involved in one and two soldiers in the other.

The sailor pleaded innocent before a United States military court on charges involving what are believed to be the Pacific war's earliest atrocities.

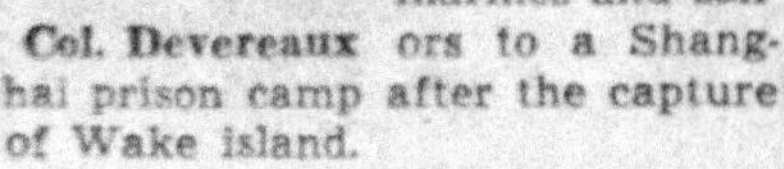

Col. Devereaux

Four defendants are accused of beheading Americans aboard the transport Nitta Maru, which took some 1,500 American marines and sailors to a Shanghai prison camp after the capture of Wake island.

The fifth Japanese is charged with ordering subordinates to bayonet an American sailor aboard the ship.

* * *

Among the prisoners on the voyage was Marine Col. James Devereaux, commander of Wake when it fell to the Japanese after a heroic defense. Trial specifications list the victims as Marine Sgts. Earl R. Hannum and Vincent W. Bailey (addresses unknown).

In the other trial, former Lt. Toshio Toda and former Cpl. Chomatsu Tamura denied they committed atrocities which contribute to the deaths of numerous prisoners of war in a Japanese camp at Toyama.

Their victims, according to the charges, were members of the British army from Australia, India and England.

Civilians on Wake headed to the Nita Maru

National Archives photos
Teeters, Cunningham, some marine officers, and civilians onboard the Nita Maru. Japanese propaganda photos

Chapter Six: The Defenders Of Wake Island In POW Camp

Their Time Spent in Hell

December 23, 1941 – September 16, 1945

Much of this chapter is from research I did on the website of Roger Mansell, who did extensive studies on Allied POWs of the Japanese.

After the surrender, all the military men and the civilians were rounded up by the Japanese and tied down with the leftover abundant communication wire. It was here that all of them escaped execution by a sudden rain squall delaying what they thought would be their last moments. A Japanese officer then appeared and called off the execution. For the next two weeks, this would be their initiation to captivity. No clothes, very little water, and food. My dad would tell the story of them lying at night next to the runway in cold temperatures. One night a marine asked one of the guys lying next to him, "say the lieutenant is kind of cold. Could you pass the tarp you have over to him?" The marine replied, "Tell the lieutenant I am just as cold as him!" Finally, after two weeks, they were moved to the old barracks, now surrounded by barbed wire. I am sure during these days they were wondering, "What in hell is going to happen next!"

As mentioned in my father's account above, they were loaded aboard the Nita Maru on January 12, 1942. Of all the stories my dad, fellow marines, and civilians tell, this was the most horrific experience they faced during their entire time in captivity. Just hearing the name "Nita Maru" sends chills up my spine. My dad spoke of it often with graphic descriptions.

Some officers and civilians were offloaded in Yokohama. The rest and vast majority of them now headed for Shanghai, China. After arrival (Jan. 24, 1942), they were marched a few miles to their camp (Woosung). There they were introduced to the new camp interpreter Col. Ishihara or from that day forward, named "Beast of the East" by the prisoners he flogged, kicked, and abused. It was January, and they were dressed in cotton Khaki. It was bitter cold, with temperatures below freezing. The days and nights became one long misery of wet and cold. The shivering became so prolonged that muscles ached and grew tired. These were very hard days for the survivors

They had not been there only two weeks when the first escape was attempted. Commander Cunningham, Wake construction head Dan Teeters, and a couple of others eluded sentries and dug under the electrified fence. They had a few hours of freedom before they were turned in by local Chinese, who were threatened with execution if they did not turn in escapees. A few days later, they were paraded through the camp with their hands wired behind their backs and with the wire looped up around their necks. This whole show did warn the prisoners not to try to escape again. A couple of the escapees still managed a spirited thumbs-up gesture to tell them they had not been broken. It became apparent that escape, at this point, was not a good idea considering the lack of assistance from the local Chinese. This would change later when they would travel further into the interior of China, where they could expect assistance from the Chinese Communists.

A couple of months after arriving, the original commander Col. Yuse died and was replaced by Col. Otera, a more genial appearing person with a large mustache. Known as Handlebar Hank to the prisoners. His geniality was deceptive, for he was so relaxed that he usually relinquished his command to the unstable whims of Ishihara, "The Beast of the East."

In his book (Wake Island Story), General Devereux writes: "The guards were brutal, stupid, or both. They seemed to delight in every form of abuse, from petty harassment to sadistic torture, and if the camp authority did not actively foster this type of treatment, they did nothing to stop it."

Devereux again would write in his book:

"That was our routine, our way of life for almost four years--except when it was worse. But that is only part of the story of our captivity, the easiest part. Hidden behind the routine, under the surface of life in the prison camp, was fought a war of wills for moral supremacy-an endless struggle, as bitter as it was unspoken, between the captors and the captives. The stakes seemed to me simply this: the main objective of the whole Japanese prison program was to break our spirit, and on our side was a stubborn determination to keep our self-respect, whatever else they took from us. It seems to me that struggle was almost as much a part of the war as the battle we fought on Wake Island."

"Living conditions at Woosung were not particularly good, nor was Japanese treatment of the prisoners gentle. Each morning and evening, the POWs fell out in sections of approximately 36 men for a roll call. Invariably one or more of the men would be slapped or beaten for such minor offenses as not standing at attention or appearing to be inattentive."

I will mention here that in an upcoming chapter, you will see the Astarita Sketches. A Wake civilian drew them while in POW camp and depicted many of the people mentioned here and the conditions they lived under. They are totally amazing!

In December of 1942, the prisoners of Woosung POW Camp (400 Marines of Wake Island, the 203 North China Marines, and some 800 civilians from Wake) were moved to Kiangwan, another suburb of Shanghai. In August 1943, 525 men were shipped to Japan and forced to work in the Japanese war effort.

At Kiangwan, as at Woosung earlier, the POWs continued the dull, uneventful routine of prison camp life. Evening roll call was held at 8:30 pm, and depending upon the season, between 9:00 pm and 11:00 pm, when taps were sounded, the lights went out in the barracks. Then the hungry, weary prisoners lay in the dark, trying to forget the thoughts a man cannot forget, hoping to sleep until the bugle called them out to slave again."

At Kiangwan, Colonel Ashurst agreed to have the officers work on a prison farm. The officers labored for approximately 8 to 10 hours daily, from 7:30 am until 12:00 and then from 1:00 pm to 5:30 pm in the summer. Enlisted prisoners worked about the same hours, but their duties were more onerous. The six-acre farm produced vegetables intended for the prisoners, but the produce was occasionally confiscated by the guards.

The enlisted POWs at Kiangwan worked on a rifle range north of the local military airport from about the beginning of January 1943 to September 1944. This work consisted of burdensome labor, and this, added to their poor diet, resulted in many cases of malnutrition and tuberculosis. In September 1944, the enlisted men were put on other details, such as digging ditches and building emplacements and gasoline storage dumps.

The health of the prisoners at Kiangwan could not by any stretch of the imagination be categorized as good, it was not critical, and the death rate was very low. A primary reason for this condition was that the POWs were not in a tropical climate and the weather, by and large, was not too bad. Overwork and malnutrition, however, contributed to the high incidence of diarrhea, dysentery, tuberculosis, malaria, influenza, and pellagra. During their more than three years at Woosung and Kiangwan, the prisoners received from the United States three shipments of Red Cross food parcels and medical supplies, which undoubtedly sustained the men, although Japanese soldiers pilfered from these shipments and sold the stolen items in Shanghai. My dad told the story about receiving the Red Cross boxes that were sent on the Swedish ship MS Gripsholm. The amazing photo below of the packages being loaded onto the ship.

Red Cross Supplies on Way to Far East

—Acme.

Repatriates returning from Far East internment camps have had one message which resounded above all others; the need of supplies on the part of those left behind. The Gripsholm herself gave one answer to the cry, an answer portrayed pictorially above wherein are seen Red Cross supplies being unloaded at Mormugao for transshipment aboard the Teia Maru for distribution to internees and prisoners of war.

On our reunion trip to Wake, the marines made it very clear that the Devereux's insistence that military discipline is maintained helped them survive the ordeals of POW camp life. I vividly remember these conversations that second night at Drifters Reef.

Colonel Ashurst (North China Marine), the senior officer prisoner, continually protested the treatment the POWs were receiving and attempted to get the Japanese authorities to recognize the Geneva Protocol as the basis on which Woosung should be run but to no avail. A representative of the International Red Cross visited Woosung after the POWs had been there for eight or nine months and managed to arrange for a few shipments of food and supplies to the prisoners. The general attitude of the Japanese captives was that without these Red Cross food and medical parcels, many more prisoners would not have survived the war. This fact was discussed numerous times by the survivors, and unequivocally they agreed that the Red Cross played a major part in the survival.

Ironically, my mother, for over 20 years, would work and retire from the American Red Cross. She was so proud of her work and the fact that the organization had helped save her future husband's life.

PRISON CAMP FIFTY YEARS AGO.

The Christmas of 1944 by Edward Pearsall sent to the Eveleth Scene Newspaper – 1994 (newspaper in Eveleth, MN)

"The mood was solemn. Christmas was near, and we Marines would all spend it together. We were family, and the glue that held us together was uncommon, yet the fourth Christmas as Prisoners of War. So, when Wake Island was overrun by the Japanese after fifteen days of constant bombing, we were all thankful that our lives were saved.

Memories of family times and remembrances of Northern Minnesota pines, and very special memory of Swedish meatballs and lutefisk at Grandmother Nelson's home with all the aromas were as sweet as they could be. It was the last and yet most significant Christmas that we would all be together in our camp outside of Shanghai, China.

On December 23, 1941, when our Island was overrun by the Japanese, the stark reality was that we all were soon going to be executed! Our lives were spared. We were gathered along a gravel road, stripped naked, and marched to the airport. There on Christmas Eve, we lay in the gravel, hands, and legs bound.

From Wake Island, we were transported to China, which would be our home for the next 3 ½ years. These arduous years brought us the Christmas of 1944.

On Christmas eve, 1944, we returned to our barracks after a long, hard day's work as slave laborers. Each one of us was given a new pair of shoes after going barefoot for two years and the best gift we could have had. The 1200 pairs of shoes were a gift from the American Red Cross. They also gave us an eleven-pound Red Cross food box filled with good old American chow, which was a great gift compared to the soup and rice, which had been our steady diet.

The reason the Japanese were so generous with us was that the war was not going well in Germany or in the Pacific. They even allowed some of us to sing Christmas carols. Many a tear was shed that night as we slept on the floor.

On Christmas Day, the Japanese announced that there would be a religious service after no such service for over five years. The minister who greeted us, to our surprise, was Japanese. He had become a Christian as a young boy. He said, "I can see that my people have treated you badly as Prisoners of war and that this terrible war will soon be over, and you will be able to return to your home."

It was months later that they were moved from China through Manchuria and Korea to the Japanese island of Hokkaido."

On August 15th, 1945, after President Truman decided to drop the atomic bomb, the Emperor of Japan decided the war and fighting were hopeless, and he surrendered. We were now hostages, not POWs.

On September 2, 1945, when the peace treaty was signed, we took our camp, disarming the Japanese. You can imagine our surprise when the Japanese soldiers were bowing to us. We then had a flag ceremony and raised our United States flag!

As we went out in the villages near our camp, the Japanese were at first afraid of us. We made friends with the civilians and shared the newly gained wealth that we had received. We made many new friends over the months we were there.

We returned to the good old USA as heroes for the short stand we made against Japan on Wake Island. However, in my own heart, we were far greater heroes for what we had done back on the Island of Hokkaido. We returned home to Minnesota in October 1945, and it made me proud that the Wake Island Marines had abided by those memorable words, "Do onto others, as you would have others do onto you." Throughout the years, my dad loved to tell his POW stories.

By March 1945, the POWs began hearing numerous rumors to the effect that they were to be moved from Kiangwan. Although the prison guards insisted that nothing like that was to take place, the POWs began preparing for a journey by discarding possessions they no longer needed and hoarding food and the like for what might turn out to be a difficult trip. Still, other prisoners began preparations for an escape during the move. One of the Wake prisoners recalled:

On 8 May 1945, the Japanese organized a working party to go into Shanghai to prepare railroad cars for the move of the prisoners. Two Marine Officers volunteered to accompany the working party in the hope that something could be done that would assist in an escape during the trip. It was well known from information gained from recently captured aviators that the 100-

mile stretch of the railroad north of Nanking was virtually in the hands of the Chinese. On arrival at the railroad yard in Shanghai, it was found that the cars to be used were standard Chinese boxcars with sliding doors in the center and windows on either side of the ends. The Japanese instructions were that barbed wire was to be nailed over the windows and barbed wire put up to enclose the ends of the boxcars, leaving a space between the doors free for the guards. It was obvious that the only means of escape would be through the windows and that this would be impossible if within full view of the guards. Also provided by the Japanese for each end of the car was a five-gallon can be used as a toilet during the trip. After considerable discussion with the Japanese, they finally agreed that the Officer's car should provide some privacy for the toilet. This was to be accomplished by removing doors from a nearby Japanese barracks and installing these in the corner of the boxcar, thus enclosing not only the toilet but the window. The barbed wire was carefully put on the window so that it would be easily unhooked. Directly outside of the windows were metal rungs that would provide a ladder to descend prior to jumping to the ground. With this arrangement, it appeared that certainly one person could make an escape, and if the guards were not alert, it was possible that several might escape before the decreased numbers would be noticed."

The main party of 901 prisoners left on 9 May; remaining behind in Shanghai were 25 seriously ill and wounded men. The first leg of the trip, Shanghai to Nanking, approximately 100 miles, took 24 hours. Upon arrival at Nanking, the POWs were taken from the train, marched through the city, and boated to the other side of the Yangtze River, where they reboarded their trains, which had crossed the river empty. On the night of 10-11

May 1945, First Lieutenants John F. Kinney and John A. McAlister were taken prisoner at Wake Island, First Lieutenants Richard M. Huizenga and James D. McBrayer were captured in North China, and Mr. Lewis S. Bishop, a former pilot with the Flying Tigers, escaped from the train. The next night, also on this same train, Wake civilian Bill Taylor and one other made a similar escape and were successful at reaching allied lines.

On 14 May, the prison caravan reached Fengt'ai, slightly west of Peking, where there were fewer facilities, less food, and more miserable conditions than at either Woosung or Kiangwan.

Approximately a month later, on the 19th of June, the POWs began another trip by boxcar, this time to the port of Pusan in Korea, which had an infinitely worse camp than the previous ones the prisoners had been in. After three days here, they were packed into the crowded lower deck of a ferry steamer, which transported them to Honshu, Japan. When unloaded, the POWs again crowded into trains and sent around the island of Honshu via Osaka and Tokyo by train and ferry to the island of Hokkaido, where they were regrouped in various camps in the mining area.

The prisoners had great fear after arriving in Hokkaido that they would be used as pawns between the advancing allied forces and the desperate Japanese. I think these fears were later collaborated by many on both sides.

After arriving on Hokkaido (Hakadate), the officers were separated from the enlisted men and civilians and sent to separate camps. Three officers and Devereux remained with the enlisted men. There they learned that they would work the coal mine. The men, after their long journey from China, were tired, very sick, and malnourished. The camp commander received orders to cut their rations to below starvation levels. Finally, it ended up with the guards telling the prisoners they must feed themselves. It was now nearing the end of the war.

In northern Hokkaido, where Major Devereux and other Woosung prisoners had been taken, it was not known that an atomic bomb had been dropped. Also at this camp were some British soldiers, one of whom cryptically told Devereux that "We're having a bowl of caviar tonight," and another officer was told, "Sir, Joe is in." In this manner, it was learned that Russia had entered the war against Japan. Following this news, the guards began treating the prisoners with kid gloves. On 14 August, all the Japanese in the camp gathered at the main office to listen to a radio broadcast, which appeared to have been an official announcement of some kind. When it was over, all the Japanese appeared stunned; they had just heard that their country had sued for peace. None of the prisoners were told, but they were informed that there would be no need for working parties the following day. All rations were increased, and little by little, the restrictions were relaxed.

Some of the men walked into town. The Japanese bowed to them. They heard a radio broadcast from General Eichelberger advising the POWs to stay put and paint large PW on the roof of their barracks so they could be identified. They went into town and found some yellow paint and painted on the roof of the barracks. Provisions were being made for their repatriation, and food would be dropped by plane.

The first relief supply drops on POW camps in mainland Japan was around August 25, 1945. Only those who were there can really describe the elation and fulfillment of hope... a dream that had truly come true. The sight of those planes dropping supplies was an immense morale booster and would forever be etched in the memories of the POWs. The men and women involved in the search, supply, evacuation, and recovery efforts are among the many unsung heroes of WWII.

Ironically, right before the Japanese surrender, a B-29 had dropped a food supply into the middle of the camp. It was a free-fall drop, and many of the containers broke open, scattering the contents. Many of the extremely malnourished prisoners began feasting on the scattered food. My dad bent over and shoveling a bunch of peaches into his mouth, was shot in the ass by a Japanese guard. Luckily it was not too severe but left an ugly 4-inch scar across his bottom. Long after the war's end, he did finally receive a purple heart.

The incredible picture below is at camp Hakadate 3 at the war’s end. It is a mixture of marines and civilians. Devereux is on the far right.

The survivors of Wake Island—Marines, men of the Merchant Marine, and Army personnel—line up in the prison camp at Hokkaido. The slender, emaciated officer at the extreme right is the author.

One former Wake marine wrote: “It’s not pleasant to recall the humiliation, degradation, and endless days of monotonous drudgery, and looking back on it now, the whole experience has an unreal aspect as though it may have happened to someone else I read about it somewhere. I suppose it's human nature to suppress unpleasant memories, and there are very few bright spots to remember from 44 months in a prison camp.”

On the other hand, VMA commander Paul Putnam wrote:” True there were some tough times and rough times and hungry times for all of us. But there were also times, at least in some camps, when a man could laugh heartily at a truly humorous incident or situation. And there were even times, short times, I grant, when a man could almost enjoy life if only, he would try broader recognition [should be given] to the surprising number of Japanese who went far out of their way, and even risked their own safety, to make things a little better for the prisoners."

From everything that I have read, the Wake Island POWs had the highest survival rate of any group of allied prisoners of Japan. This is a testament to their discipline and perseverance to just survive and go home. It is also said that this was somewhat due to better camp conditions for their 3 ½ years spent in China.

No Wake Island POW story could be without hearing about Sasebo and the Soto Dam.

"Soto Dam has served as a vital water source for Sasebo since its construction during WWII by approximately 265 American civilian construction workers imprisoned by the Japanese after the surrender of Wake Island on Dec. 23, 1941. The group was then transported to Japan to complete construction projects like the dam alongside Japanese laborers. The 53 American POWs and 14 Japanese laborers who died building the dam are memorialized today at the site by a large memorial tower, which was erected by Sasebo City and its citizens in 1956. On prominent display inside the tower is a brass plaque on which their names are engraved."

On September 20, 1942, 200 of the remaining civilians on Wake Island were transported aboard the Hell Ship Tachibana Maru, arriving in Japan on September 30. We know what happened to the remaining 98 left on Wake. They were then taken to Fukuoka near the dam and became slave laborers of the Japanese. Very harsh conditions, malnutrition, and poor housing caused an excessive death rate.

"We arrived at Camp No. 18 on the 14th of October 1942 and stayed there for eighteen months. Most of our fellows died there. We lost thirty-five men in March 1943. We were divided into groups of twenty men. In March 1943, we lost six of our group. They all died of pneumonia. The Japanese worked us terrifically long hours. One time they worked us thirty-six hours without sleep. We worked in a rock quarry". From - Warren O. Rogge, civilian, Watsonville CA

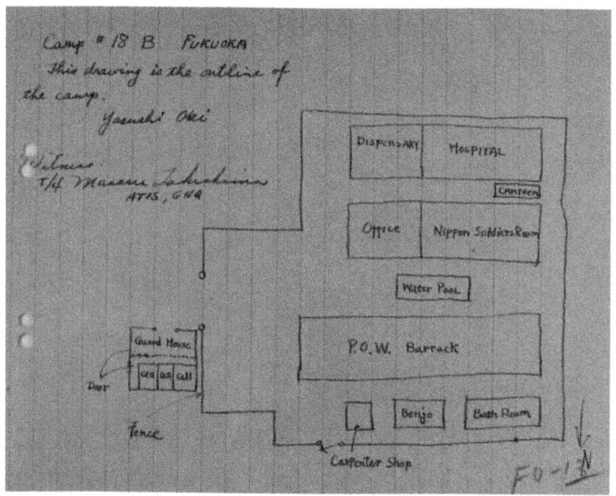

POW Camp 18B, Yunoki, Kyushu, Japan.
Soto Dam where prisoners from POW Camp 18B worked.

"AN INDESCRIBABLE SCENE OF JUBILATION AND EMOTION"

The USS Ozark arrives in San Francisco end of September 1945, carrying a thousand Wake Island Marines and Civilian POWs. My father described sailing under the Golden Gate Bridge as one of the most cherished moments of his life. Sixty busses and ambulances await their arrival. Can you imagine how they felt??

Upon arrival in San Francisco, my father telephoned home. He said, “Dad, this is your son Ed!” My grandfather was so shocked he dropped the phone and collapsed.

They are home now. It was a surreal moment for all of them. Most of them had contracted numerous diseases that would affect them for the rest of their lives.

A welcome home letter from President HarryTruman

THE WHITE HOUSE
WASHINGTON

5 December, 1945.

Dear John E. Pearsall,

It gives me special pleasure to welcome you back to your native shores, and to express, on behalf of the people of the United States, the joy we feel at your deliverance from the hands of the enemy. It is a source of profound satisfaction that our efforts to accomplish your return have been successful.

You have fought valiantly and have suffered greatly. As your Commander in Chief, I take pride in your past achievements and express the thanks of a grateful Nation for your services in combat and your steadfastness while a prisoner of war.

May God grant you happiness and a successful future.

Harry Truman

The below article was from October 5, 1945.

—★—

Pfc. Pearsall Sends Message To Parents

A message from their son, Marine Pfc. John Edward Pearsall, who, they were informed last week, had been liberated from a Japanese prisoner of war camp, was received today by Dr. and Mrs. R. P. Pearsall through the Marine Corps headquarters, Washington, D. C., and Great Lakes, Ill.

"All well. Hope to be home soon," the message said.

The information was augmented by a postal card which the Pearsalls received from Mrs. O. Hendrickson, Duluth, informing them that her son, Russell, who had been in a Jap prison camp had telephoned her Thursday and asked that she inform the Pearsalls that Edward "is fine and say hello."

Mrs. Hendrickson said her son told her the liberees were leaving for home "in a day or so."

—★—

Marine, Russell Henrickson, and my dad were good friends. His wife Betty still resides in Duluth, MN.

Chapter Seven:
The POW Diaries Of John Edward Pearsall

These diaries were written by my father in China between early 1942 through May 1945. These diaries were smuggled out of China to Japan, where they were finally liberated in September of 1945. How he managed to accomplish this is a story in itself. Growing up, I can vividly remember trying to read them, especially considering their frail condition. Each one of the entries tells a unique story as to what was either going on in his mind or in the camp. I will try to explain each one or at least a guess as to what they meant. In the early 1990s, my dad donated the diaries, his letters to/from his parents, and some eating utensils to the Marine Corps Museum in Quantico, VA. They are proudly displayed there today. I want to thank the Museum for digitizing these documents for me and this book. From what I am told, this is one of two diaries that survived the war.

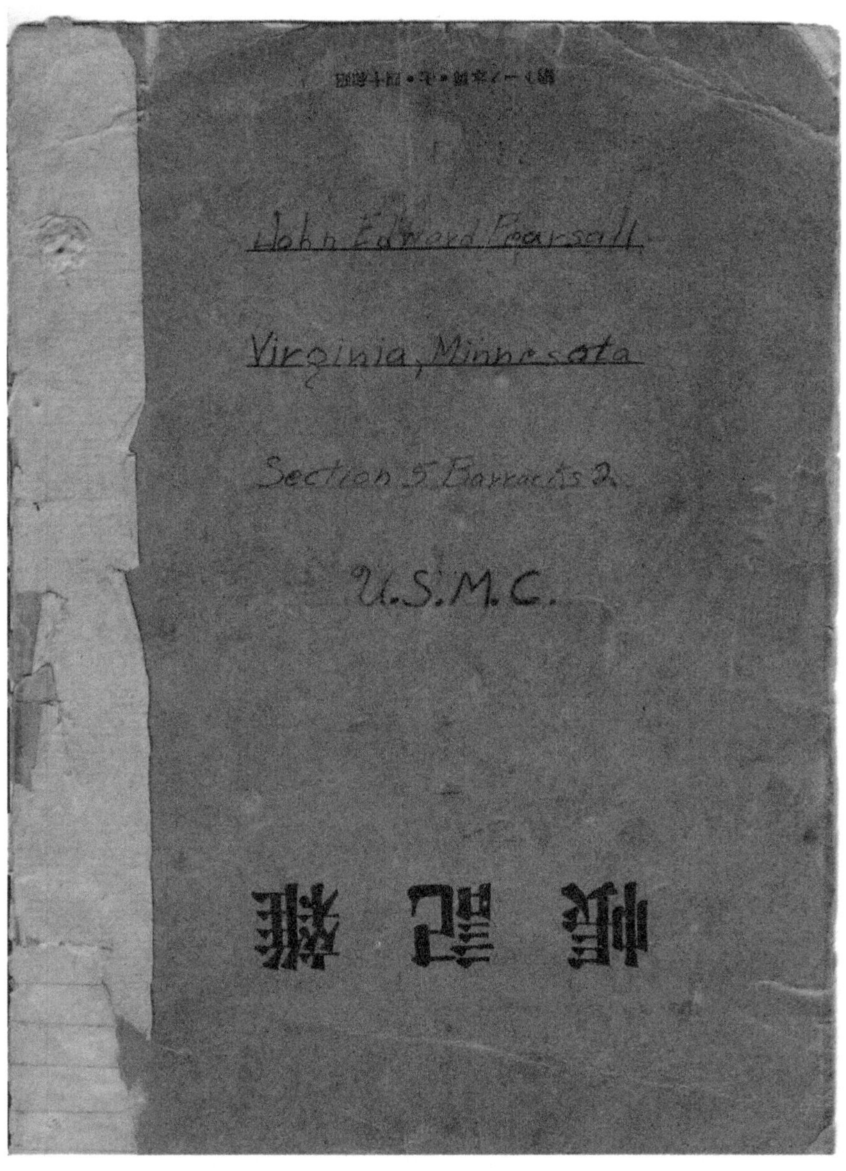

My dad loved his canoe trips into the Boundary Waters Canoe Area of NE, Minnesota. I am sure when he wrote this, he was dreaming of those days.

Camping

1 Tent
1 Cooking set
1 Gas stove
13 Thermos bottles
1 Ice box
Blankets
2 cots
2 matteresse
1 Axe
Spare rope
1 Fireless cooker
1 Dutch oven
1 hunting Knife
2 water buckets
1 wash basin
1 gas Lantern
Electric Wire
First Aid Equipment
Camera + Films
1 FOLDING OVEN
2 " CHAIRS

Spare Parts

1 Fuel pump
6 lights
1 Tire repair Kit
Gaskel material
1 jack
1 pump
1 Toe chain
cutter keys & nuts & Bolts
Fan Belt
grease gun
1 ditributor
1 oil can
1 Troublelight
1 Flashlight
2 rolls tape
1 connecting rod
4 spare plugs
Valve cores
Fuses

Transportation

1 stationwagon

Tools

1 Box tool

1 set Box wrenches

1 " Open End wrenches

1 " socket "

3 hammers

3 screwdrivers

1 Ford rod wrench

2 Pliers

1 Sitecutters

2 cresent wrenches

1 monkey "

1 chisel.

1 Punch

Tire Tools

Valve Box

Hack saws

1 PAIR CHAINS

Diary Of My Last Year 19-42-43
a United States Marine.
Nov. - 42

t rained, no work. Played polker
ll day. The AXIS Powers bought
wo decks of cards for fourhundred
nd fivety weeds.

nice day to go hunting if back
ome. Worked in the bean patch all
ay. Made a hot bread-tomato sand-
witch for a midafternoon snack.

erron & I made my self a hat
for winter. Late chow as there was
o Power. Shave & haircut took
f the rest of the day

School - Test in History which I
didn't know much about. Tryed to
get to the dentist but to much
ten per cent compitition. Was in a
snake game in the evening when
the lights went out. Stood inspection
in the dark.

Road gang - nice walk but the smell
of human excreation being spread is

3- Civilian [illegible] [illegible]
a bunch of tramps. [illegible]
a few yen in ~~[illegible]~~ saw
things all quite [illegible]
for a good while.

4- A cold morning - played
polker. Nazie Smith took
a shower outside with ice
on the ground.

5- Up early in preparation to m[illegible]
Every thing was [illegible] up as [illegible]
A ten mile hike which [illegible]
[illegible] well except for the co[illegible]
New camp has a brick wall
around, built for us. The Ja[illegible]
who left hear certainly [illegible]
a dirty lot. [illegible] all th[illegible]
way though. Put right to [illegible]
cleaning up.

6- Went to work [illegible] [illegible]
[illegible] is in the rampage a[illegible]
We had to move after da[illegible]
lots of fun.

7- Continued are work around cam[illegible]

11- School - Also tried again to see the dentist but again the Ten Per Cent boys won out. Arrile and I made a ten loaf bread bet on Snake till Dec. 25. Some of the boys recieved packages from Stateside.

12- Road gang. Saw a few nice Saguna's pase by. Had a few chink Kids follow us all day after the commander gave them some salamy

13- Friday the 13th - School in the the morning. Rained in the afternoon so we layed around the barracks. I played some polker and lost, also got a mad on so made the same bet with Arrile that I had with snake. Ben. lost heavily in snake so he took 83 of are hands on the next exchange.

14- Missed the road gang - good thing as it was darn cold - worked the day for Dave J. around the water sterilise.

15- Sunday - Saw football game between five & three - Three won the game also the camp championship. Stayed around the rest of the day doing nothing.

16- Power went off sometime during the night, so we had a late breakfeast. Ispection by some Buda Priests. The also had services in are recreation room. Life in prison camp is certainly miserable

17- School - The math is getting stif recieved are papers back in History my grade was 87% Math 92%.

18- Road gang - worked as far out on the road as possible. Life is very discoureging. We have more number of moving again.

19- School - cut Spanish class - got over in snake and paid off what Smi lowed.

20- Road gang - went to work in Truc for a change. Worked on the road in Woosong. The Chinese forced Labor gang working on the docks in Woosu certainly is depressing to see.

21- School - Cut class again to wash cloths share and take a cold shower.

22 - Sunday - Watched football game be tween allstars. Played some ~~ba~~ bas ball awhile.

23 - Road gang went to work in truck again. A long day but the day w nice and warm. This area certain is well occupied by Jeep troot Truck broke down coming home, so got home after dark.

24 - Tryed to see the dentist again w cloths. Were moving again to the do,

25 - Road gang a nice day for a ch Worked next to a Japanese Gesh house. Talked a little with the Lim who were ~~the~~ on the Jap ship was torpedoed.

26 - Layed around the barracks doing nothing. A very lonely Thanks giving - menu - Rice - slum - and a Red Cross Apple.

27 - Road gang - avery cold and miser able day - Had a chance to see Chinks living first hand. Boy am I glad I was born in good old U.S.A.

We were all very glad to get back to the barracks that nite.

28 - Tryed to make a pair of mittons not much success - everyone is busy sewing getting ready for winter & the road gang.

29 - Sunday - The days are getting colder & miserable. The red cross is trying to outfit us in winter cloths ut so far only a few have made t.

Rained during the night so we idnt go to work although the ay turned out fair. Apple & urnover for lunch so we all e a heck of time.

Decmber

Went to work, a very nice ay. All of the sick bay men ad to go out because we miss d Monday

layed around the barracks. ivilians prepared to move to

f barracks we were in the first
night.
It was just a year ago but I'll get
by some how. Itchy racked a few ten
cent officers. The pilots shot down
over Canton passed out a little good
news on how the war was progressing

- Holliday - had a queer dream last
night. May 23, 1929 seamed to be an important date. Worked most of the
day

-Road gang again recieved Red Cross
boxes seven per section Five men
to a box. Boy is that State side
chow ever good. Sat around all
nite eating chocklate rasins etc.

- Stayed in camp to get blood
typing The neddle wasn't to bad
Layed around the barracks in the
afternoon and Watched the officers
Work. Turned tables.

-Road gang - came in that nite
find a Canadian red cross Parcel
... bunks. Ate my candy first

13- Sunday - Worked half a day bank[ing]
up the side of 38 are happy home[s]
plenty of chow for the first t[ime]
since the war began a year
ago. Boy is it ever a good feeling
to have a full gut.

14- Road gang took along a
stateside noon lunch. Still plenty
of chow to eat.

15 - Road gang as usual

16- One day to work around camp.

17- Road gang - recieved another
Canadian red cross box also caps
socks & gum drops from the local
red cross.

18- Road gang we started to st[ay]
in but the Japs changed there
minds. A very cold day. A few thousand
Jap troops left this area in summer
uniform. Feel sorry for the privat[e]
in Nippons army the war & how t[...]

19- One day to work around ca[mp]
[...]

played not so good Worked in the afternoon around camp.

22- Worked around camp getting anxious for Xmas.

23- Stayed in to go to sick bay for my back which is darn sore. Dr. couldn't do much for me.

24- Day before Xmas worked on the canal - went to work in a train walked thru a village very interesting. Suppose to come home early but trains were mixed up. Recieved a box of candy American Red cross box ECC Kit Smokes & chewing for Xmas. Sang Carols till eleven.

25- Awaken by carolers at six. A card from Rose E. Haran of Americans in Shanghai (very nice) A very merry Xmas from what we had last year. Delicious turkey with a few trim-

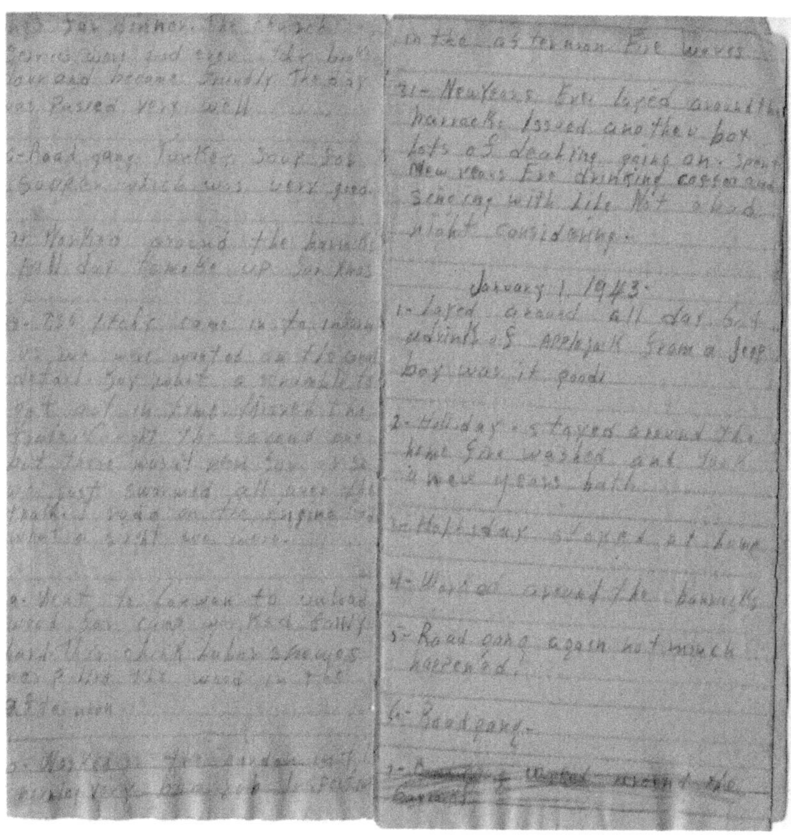

[illegible]

5- Road gang. Turkey soup for supper which was very good.

[illegible]

in the afternoon. Eve [illegible]

31- New Years Eve layed around the
barracks. Issued another box
lots of [illegible] going on. Spent
New Years Eve drinking coffee and
[illegible] with [illegible] Not a bad
night considering.

January 1, 1943.
1- Layed around all day. [illegible]
[illegible] of applejack from a Jeep
boy was it good.

2- Holiday - stayed around the
[illegible] washed and took
a new years bath.

3- Holiday stayed at home

4- Worked around the barracks

5- Road gang again not much
happened.

6- Road gang.

7- [illegible] Worked around the
barracks.

A favorite pastime was poker playing. Here he is keeping track of scores.

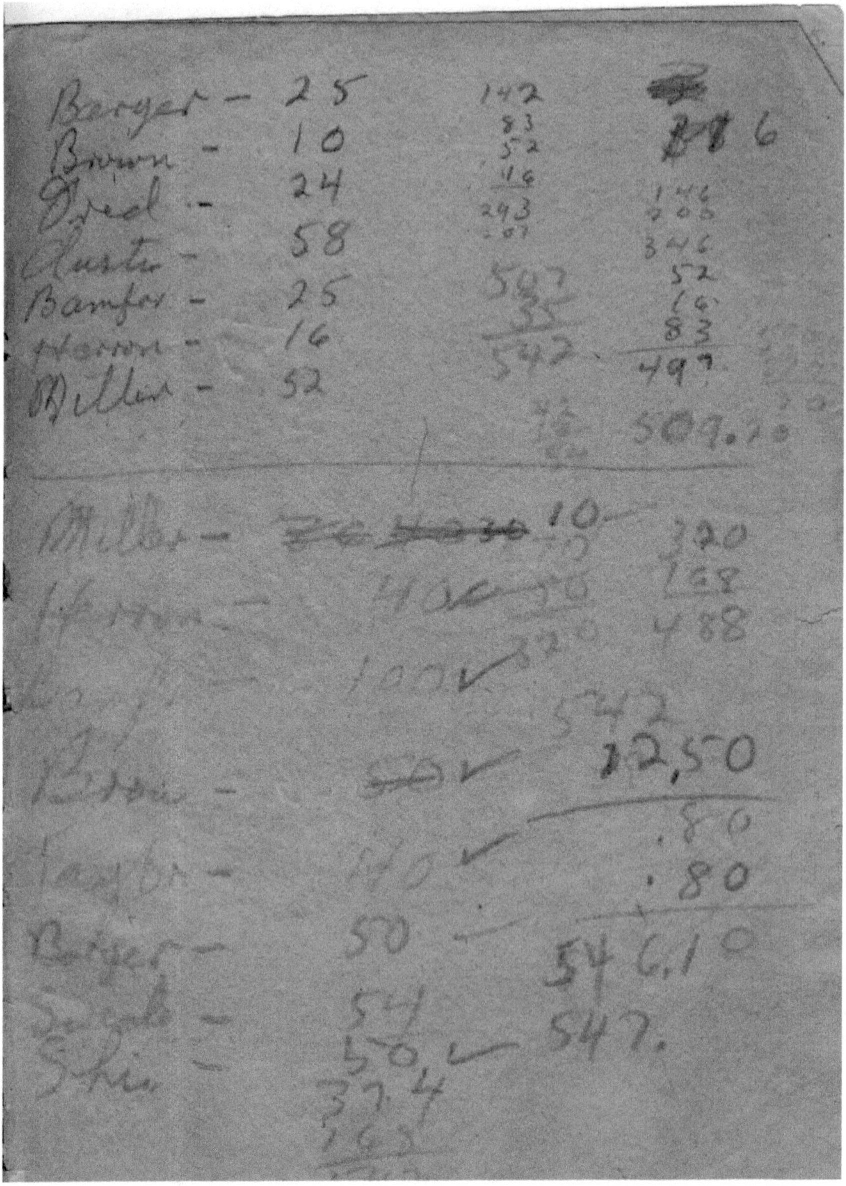

Barger – 25
Brown – 10
Fred – 24
Custer – 58
Bamford – 25
Herron – 16
Miller – 52

Miller – 10
Herron – 40
100
50
40
Barger – 50
54
50
37.4

320
168
488
542
12,50
.80
.80
546.10
547.

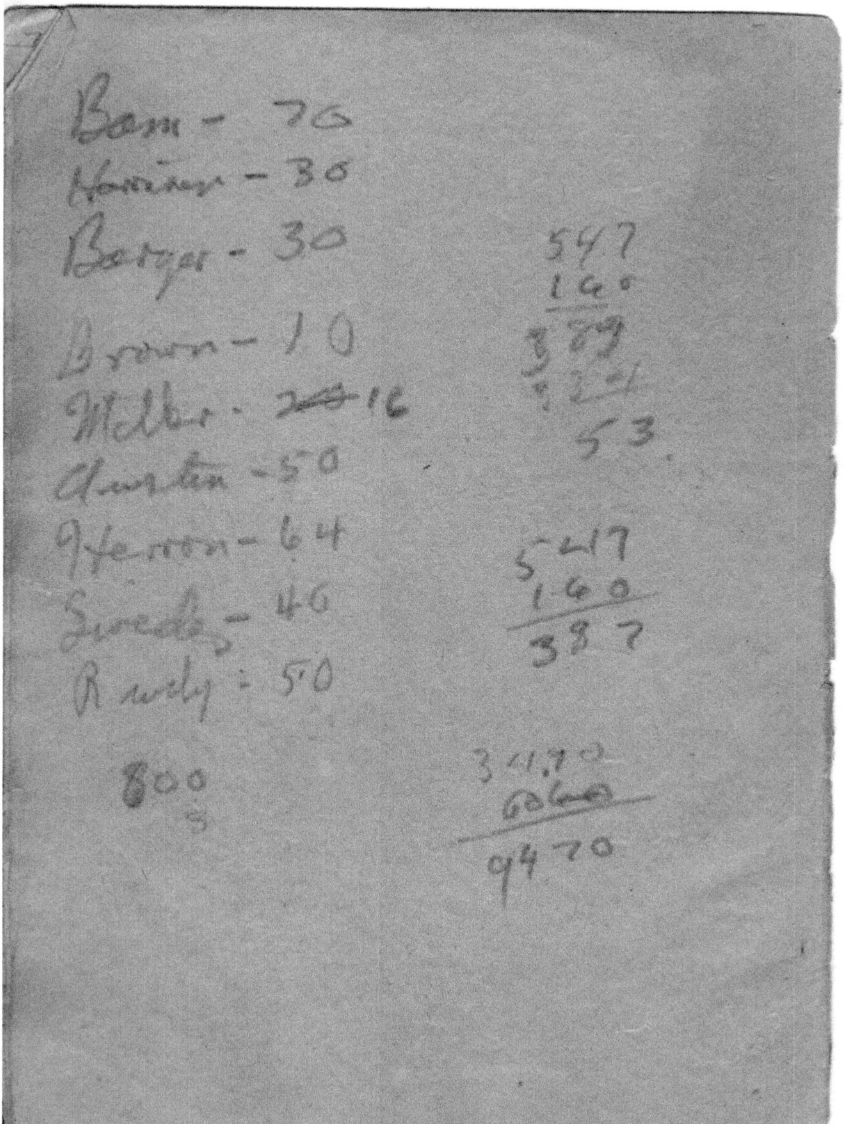

Bam - 76
Harring - 30
Berger - 30
Brown - 10
Miller - ~~20~~ 16
Austin - 50
Heron - 64
Swede - 46
Rudy - 50

800

547
160
53

547
160
387

3470
60
9470

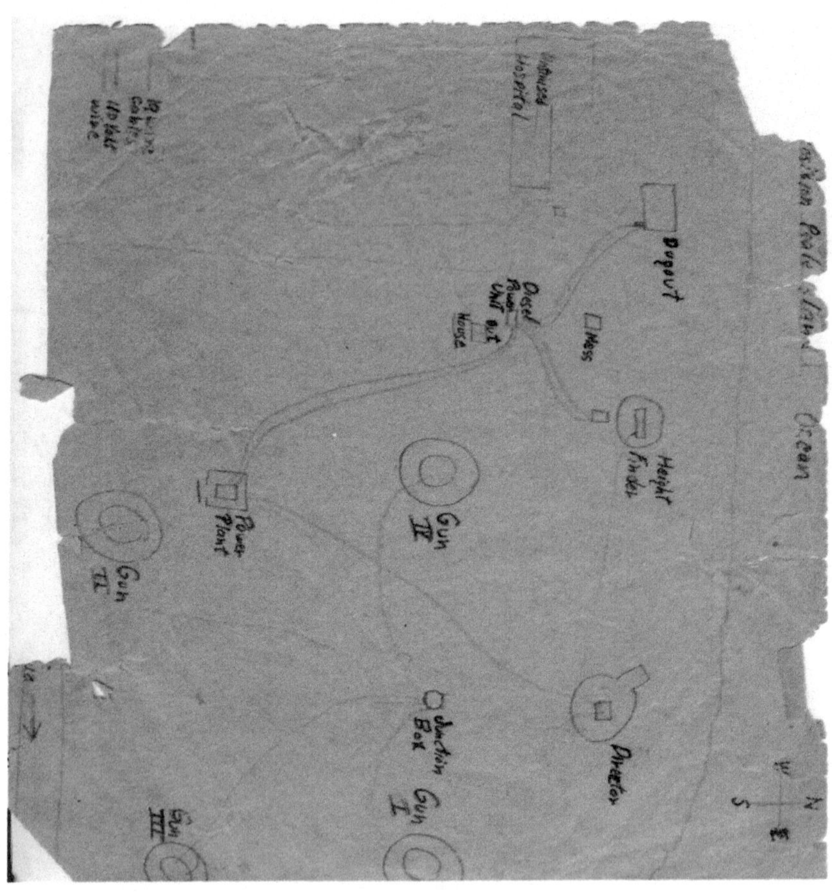

Drawing of his 3-inch gun position on Peale island – 8 -23 December 1941

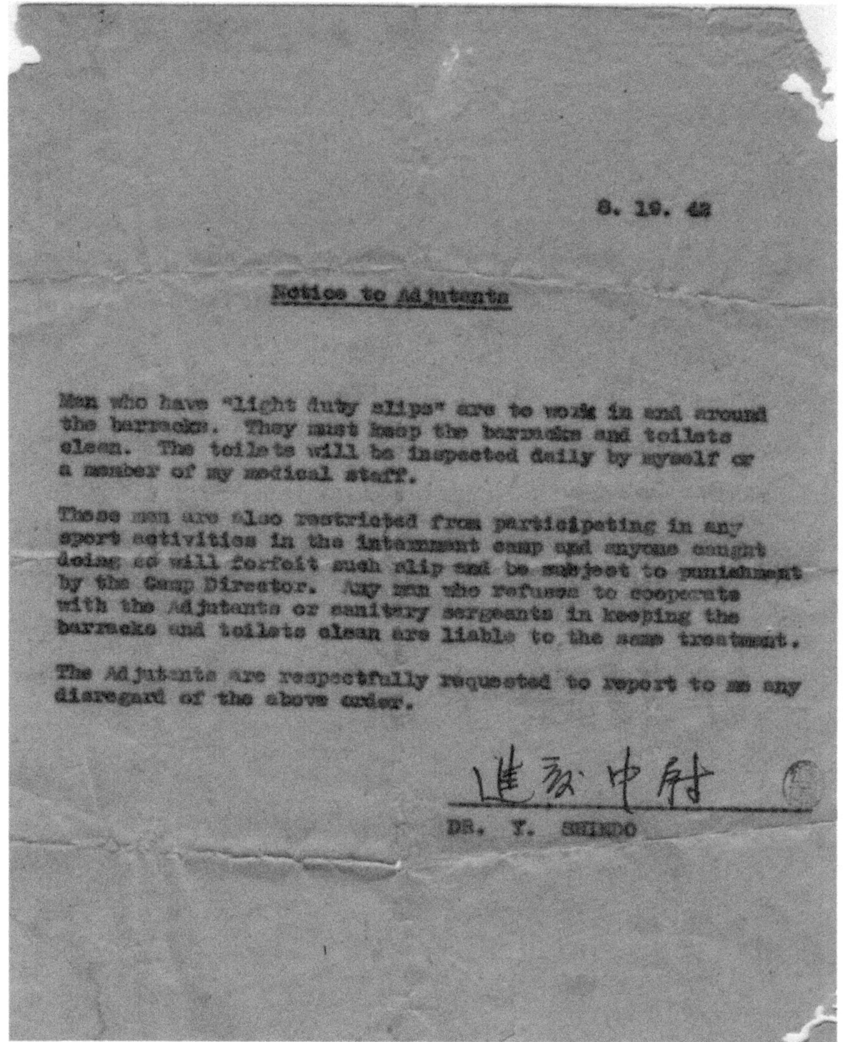

8. 19. 42

Notice to Adjutants

Men who have "light duty slips" are to work in and around the barracks. They must keep the barracks and toilets clean. The toilets will be inspected daily by myself or a member of my medical staff.

These men are also restricted from participating in any sport activities in the internment camp and anyone caught doing so will forfeit such slip and be subject to punishment by the Camp Director. Any man who refuses to cooperate with the Adjutants or sanitary sergeants in keeping the barracks and toilets clean are liable to the same treatment.

The Adjutants are respectfully requested to report to me any disregard of the above order.

進藤中尉

DR. Y. SHINDO

Directions on light duty

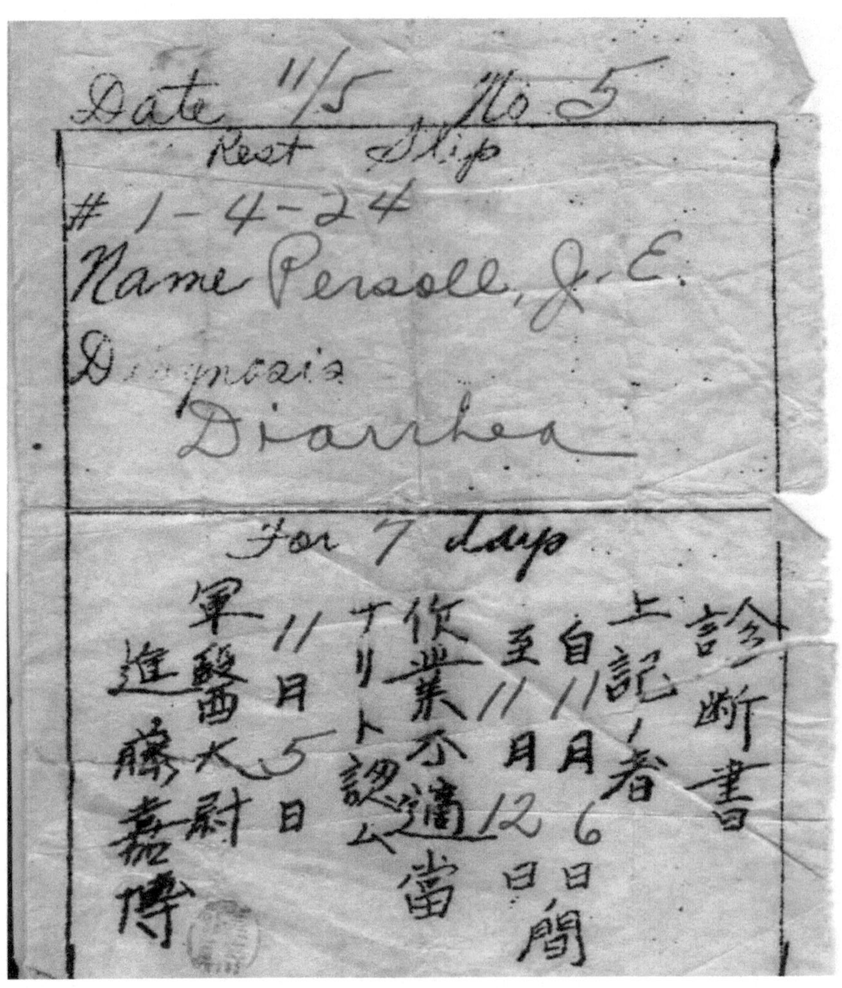

Date 11/5 No 5

Rest Slip

1-4-24

Name Persoll, J. E.

Diagnosis

Diarrhea

For 7 days

診断書

上記ノ者

自11月6日

至11月12日間

作業不適當

ナリト認ム

11月5日

軍醫大尉

進藤嘉傳

Light Duty Slip

CHAPTER EIGHT:
THE ASTARITA SKETCHES

SKETCHED OF POW LIFE BY
JOSEPH J. ASTARITA

Joe Astarita was a civilian worker born in Brooklyn, New York. I haven't been able to find out much about him. Apparently, he never married or had children. He was able to get these sketches out of POW camp rolled up hidden in two Red Cross shaving cream tubes.

They are absolutely remarkable. The sketches tell a story of both Wake Island and their lives as POWs. Fortunate to share them with you!

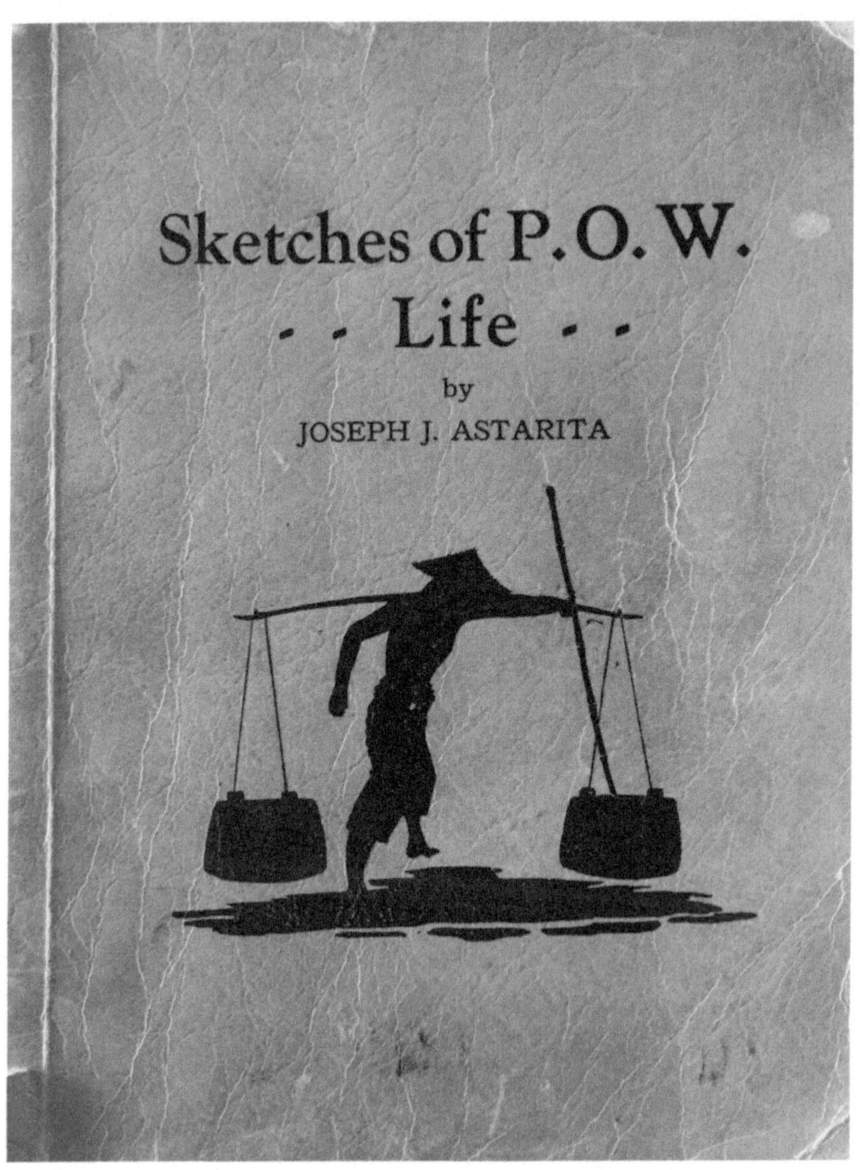
Sketches of P.O.W.
- - Life - -
by
JOSEPH J. ASTARITA

Introduction

THE sketches on the following pages are from real life. Not as they might have occurred but actually as the artist and his fellow prisoners lived them for three years and eight months. They were first sketched under abnormal conditions. In freezing winters, without heat, and the stench of China summers. Constant barrack raids by the Nips, not to mention the forty-four months of perpetual hunger. These were the conditions under which the drawings were made.

THE originals were done on any kind of paper the artist could lay his hands on. To keep them from being discovered by the Nips. the drawings were rolled up and concealed in two empty Red Cross shaving cream tubes. By unwrapping the bottoms of the containers, the sketches were stuffed into the tubes. Re-sealed, they were as light and soft as though the original shaving cream was still in them. Through many a shakedown (searchings) the tubes survived, actually being handled by the Jap officials then thrown back into the small bag which held the artists meager belongings.

IN this manner the sketches traveled from camp to camp as the artist and his fellow prisoners were moved from China to Japan.

TABLE OF CONTENTS

WAKE ISLAND — Just a tiny atoll — but it took a terrific pounding in the early stages of the war. The men defending the island put up a wonderful stand.

Page One

For sixteen days the Japs pounded away at the rock from the air and sea. The Nips were thrown for quite a loss all the way. At lower right is a Japs eye view of our little island.

Page Two

The Pan American Clipper Base was wiped out during the first days of the siege. The Clipper took off shortly after the raid and arrived safely at the Hawaiian Islands.

Page Three

Across the emerald green lagoon from Pan Air, can be seen our large fuel tanks which were also hit early in the war. The fire burned for three days.

Page Four

The Contractors camp was well demolished. Shown above is the Contractors warehouse. Behind and to the left, can be seen the conveyor belts and gravel piles where many of the men were able to take shelter. At the extreme left lies the remnants of the garage and machine shop.

Page Five

Our small Contractors hospital was completely destroyed. Many of the men wounded the first day were in the doomed building when it was hit.

Page Six

Our plane squadron was hit the heaviest. We lost seven in the first raid. The few we had left were without maintenance for the duration. Above can be seen the Gruman fighters after the raid.

Page Seven

During the fighting, two Jap destroyers were heavily hit and set afire. To save the men on board the Jap destroyers rammed our beach where they unloaded their troops.

Page Eight

After our capture on Dec. 23, 1941, we were marched off to the airport. As we trudged along the beach road we could see Jap ships plying around our tiny atoll.

Page Nine

As cattle herded for slaughter, we were brought to the airport. The tired, weary men were kept there for two days in the blazing sun and cold nights. Gasoline tainted water and a bit of stale bread was our fare. On Christmas day we were taken to the barracks which by this time were encircled with barbed wire.

Page Ten

Going out on various work details we were able to smuggle in a bit of food now and then. On Jan. 12, 1942, we piled into Jap landing barges. We were leaving our former peaceful home.

Page Eleven

From the landing barges we could see the grey prison ship on which we were to be taken first to Japan without getting off then on to China. Sixteen days with barred and bolted hatches, sixteen of the worst days of our lives. The artist had been eating unground black pepper seeds and bits of rice mixed in among the dirt in the hold of the ship.

Page Twelve

From barges we boatded the Nita Maru, a former N.Y.K. luxury liner. Lining up in the companion way we were searched from head to foot. Eye glasses were ripped from those who wore them and dashed to the deck."

Page Thirteen

In the hold of the Nita Maru sixteen days of hell were experienced. Beatings. Starvation. From sub-tropical weather to freezing January within forty-eight hours. The shock was terrific. After our debarkation at Woo Sung, China, we had to run all the way to the prison camp about four and a half miles away.

Page Fourteen

Worn out, hungry and weary we were given some wet blankets, some rice and stew. It was just slop but one of the best meals we had. They also brought in hot (tea?) The most welcome thing was sleep.

Page Fifteen

When "come and get it" was sounded chow details would go to the galley. At the right is the tea house. The only safe way to drink China water was to boil it first.

Page Seventeen

The galley was a filthy, smoked-filled room. Flies, rats, mosquitos, etc. The food was cooked by our own men. It was filthy but our cooks cleaned it as best they could.

Page Eighteen

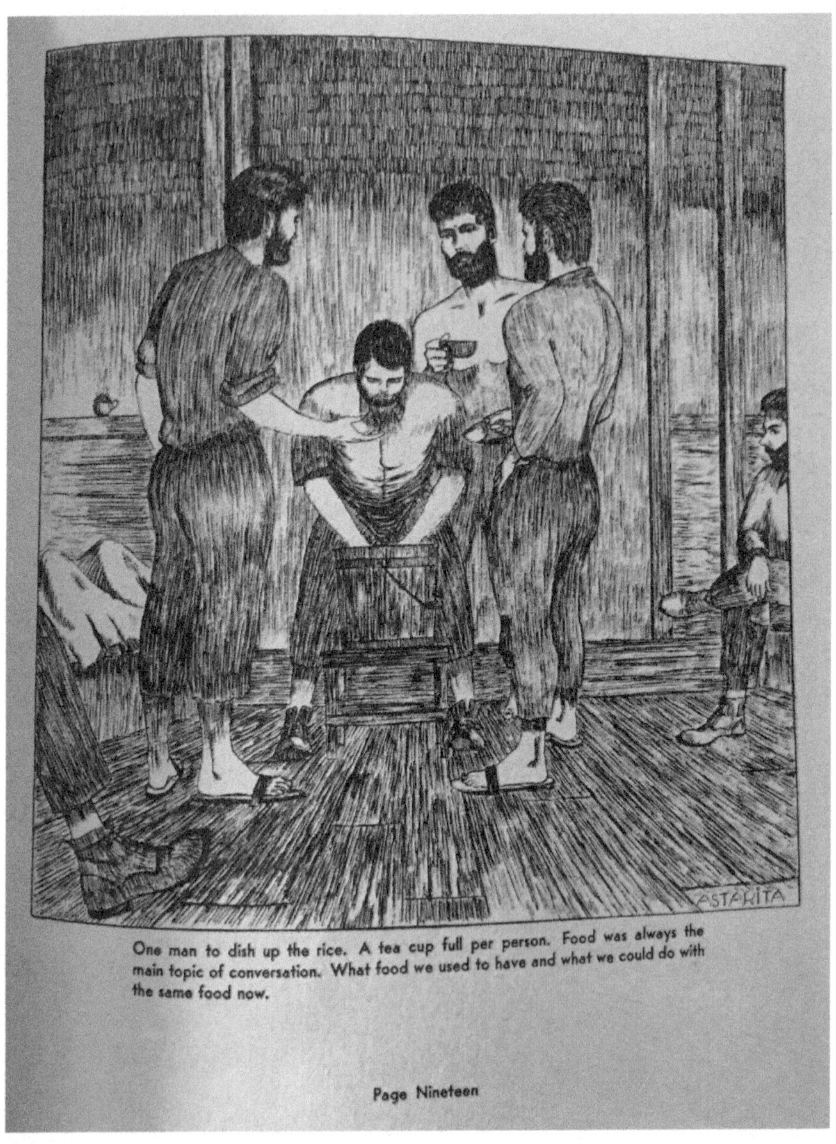

One man to dish up the rice. A tea cup full per person. Food was always the main topic of conversation. What food we used to have and what we could do with the same food now.

Page Nineteen

Extra stew would be divided by sections as was the burnt rice that would be scraped up from the bottoms of the pots.

Page Twenty

The water for the entire camp was piped from this old and leaky tank. Often the pump would break down and we would be without water until the pump was fixed. Our food depended on the water supply. Many a meal was postponed and no rain-checks either.

Page Twenty-One

The same water tank in the winter time. It can get mighty cold in China. In the background can be seen a Jap army radio tower just outside the compound.

Page Twenty-Two

We worked under slave labor conditions. A terrific strain on us. We were all in a state of perpetual hunger and to preform strenuous work under these conditions was sometimes maddening.

Page Twenty-Three

A large project was the Woo Sung Canal which many men will remember. The hard work and freezing weather we had to contend with along with the skimpy amount of food was more than we could bear. Jap guards would stand at points of vantage such as Chinese graves (background) which were placed above the ground.

Page Twenty-Four

While tramping to work one cold morning we could see Jap soldiers torturing a Chinese coolie slave. They would rope the poor devil to a post and pour hot water over his naked body. A broken bottle was tied around his neck. The hot water treatment was given on very cold days.

Page Twenty-Five

The camp Commandant was Col. Yusi, better known as "Useless Yusi" A pesky old goat, always out on the jobs to get the most from us for "Die Nippon." The old man died just before the artist left for Japan. This picture was made just before he died.

Page Twenty-Six

"Useless Yusi's" successor was Col Otera or "Handlebars." ' So named because of his large white mustache. He would strut around camp just happy about the whole thing.

Page Twenty-Seven

One of our first jobs was the old ditch at the Woo Sung prison camp. Above is the mosquito infested canal before we tackled it. The lower picture is the same section after completion. The artist will well remember this project. He was tossed into the Jap guard house without food and was smashed around a bit for refusing to work.

Page Twenty-Eight

One of the largest details was the Mount Fuji project. The big stick was Ishihara (above) better known as the "Screaming Skull." A wild and vicious fanatic. He was head interpreter of the Shanghai camp. Hated by all, he would think nothing of smashing one in the adams apple with his riding crop or beating up our officers. In the background can be seen his pet project "Mt. Fuji."

Page Twenty-Nine

The "Screaming Skull's" sidekick "Handsome Harry" Morasako. Better known as "Mortimer Snerd" number two interpreter. A moronic sort of fellow. Had a mania for taking personal pictures of the folks back home from prisoners mail (when we got it).

Page Thirty

The camp barber shop. Just a small room that would ordinarily hold a few men at a time. It had to accomadate 1700 men. The elder prisoners doing the barbaring and a mighty fine job too for the equipment they had. They used old razors that had to be sharpened on a brick.

Page Thirty-One

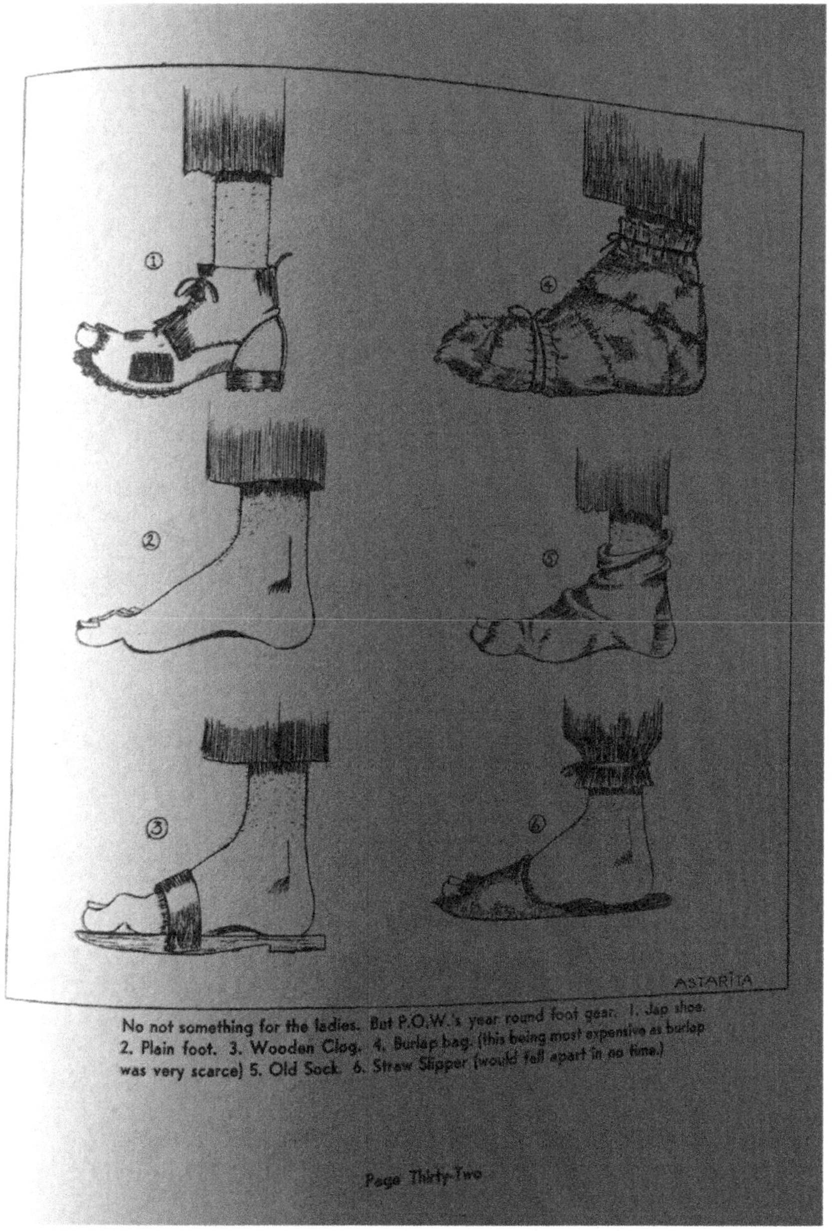

No not something for the ladies. But P.O.W.'s year round foot gear. 1. Jap shoe. 2. Plain foot. 3. Wooden Clog. 4. Burlap bag. (this being most expensive as burlap was very scarce) 5. Old Sock. 6. Straw Slipper (would fall apart in no time.)

Page Thirty-Two

The prison camp from within. -This was called the Kiang Wan camp a short distance from Shanghai. A filthy stinking hole when we moved from Woo Sung. In the foreground can be seen the electrified fence which runs around the prisoners barracks. In the background an eight foot brick wall with another electrified fence on top. Lower right can be seen water pits in case of fire. Jap guard tower upper right, one at each corner. Jap barracks beyond wall.

Page Thirty-Three

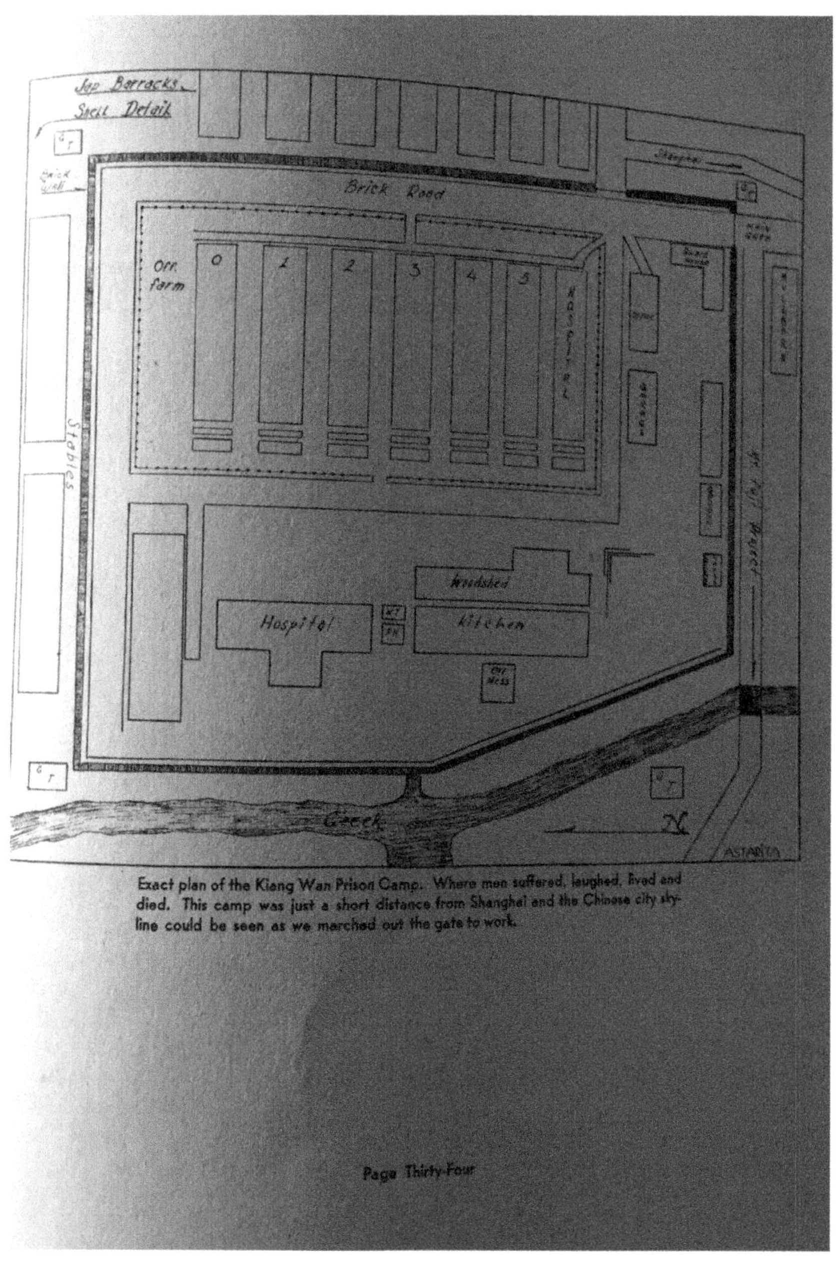

Exact plan of the Kiang Wan Prison Camp. Where men suffered, laughed, lived and died. This camp was just a short distance from Shanghai and the Chinese city sky-line could be seen as we marched out the gate to work.

Page Thirty-Four

One of the pet projects of the Japs was the shell polishing detail. This work was despised by all the men yet forced to continue. After polishing each shell we would bang it up as much as possible before turning it in.

Page Thirty-Five

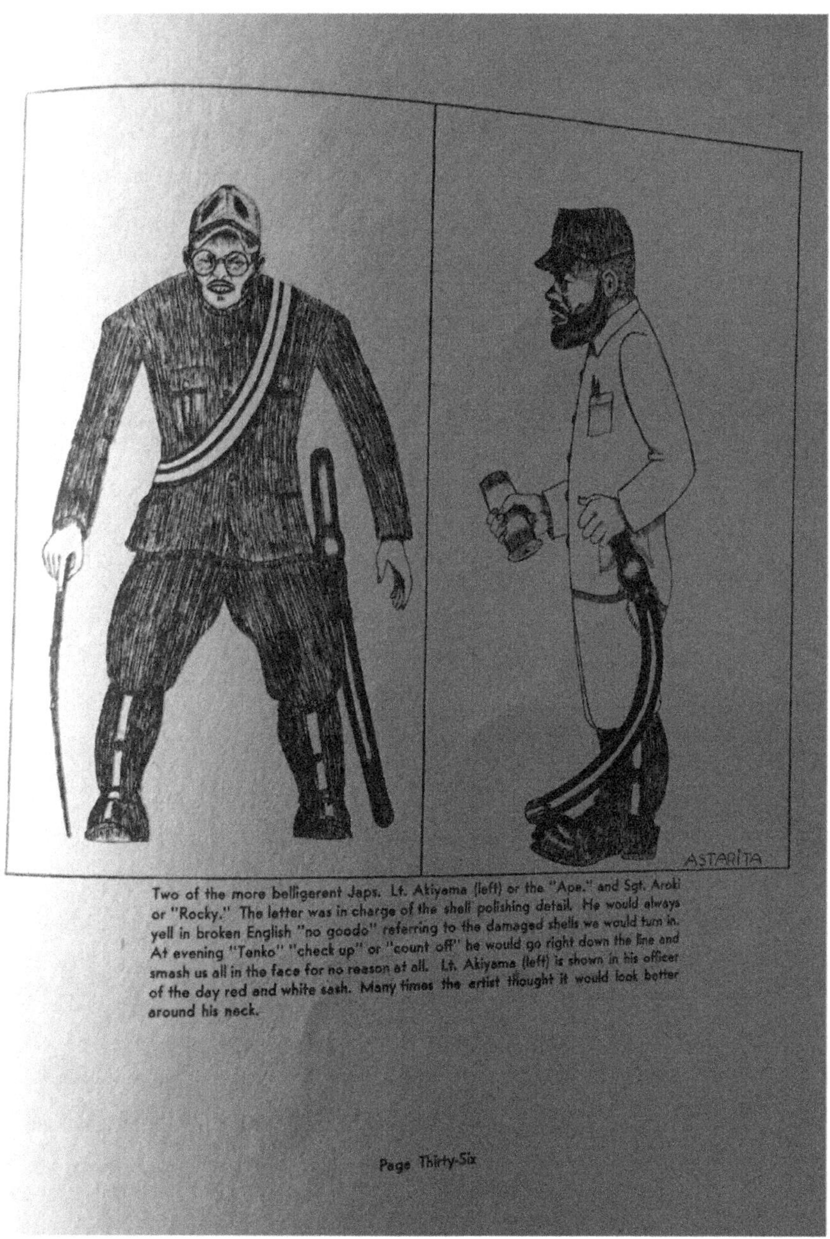

Two of the more belligerent Japs. Lt. Akiyama (left) or the "Ape." and Sgt. Aroki or "Rocky." The letter was in charge of the shell polishing detail. He would always yell in broken English "no goodo" referring to the damaged shells we would turn in. At evening "Tenko" "check up" or "count off" he would go right down the line and smash us all in the face for no reason at all. Lt. Akiyama (left) is shown in his officer of the day red and white sash. Many times the artist thought it would look better around his neck.

Page Thirty-Six

A member of the supply organization. The only thing wrong with it was that there was nothing to supply. Cpl. Tujioka (above) with his longer than he sword and very large boots. Always wanted to ride a horse. I guess he is still trying.

Page Thirty-Seven

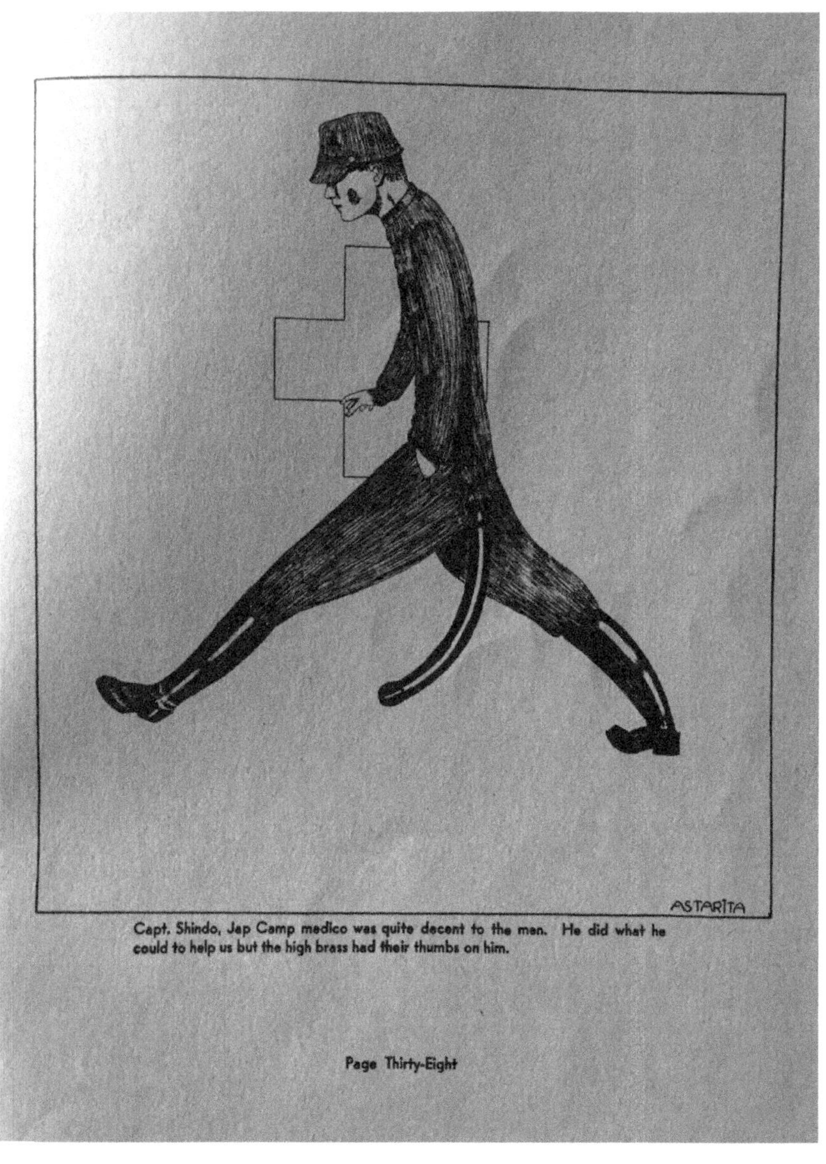

Capt. Shindo, Jap Camp medico was quite decent to the men. He did what he could to help us but the high brass had their thumbs on him.

Page Thirty-Eight

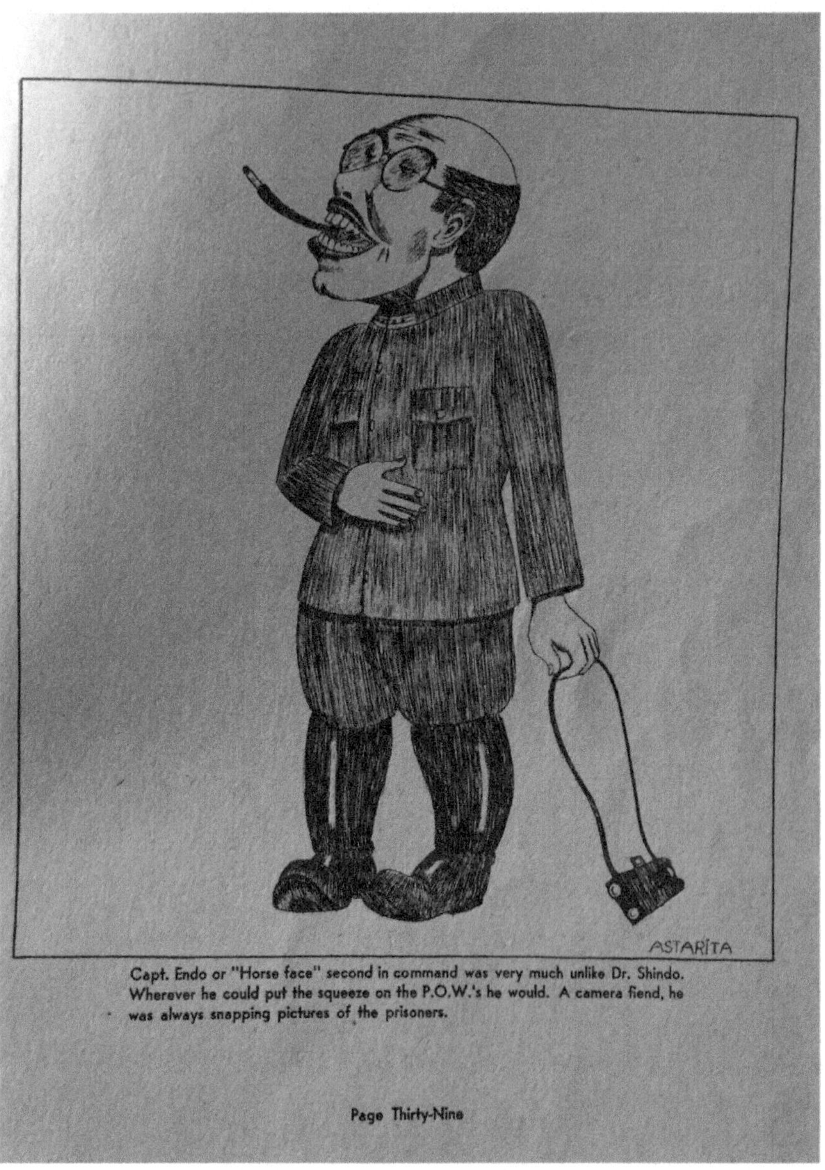

Capt. Endo or "Horse face" second in command was very much unlike Dr. Shindo. Wherever he could put the squeeze on the P.O.W.'s he would. A camera fiend, he was always snapping pictures of the prisoners.

Page Thirty-Nine

Work was hard and food was scarce in China. But we who had been shipped to Japan really found out what work and no food meant. Jobs such as unloading coal from barges, pig iron and iron ore. Working in filthy dry docks, ship yards, railroads etc., all through the air raids. They were the hard times. And we who have been fortunate enough to return to our loved ones can thank God for coming back from hell.

Page Forty

CHAPTER NINE:
THE LAST REUNIONS

MARINES - SAN DIEGO, CA – 1995

I had followed the discussions on the Wake Island Wig Wag about having another and perhaps the last reunion get-together. My dad kept me posted on the planning progress. They finally settled on San Diego. I know for a fact that the marines loved San Diego. Most of them had gone through boot camp there in 1939. It was a great place to end where it all began. I believe there were approximately 35 marines in attendance. Some had been with us on Wake in 1985 or 88 or both. It was so good to see these guys again. Some I had never met before, such as General John Kinney. I was fascinated by his stories. That same year he wrote a book "Wake Island Pilot." (See amazon synopsis below)

Wake Island Pilot is the story of John F. Kinney - hero, POW escapee, and aviation pioneer. It contains the first full-length account of a successful escape by a Marine captured in one of the great battles of World War II. Within hours of the Pearl Harbor attack, the Japanese struck the small U.S. garrison on Wake Island. As his squadron's engineering officer, young pilot John F. Kinney used all his considerable ingenuity to oversee the cannibalization of crippled planes for spare parts when he himself was not in the air fighting off the Japanese assault. His gallant efforts helped enable the desperate Marine and Navy defenders to hold out for an incredible two weeks, a truly epic struggle. After the island's inevitable surrender,

Kinney was a Japanese prisoner in China for the next three and a half years. During this time, he put his amazingly inventive mechanical skills to work, creating from scratch numerous items, including radio, to improve his fellow POWs' situation. Toward the end of the war, Kinney escaped from a prison train and, with the assistance of both Nationalist and Communist Chinese troops, made his way to an American airfield. He was thus one of the few Americans to escape from Japanese captivity outside the Philippines. General Kinney's subsequent Marine Corps career was equally distinguished: He flew fighters in the Korean War and helped develop the classic A4-D Skyhawk.

My wife Carole and I drove down from Huntington Beach to join the reunion. It was so great to see many of them after nearly ten years and the Wake trip. This would be the last time my mom and dad would also see them. My mom was especially delighted to see a few of her fellow wives that she had gotten to know from the many reunions she attended. I could tell she was really enjoying herself. One afternoon we all gathered in one of the meeting rooms for refreshments and conversation. After a short time, Carole came up to me and said, "I've been talking with General Kinney. He is a fascinating man! He escaped twice, in China and then in Korea." I am glad Carole had the chance to meet some of the marines. Then and to this day, she has heard her share of their stories. In attendance at the reunion was a film crew from the National Archives, doing interviews for the World War II Remembrance project. I have seen some of the interviews done for this project but am unable to find these Wake interviews done during this last reunion. As the reunion was winding down, I had the very sad realization that this would be the last time I would see them. I made use of every moment. Talking, joking, and reminiscing with all of them. I could feel that they knew this too. I felt very good. I felt a sense of accomplishment. After all, I am a "Son of Wake Island." Good-bye, my dear friends, Good-bye my heroes! I have been more than blessed to have all of you a part of my life.

My dad passed away peacefully in 1998. He did not suffer. He went to bed one night and just didn't wake up. His funeral was at our church in Virginia, MN. I can only relate it to a State Funeral in Washington, D.C. People came from all over the state to attend and pay respect to a man they so admired.

To my father, I dedicate this ending to you. Thank you for all you have given to me, our family, and our country. I will love you forever and be in my heart always.

THE FINAL REUNION – CIVILIAN WORKERS OF WAKE ISLAND

SURVIVORS OF WAKE-GUAM-CAVITE, INC.

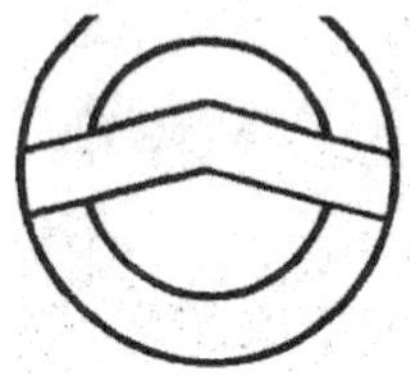

Dear Friends,

Our 2017 reunion will meet September 8th and 9th at the Riverside Hotel- Boise, Idaho for our final reunion.

A Note from Bonnie Gilbert:

After much thought and discussion with family and friends, we have decided that the reunions will end with the last gathering in Boise, September 8-9th, 2017. The "Survivors of Wake, Guam, and Cavite" officially disbanded in 2003, but we continued the tradition of annual reunions and other get-togethers so that our survivors and families could retain that special bond. Sadly, the number of living Wake Island survivors has declined rapidly in recent years, and few have been able to attend. We would like to honor all of our Wake men - the living, the deceased, and those who never made it home from the war - with this final · reunion. In order to plan ahead, we are setting a reunion reservation deadline of August 1, 2017, and request that you submit your form and payment by that date.

All good things must come to an end! Wake, Guam, *and* Cavite group have had quite a run; 1945-2017.

A priceless photo – Workers of Wake, Guam and Cavite, 9th annual reunion, 1953, Los Angeles. Photo from Brent Scott, grandson of Allan Asbury O'Guinn

9th Annual Convention
WORKERS OF WAKE, GUAM & CAVITE
Hotel Statler - Los Angeles, Calif.
December 4-6, 1953

Recording Wake Reunions and Special Events

J.O. Young left, and Marshall G. Sturdevent former Japanese P.O.W.'s display the American flag that T. Bailey Lee Jr., and John E. Sclutz who were in a Japanese P.O.W. camp at the time of surrender, 14 August 1945.
They set to work finding material to make an American flag. Two Australian P.O.W.'s gave them a pair of blue jeans for the background for the stars and a bed sheet for the stars and white stripes. The red stripes came form a red quilt, and the thread was made from unraveling a white sock, the whole thing was hand stitched. The next morning Old Glory was flying over the compound.

FAMILY OF
WAKE ISLAND
DEFENDERS
THE BATTLE OF
WAKE ISLAND
DEC. 8-23 1941
80
YEARS

By Bonita Gilbert for Family of Wake Island Defenders

Dusk is brief and dark falls fast on Wake Island. During my visit there ten years ago I took late night walks, imagining my father and all of those men under that same star-studded canopy during the sixteen day siege in December 1941. But where I found inspiration and awe, they faced unimaginable peril.

Japanese bombers first targeted Wake at noon December 8, raining death and destruction on the remote atoll. Trained and disciplined for war, Marines manned gun positions, dug foxholes, and organized for war. Stunned civilian workers sorted into groups, grabbed canned food from the storehouse and dragged mattresses out of bunkhouses into the brush. Some stepped up to aid the Marines, some helped with casualties and damage, and others just sat back waiting for Uncle Sam to rescue them.

The siege stretched into days as the defenders held out against attacks by air and sea. At nightfall the island kicked into gear: under strict blackout rules cooks churned out hot food to deliver in the field, work details moved shore gun batteries to outfox the enemy, mechanics patched up the fighter planes, and sentries patrolled dark beaches. Doctors worked around the clock in makeshift field hospitals. Daylight found exhausted men scanning the skies again for the next attack. When the bombers swooped in men leapt into their camouflaged dugouts or under whatever was nearby to escape the lethal barrage. As time went by the constant torment of rats, ants, and flies came to rival that of bombs and bullets.

In the end Uncle Sam did not come to the rescue of Wake Island. The Japanese invaded in the early hours of December 23 under heavy cloud cover that obscured the canopy of stars and rendered the battlefield a pitch-black canvas. The waiting was over, and a whole new hell on earth began.

Bonita (Bonnie) Gilbert teaches history at North Idaho College in Coeur d'Alene and is the author of Building for War: The Epic Saga of the Civilian Contractors and Marines of Wake Island in World War II (Casemate, 2012). Bonnie has an MA in history from the University of Oregon and taught in Colorado before moving to North Idaho in 2006. For more information please visit https://bonitagilbert.com.

By Gregory J.W. Urwin Ph.D. for Family of Wake Island Defenders

Major James Patrick Sinnott Devereux, who commanded the Wake Island Detachment, 1st Defense Battalion, ranks as the best-known officer in the outnumbered American garrison that held off repeated Japanese attacks from December 8 to 23, 1941. Most of his Marines did not begrudge him his fame, but few expressed any fondness for him. Before they occupied Wake Island, they feared him as an unfeeling martinet. After they reached the atoll, they resented him for working them twelve to sixteen hours a day, seven days a week, to fortify their outpost. Once hostilities commenced, the Wake Marines came to respect Devereux for his skillful repulse of the first Japanese landing attempt on December 11. Devereux also won praise for maintaining the discipline that helped most of his men survive three-and-a-half years as POWs. Despite all that, the major's aristocratic aloofness made him difficult to love.

The Wake Marines respected almost all their other officers, but if asked to name the one they truly admired, most replied "Captain Platt." Wesley McCoy Platt was a twenty-seven-year-old South Carolinian who had spent six years in the Marine Corps before landing on Wake. Fond of athletics and wisecracks, he preferred to lead by example, rather than rule by fear. As Corporal John S. Johnson, Jr., described Platt's command philosophy: "Never ask a man to do anything you would not do yourself. If in doubt, you do it and the men will follow." Pfc. Henry H.W. Chapman claimed that if Platt ordered his men to charge hell with buckets of water, they would not only do so, but "we would argue about who was going to carry his bucket." Nearly forty years later, Pfc. Erwin D. Pistole declared, "Hell, we would have died for him."

These sentiments explain why Platt, who commanded the Marines and American civilians stationed on Wilkes Island, could execute the counterattack that wiped out the Japanese troops that stormed ashore there before dawn on December 23. He led his followers grasping a pair of .45-caliber Colt automatic pistols and remained in the thick of the action until all but two Japanese had been killed, sparing them to extract intelligence. That little victory on what became a day of defeat would help sustain the Wake Islanders during the years of hell they faced in Japanese prison camps.

Gregory J. W. Urwin is a military historian whose work spans the American War of Independence through World War 2. He holds his Ph.D. from the University of Notre Dame, and taught at Saint Mary of the Plains College in Dodge City, Kansas, and the University of Central Arkansas before joining Temple's History Department in 1999. Urwin has published nine books, including Facing Fearful Odds: The Siege of Wake Island, which received the General Wallace M. Greene, Jr., Award from the Marine Corps Heritage Foundation, and Victory in Defeat: The Wake Island Defenders in Captivity, 1941-1945.

Chapter Ten:
Tributes from the Families of the Wake Island Defenders

In the fall of 2021, I reached out to the families on our Facebook page and asked them to submit a tribute to their Wake hero for my upcoming book. I was very proud and moved to have received so many. To those of you, my heartfelt thanks! May these memories be handed down to future generations to never forget your beloved defender.

From The Pearsall Family

Tribute To Ed Pearsall By Daughter Carol Brankin

Growing up, I do not remember much about my dad telling us about his war experiences. As I got older and he became Mayor of Virginia, MN, more of his war stories started to come out.

He always reminded me of what happened on December 7, 1941. He was happy to tell me about this day. He was having a pancake breakfast when the sirens went off, and suddenly, he was sent out to be ready for the threat of the Japanese Attack! For many days and nights, he was out as a gunner on the beaches, dug into trenches fighting the Air Attack and from the ships sending men to attack the ground.

The Marines fought a Long hard battle, but they ran out of ammunition and had no choice but to surrender! This was never anything the Marines were accustomed to, but their General knew they all would never have survived.

That Christmas, they spent in captivity wondering if they would live or be executed. The emperor decided their fate. Thus, they spent the next four years in prison camps in Japan and China, doing forced labor and living on dirty rice filled with bugs, eating spiders, grasshoppers, and whatever insects were available for protein. The prisoners all suffered terrible GI diseases from diarrhea to severe malnutrition. All that I know now as a Nurse, I cannot imagine how anyone could have survived, but my dad kept up his hopes, and mental, and emotional health from deteriorating by planning his canoe trips into the Boundary Waters, something he did while he was in High School.

After I moved away, got married, and had four children, I frequently went back to Northern Minnesota so the Grandchildren could know their grandfather and grandmother and the beauty of being at the Lake in the Boundary Waters. My parents built their cabin on Crane Lake when I was four years old, which they had for over 40 wonderful years! My children loved to visit grandma and grandpa, spending time at their cabin. He loved to sing the Marine Hymn and teach the grandchildren how to march and salute. My oldest daughter, Catie decided to join the military (Navy) while in Medical School after learning so much about the military from her grandpa.

My parents sold their cabin when it became too much to maintain for them. Near the end of my dad's life, my parents and I and my two sons stayed at Nelson's Resort on Crane Lake.

Before we left for home, my dad gave his grandsons his favorite Marine hats. He must have known something we didn't, for soon after that, he passed away in his sleep while taking a nap. My son Philip played his Trumpet for Military Taps at his funeral service, a very touching farewell to grandpa! That beautiful day in July, we were there at his funeral when we should have been with him at the lake. Now he will spend his days in heaven always at the Lake.

Submitted with Love, Carol Pearsall Brankin

From - John Pearsall – Son - The Story of Primo Carnera (the Goat) – circa 1934-35

The old homestead housed a variety of animals in the barn, including an exceptional goat. This goat had quite a reputation on the south side of Virginia. Our goat's name was Primo Carnera, appropriately named after a famous Italian boxer by the same name. Instead of running or playing, Primo would rear up on his hind legs and "box" anyone who came near him. Many days, he got out of the barn or was let out, as might have been the case. One day, due to the proximity of the homestead and barn to the school, Primo Carnerar followed the kids down the alley and ended up in the school and wandered into the Principal's office. Shortly after, an announcement over the loudspeaker said, "Ed Pearsall, come to the office and get your goat." Primo was obviously a fairly resourceful goat, as the principal told my father that his goat had eaten some very important papers in the office.

This story has remained in the family archives and is still told with much humor many years later. It was pretty obvious that the kids liked to play with Primo and get him to box with them. They also let him out of the barn to see what mischief he would get into before they could catch him. Every student in the school that day will remember Primo Carnera and his antics. It brings a smile to our grandchildren's faces when we think of the importance of family, neighborhood friends, and beloved pets and animals. So remains the story, now a family legend, of Primo Carnera.

From – Samuel Pearsall - Grandson

Grandpa Ed

Growing up, I spent many days hanging out with Grandpa Ed on the back porch, at Crane Lake and in the boat with him and Felix, his beloved dog. Nowadays, people don't leave home without a cell phone. Well, for Grandpa Ed it was a box of half and half and his pipe. Anytime I smell pipe tobacco I think of him, and it takes me to the back porch and the cabin on Crane. He didn't really do much on that back porch but sit on the couch with Felix smoking his pipe, and I'm sure reflects on how he ended up alive and try to forget the misery of being a POW in Japan. He told many stories about his military days and time as "a guest of the Japanese government," as he would say. He had Semper Fi bumper stickers all over his house along with numerous military artifacts and mementos from his service days. He deserved every second of peace out on that back porch and the right to just sit there. I wish I had been a little older back then to be able to understand the sacrifices and tribulations he went through and what made him who he was. Eventually, we kids would come out there and grill him with questions and disturb the peace, but grandpa would always answer our questions whatever they were and boot us out the back door when he'd had enough. I was always fascinated with his huge Amberjack fish mount he had out there and hoped that someday I could catch a fish that big, so I'm sure I asked many times about it. My cousin Chris and I would always try to catch the big fish when we went to my grandparent's cabin on Crane Lake. We eventually did catch that big one up at Crane in the form of a 40-foot tree on shore one day. Chris and I were tired of casting off the dock, so we decided to launch lures up onto shore.... most of them ended up in the trees. As we were tugging, trying to get one out of the tree's grandpa Ed came down the path and was not happy, proceeding to chase Chris and me down the beach to the neighbor's dock! Little did we know how expensive fishing tackle actually was. Grandpa would take us out in his old fishing boat and troll around the "Crappie Rock" at the end of the bay. Most of the time, he spent untangling our lines and tying on new ones. When there wasn't a major catastrophe with Chris and me, he would sit there, smoke his pipe, drive the boat, and seem to not pay any attention to the fishing rod in his hand. Most of the time, he had a good 2-3 feet of his rod underwater trolling around with the boat. Chris and I would always laugh and make fun of him for it, but he always ended up catching the fish when we'd go out. Back at the cabin, grandpa taught us how to play cribbage and solitaire, so many games were played over the years. He'd sit in his recliner, keeping the fire going, smoking his pipe, and sipping on his E&J Brandy. Most of the time, he'd fall asleep in that chair. I'd wake up the next morning to the crackling of the fire and the smell of grandpa's pipe and he'd be sitting in the same spot. Being older now with kids of my own, I realize how much work it must have been to take us kids up to Crane Lake for the weekend, but he loved it and we loved it, so I think that took a little of the work out of it. It was his happy place up there being out in the woods, in the cabin, or out in the boat. I'm sure he's watching down on us... pipe in hand, a glass of E&J on the end table, and Felix at his side.

Grandson-

Samuel Pearsall

TRIBUTE TO J. EDWARD PEARSALL: BY GRANDSON CHRIS PEARSALL

My Grandpa - J. Edward Pearsall

I grew up in the same small town as both my grandfather and father in Northern Minnesota. Virginia, MN, was our hometown on the Mesabi Iron Range. It was awesome growing up in the same town as my Grandpa Ed, Grandma Marge, and their black lab Felix. A lot of my greatest memories were spending time at their cabin on Crane Lake, an hour of Virginia north on the MN/Canadian border. We would fish, walk through the woods, chop wood, swim, and watch my grandpa play Solitaire. And he always loved taking a good nap at the cabin, as did I!

Every summer, our Grandparents would load us up in their blue station wagon and bring us up to the lake. My Grandpa loved making blueberry pancakes. He would go up to the cabin to relax and unwind and enjoy his pipe overlooking the lake. On one of the trips, my cousin Sam and I were fishing down on the dock. We got bored of casting off the dock and decided to cast into the pine trees on shore. One by one, we cast lures into the trees and would cut the line when it got stuck on a branch and then retie it with a new lure. Eventually, we ran out of Grandpa's lures in the tackle box, and all the line blowing in the wind looked like Christmas tree tinsel. Sam and I were proud of our work that afternoon, but Grandpa Ed came down the hill and was unimpressed! He chased Sam and me up and down the beach. I have never seen Grandpa run so fast! We had to chop a lot of wood to make up for that mistake.

Whenever I think about my grandpa, Eddy, I can still picture him wearing his Marine Corps hat and singing the Marine Corps hymn. "From the Halls of Montezuma to the shores of Tripoli" … while marching around their house. I would give anything to spend one more afternoon with him on the back porch of their house or sitting on the dock at Crane Lake just listening to his stories. I take the lessons he taught me as a young kid and carry them with me in both my personal and professional life today. To be able to endure everything he did and still have a positive outlook on life, great sense of humor, passion for the outdoors, raise a family with three kids, have a cabin in God's Country, and become mayor of our town, it shows me that anything is possible, and we are truly blessed because of what this generation did for our country.

I didn't truly understand what sacrifices my grandpa went through until I was in 5th grade. Mr. Holmes, my teacher, had my grandfather come into his class to speak about WWII and his life as a POW. He talked about it occasionally, but this was the first time I heard all the stories about survival and perseverance. That generation of young men and women sacrificed everything to preserve freedom around the world.

There is a postcard my Grandpa Ed sent home on New Year's Day 1945. He wished his parents a Merry Christmas and Best of Wishes for 1945. I cannot imagine the emotions he felt while writing this letter, as they had just passed their 36th month and 4th Christmas as POWs. My wife and I have three sons, and I also couldn't imagine receiving that postcard in the mail from a son. When he wrote that letter, the POWs would have nine more months of captivity to endure, and conditions would worsen as they got transferred from China to Japan. In hearing stories about the 2-week battle on Wake Island, the Japanese capturing the Island and almost killing all the Marines and civilian contractors, the "hell ship" Nitta Maru and the horrific conditions, and then the POW camps in both China and Japan

That's why we call them the Greatest Generation, and I am proud to call one of them my grandpa!

Honored Grandson Chris Pearsall

From - Sarah Pearsall Lambert – Granddaughter

In memory of my grandpa, my Hero - J. Edward "Eddy" Pearsall, I am known as the family historian. I am the keeper of the stories, the medals, the letters. My love of anything and everything about history is thanks to my grandpa. In fifth grade, I had a teacher, Chris Holmes, who was good friends with my grandpa. He would come to the classroom at least three times a year to talk to the class - one would be about the Great Depression and what it was like growing up during that in the small mining town of Virginia, MN; one would be about World War II, and his experiences as a Prisoner of War; and one would be to take the class to the town cemetery, to talk about the history there of our ancestors. This didn't just start the year I was in school or even the year my brother was in school two years before I was. So, there have been many children in this town who have heard these stories, and they have made an imprint on them as well. He was also the mayor of the town, and a member of the local Elks Club, where many of his stories have been told and remembered by many. It is not a fun story to tell. In fact, there were multiple times when he was nearly killed, and was saved by a rain squall, or to be brought to the bow of a boat, never to return, but he was too injured to climb up the ladder. But I am grateful he shared it with so many. I remember sitting on the back porch with us on the couch, and his beloved black lab, Felix - who had his chair to sit in, listening to stories, and me asking questions, and he would answer them all. He would always be smoking a pipe, and it is a smell I will never forget. He would sing and march around, signing the Marine Corp song, and when it would be time for us to go back to school, he would march around the house signing a song about back-to-school days. I interviewed him for a few class projects in high school and even had friends come with me for interviews for a group project we did. He was always happy to share, but near the end of his stories, he would always be ready for his nap on the couch. One spring, fifty years after the anniversary of him getting shot while being a Prisoner of War, he finally received a Purple Heart. He was so honored and proud of this and carried it everywhere he went so he could show it to anyone he would see that day. When he passed away, we couldn't find the Purple Heart at first, and my mom found it finally in the back seat of his van, ready to show it to the next person he would see. For all he endured in this lifetime, his attitude and outlook on life is something to be admired and looked up to. I have many letters from Senators and Presidents of the United States, along with letters and postcards sent and received from his family during his time in prison camp, stories he has dictated to my mom to type up for him, and multiple newspaper articles written on him and his story, and even one of his dog, Felix, waterskiing on a board between the boat at Crane Lake. I am always honored when I get to share these stories with friends and family. I also have a shadow box of his Purple Heart and his other medals in my room. It is a daily reminder of the sacrifices he went through. I am honored to have him as my grandpa and wish he were still here to tell his stories as only he could, besides maybe my Grandma Marj, who heard his stories probably more times than she cared to.

From Winai Goyadoolya – Foreign Exchange Student Son - Phang-nga, Thailand – 1967-68

I have to thank the AFS organization that selected me to put in the Pearsall family. I warmly lived with them for one year. It seemed a short period of time, but Pearsall's family gave me a lot experiences and advice and opportunity for me. I hardly find such a word to say in order to cover all the good deeds that Pearsall's family gave to me.

Especially my dad, Mr. Pearsall, gave me a big time to learn such a things that the American kids should do and should know. My dad was very kind to me. He told me stories of Wake Island. He took me every place where he had a chance to go and it good for me to participate. For example, my dad took me to the Toast Master club meeting to hear the speech that each one presented. Furthermore, my dad took me to the graduation ceremony of

Cook High school and introduced me to the ceremony. My dad still took me to the City Hall of Virginia to meet with the officers and also introduced me to the officers. There were still my events that I could not mention in my writing. Many weekends we went to Crane Lake cabin for recreation.

I have to thank the Pearsall family, my mum, John a big brother, Dave my brother, and Carole my sister who gave me a happy and warm life while I was in Virginia. It is still keeping in my mind forever.

Tributes from the Families of the Wake Island Defenders

From Roberta Curry – daughter of marine Robert (Big Mo) Curry

Pearsall was a name I have known since birth. To say that John Edward Pearsall was an important part of my dad's life is an understatement. Robert Eaves Curry from Parnell, Missouri, was my dad and my hero. He enlisted in the Marines, while his five brothers were all in the Navy. He met John Edward from Virginia, Minnesota, in boot camp in San Diego, California, and an unbreakable bond was created between Swede (Pearsall) and Big Mo (Curry). The first time I can remember seeing my dad cry was at a Wake Island Reunion in Wichita. I was around ten years old. I watched as these larger-than-life figures hugged and cried. The joy of being reunited was expressed on their faces. Through the years, Swede and Big Mo would visit each other in California or Minnesota. To watch my dad, light up while spending time with Swede is a memory, I keep close to my heart. My Dad passed away in 1996 in the Jerry Pettis Veterans Hospital in Loma Linda. He had Alzheimer's, Parkinson's, and fell while in the hospital, and had his leg amputated as they found cancer. The last time Pearsall came to visit my dad, he broke down. After all the horrors these two men faced together - seeing my dad in the state he was in was just too much. It took years for my dad to share any of what happened while they were held in Japanese Prison Camps. There were funny stories of how they would steal the watermelons and other items from the Japanese officers' garden. It was not until my dad helped form the first POW support group at the VA that some of the more difficult things they faced were talked about. The civilian contractors who picked up weapons and helped fight the Japanese were invited to join the group. I have learned much from the friendship of Swede and Big Mo. They faced death together, and yet - both returned home to start families and careers and carry on with very little help in the transition. Pearsall went on and served in politics, and my dad worked at the Post Office and was active in groups such as the DAV, VFW and others. What I also learned from both - was the importance of a sense of humor. They were the funniest guys together. I will believe until the day I leave this Earth that it was their sense of humor that helped them survive. These men are my heroes. They walked through hell on Earth and came home and built lives. Not all were as lucky. David Pearsall spoke so beautifully at my dad's burial and told the story of when they were captured. Swede and Big Mo were tied up on the tarmac, along with the others. They were to be executed. My Dad said to Pearsall, "Take a good look at the sun - it's the last time you are going to see it" It is beyond comprehension what they all went through. Semper Fi Swede and Big Mo. We will see you again. There is not a day that I don't think about them.

From - Franklin W. Towler – Grandson of Archie Pratt – Wake 98

I would like to tell you our family's story of Wake Island.

My mother was Margaret Sharon Pratt (died 24 SEP 2020), daughter of Archie Pratt. Archie and Marion had three daughters and three sons. Archie was a ranch hand from Washington who moved to L.A. with his family. Archie was a pack-train driver and ranch hand. Our family has a photo of him in the Rose Bowl parade driving his mule team with Will Rogers on the seat next to him.

Archie was saving his money to buy his own ranch, which is why he signed on with Morrison-Knutson as a civilian contractor. Grandma Marion went to work for the war effort, and the children were placed in a Los Angeles orphanage to care for them while she worked. There are several photos from the L.A. papers showing Marion and her children taken around Christmas.

Archie went to Wake to help build the airstrip for the military at the age of 38, so he must have been one of the "old men" on the trip. All was going well in the correspondence with our family until the attack on Pearl Harbor.

Family history has it that Archie drew the straw to go to Japan to be slave labor, and he was afraid he would never return. So, he traded straws to stay on the island. He was one of the 98 civilians murdered there by the Imperial Army on OCT 7th, 1943.

My mother, Molly, loved her father very much. She often spoke of the difficult times they had growing up without their father. She dreamed of him her whole life and never got over his loss. Archie's legacy is now with us, his grandchildren, and his last two remaining sons, Terrance Shepard Pratt and Lorimer Bruce Pratt.

Thank you, sir, for taking on this project to keep the memories of these heroes alive. I only wish our government cared as much as you do.

With great respect,

Franklin W. Towler/Veteran, USAF

From Rod Balhorn, Mike Balhorn, Rita Merta

Our father, Marvin William Balhorn, enlisted in the Navy when he was only 17. Still very much a kid and unmarried, he left his parents, brothers, sisters, and friends in Garrison, Iowa, in the summer of 1939 to do what he could to defend his country at a time when patriotism was at one of its highest points in the history of our nation. After completing boot camp in the Great Lakes, he was accepted for training as a Naval radio operator in San Diego. Following the completion of his training, he was assigned to the U.S.S. Northampton as a Radioman 3rd class and shipped out to Pearl Harbor. In June of 1941, he was transferred to Wake Island. He found himself in the western Pacific on a piece of land with an area of less than 3 square miles surrounded by nothing but water. As isolating as it might seem for a nineteen-year-old, he always remembered and spoke fondly of his first six months on Wake. The warm water and white coral sand beaches where he often ran after ending his shift in the "radio shack" seemed amazing to this midwestern "farm boy" But only a few hours after the Pearl Harbor bombing everything changed. The capture of the island by the Japanese was the beginning of three and a half incredibly difficult years he spent as a POW as he was transported to Japan, briefly interred at Ofuna, and then moved to Kanigaya, a secret POW camp north of Yokohama.

What our father and the others on the island went through as prisoners of war after being captured on Wake Island, most of which he never talked about until much later in life, was something few in our current generation have had to endure for our country. While he had nightmares for many years following his liberation from the POW camp, the experiences he shared with us when we were growing up were the more positive ones - such as his fond memories of his early days on Wake Island, his saving and planting seeds from the rare tomato he managed to "acquire" while imprisoned, and the kindness he received from one of the Japanese guards. Much later in life, he began sharing more about his experience. But as difficult as that period of time had been for him, Dad never disparaged or showed hatred for his captors. Instead, he served as an incredible role model by teaching us to treat everyone, irrespective of their differences, the same. His stories about how he and other prisoners in the camp continued to work to turn the tide of the war by (at great personal risk) trying to disable the anti-aircraft guns they were forced to clean on a beach (using sand and salt water when the guards weren't looking) and intentionally leaving critical information out of radio messages they were forced to decode helped teach us as young adults to not give up when faced with adversity or personal hardship. His service and actions also instilled a tremendous sense of patriotism in all of us. Learning about these experiences and the difficulties he had to deal with at such an early age, and then seeing first-hand as we were growing up how he took responsibility for whatever needed to be done, engendered in each of us a strong work ethic. Life's lessons that he learned during that time were passed on to us, sparing us the need to experience them. As one consequence of his enduring years of starvation in prison camp, he always insisted we not waste food. And a poem we discovered years after his death that he had written on a scrap of paper during his time at the camp as a POW reinforced what we had learned about how he dealt with the most difficult time of his life:

"Here in times of great distress, I give thanks; and much I bless,

That my life, though no complaint might have dealt me greater pain. MWB 1944".

Rod Balhorn, Mike Balhorn, Rita Merta

DIANA NIDICK – TRIBUTE TO MY BROTHER

Donald MacLeod Williams was born May 14, 1921

He had just graduated high school in Hawaii when news of a construction project was listed. He was not yet 18, so my Father signed permission for him to join the construction company

Don went to Midway first, and from there, he went to Wake Island to build the landing strip for the Navy.

His father and my mother left Hawaii and returned to Alameda, CA. I was born in 1942.

Don had talent that poured from his every pore; he wrote stories, poems, drew, sang, and played guitar by ear. He could do it all.

When Wake was attacked, he helped defend Wake, and when they were overtaken, he was kept behind to finish the job.

When the job was finished, he and the 225 other men were taken to the ship to be sent to Japan. The Japanese kept 98 men on the island who were later shot to death on the beach. My brother was sent to Camp 18 Seasbo, Japan to build the Soto Dam.

He died from torture and pneumonia March 9, 1943; he was not yet 21.His bunk mate and friend Arnold Green lived, and when he came back to Oakland from Japan, he came to our home and met my mother. I just barely remember him as I was just a small child...He gave my mother things that Don had. My father was away in London teaching engine repair When my father returned home, he found out what had happened to his only son and never forgave himself for signing the papers to allow Don to go to work for the company

He waited from 1941 to 1945, wondering if his son was dead or alive. He only spoke to me about his son once when I was much older and married. My mother told me about him when I was youngerDon rests at the Punch Bowl in Hawaii. Father was given the choice of where he could be laid to rest and Hawaii was chosen as that was the last time my father and mother were together with Don in happy times.

My Grandson, who serves in the Navy was stationed on Oahu, and he went to the Punch Bowl, found my brother's grave and had taps played for him. Little did he know that bagpipes were Don's favorite. He was finally given peace.

Sincerely

Diana Nidick

Jody Johnson For Her Father - Mic Johnson

Wake Civilian Awarded Bronze Star

In February 1947, Mic was awarded a Bronze Star with a V clasp by the US Navy at the Spokane Naval Supply Depot with his parents by his side with these words:

> "For heroic service as a member of the civilian construction crew on Wake Island when Japanese forces landed on The morning of December 21, 1941. Volunteering to assist the men of marine aircraft squadron 211 when they went forward to make a final stand against an overwhelming enemy landing force. Johnson fought bravely for approximately nine hours in the brush along the beach, refusing to seek security in the rear despite his lack of training for combat and the insufficiency of weapons for all."

I have many memories of my dad. On a late summer afternoon, I was walking behind my dad, my uncle, and cousins as we "helped" bring the cows to the barn from the pasture for milking. Little children are more observant than you think. I watched our footprints on the dusty roadside and asked my dad why he walked with his feet turned out instead of straight like me. He replied that everybody does. It was **MANY** years later when the child learned of her dad's mistreatment by Japanese prison guards which caused a lot of damage to his knees and back, as well as post-traumatic stress.

I vaguely remember the scar on his arm from his war wound. But I vividly recall his response when supper was something my brothers and I did not like. “People are starving in China,” he would say. That statement translated to; you need to eat what’s on your plate.

The county road edges in northeastern Washington state had deep drainage ditches on the sides filled with snow that was perfect for kids to jump in and crawl out of the way home from school. We attended the same two-room schoolhouse that dad and his siblings attended a generation before. At Rice, those deep ditches led to very wet clothes when we reached home. Dad did not punish us but made a point of saying,” I don’t understand how kids walking home from school can get so wet.” The walk home was only a quarter mile from the barn/milk house between grandpa’s house and ours. If we got hurt, many adults were nearby.

I attended college on an academic scholarship but was ready to quit school. I think his face was blue when he said, “It isn’t costing you anything but time. Don’t quit.” He did not tell me that this was a great opportunity that he could not use to his advantage when he returned from Wake.

Mic was silently concerned about my children’s deployment into war zones, but he was also intensely proud of their service. Only one son is currently in the military, and I am sure Mic is watching from heaven over him. That son was recently promoted to Lt. Colonel. Due to military safety protocol, I cannot tell you his name or location.

After my children were grown, dad gave me a back-handed compliment, “You did a good job raising your boys.”

On one visit with dad, he noticed I had no hubcaps on my car and asked, "What happened to your hubcaps?" I had parked my car at fire admin when I flew to Spokane and when I returned, one hubcap was missing. (Fire admin in Phoenix is the location of the old Phoenix Brewery in an unsafe part of town). I didn't want my car to look odd, so I removed the hubcaps. Jokingly, he asked, "Does that change how it runs?" My response "Of course not!"

Dad had three knee-replacement surgeries. His knee pain was so bad that the only relief was hospitalization with his leg in traction.

Finally, he had his first knee replacement and was able to walk 10 miles a day. The second knee replacement was the other knee. He continued his daily 10-mile walks. The third knee surgery was to replace the first knee, as he had worn out the metal. That surgery took 45 minutes to replace the mechanics and 2 hours to clean out the black, deteriorated titanium. The last knee surgery had some infection, and some of the dissolvable sutures did not dissolve.

Lucy, the Chinese doctor, and wife of my stepbrother, Chris, pulled the long suture material out of the wound. I told Chris to put the suture in a zip-lock bag and take it to the doctor.

Several years later, the specialist at the VA wanted to amputate dad's leg. Dad called me for my opinion. We had a lengthy discussion, and Lucy used Chinese medical approaches to save his leg. The specialist used dad to show his medical students a miracle!

I miss his joking and teasing every day, but mostly I miss our consultations on how to repair things. Dad could fix anything - even VMF-211s, although he was not an airplane mechanic. He always saved parts, nails, screws, nuts, and bolts. I really wanted to have him teach me to change brushes in an electric motor, but by that time, his dexterity had dwindled so much, that it would have been too frustrating for him. I would have heard him swear a lot, too. I taught the young men in my home that we know all the bad words, but we **CHOOSE** not to use them in our home!

Dad had a forge in his shop by the barn, and he fashioned parts as needed for farm machinery for himself and his neighbors. He also learned to weld and mix and pour cement.

I have his 8-CD video scrapbooks and listened to his explanation of POW memories, especially the photo of the Japanese surveying the camouflaged hangars where he scavenged parts to keep the 211s flying. This is where he worked when an enemy bullet broke his elbow a day or two before Wake was captured.

The last six years, dad looked tired and became frailer. I have no photos of him in that state but have many showing him as a healthy, elderly man.

My stepsister, Linda, tells me when we talk that I am definitely Mic Johnson's daughter! NO, it isn't swearing or drinking, it's just attitude.

Tribute To Jack Fene and Elmer "Whitey" Chrisler: Great Uncles By Nicolle Salisbury

Jack Fenex and Elmer "Whitey" Christler were two of just the ten men from the Cody, Wyoming area that sought a better financial opportunity through working for MK on Wake Island. Both were my Great-Uncle's. Jack was my Paternal Grandmother's oldest brother, and Whitey was my Paternal Grandfather's oldest brother. Jack came to Wake in March of 1941 and was going to leave once his contract was over until he learned that Whitey would be coming in November. He decided to stay another nine months as they were both good friends and both dragline operators.

Jack was in his early 20s when he came to Wake, single and more or less fairly carefree. He was driven, motivated, and tough as nails. He never backed down from a fight or a challenge and valued his independence. When he was a teenager, he left home and lived life as a Hobo for a while. Traveling and adventure must have been in his veins. Whitey, who was older and married, came to Wake and wrote home that Jack had become an exceptional dragline operator. Their time on the Island together was shortened by the December 8 attacks on the island. Both men volunteered to help with whatever reinforcements they could provide. They were asked to continue construction with night work details. Both men worked side by side until they were told to stop and hunker down after the Japanese landed on the island.

Jack and Whitey were separated in January of 1942. Jack stayed on the Island with around 350(?) other workers while

Whitey was shipped to Shanghai on the *Nitta Maru*. Jack, unfortunately, never left Wake. He was among the 100 men left on Wake in 1943. In July of 1943, he was caught stealing (presumable food) and swiftly executed that same day. I can only imagine that it was hard for Jack (like all men) to take orders from the Japanese. He valued his freedom, and this swift execution without trial instead of a different punishment may have indicated a greater hostility between him and the camp commander. His family never knew what became of him and were told after the war that he was likely one of the 98 executed on the island in October of 1943. It wasn't until 2019, almost 80 years later, when the information was uncovered by historian Bonita Gilbert, that the family found out exactly what happened. By then, all those that knew him personally had already passed away.

Jack was deeply loved by his family, and they grieved his loss accordingly. My grandmother and great-aunt talked about him frequently, and we grew up hearing stories about him. We came to love him too, and his memory has never been forgotten. I learned to admire his courage and tenacity.

Whitey lived through a prison camp in Shanghai and a few other camps in Osaka. During his time there, he observed the differences in culture between Japan and America but developed a great respect and love for the Japanese civilians. He recalled that civilians risked their own lives by giving what little food they had to the American prisoners. In later years he would teach his nieces and nephews how to count to ten in Japanese. In turn, my dad taught my sisters and me! I can still count to ten! One of my sisters recalls being out to dinner with Whitey and his wife Rhea; he saw a group of Japanese tourists come into the restaurant they were eating at. He jumped up from the table and immediately started talking to them. By the end of the encounter, the group each gave him a big hug and left. His happy nature and easy ability to make friends left a great impact. When I was working in my hometown as a barber/stylist and the older men would find out my last name, they would immediately ask me if I was related to Whitey. They always had a great story to share.

Both men left a great impact on their families. While neither man had any children, their memories and stories have not been forgotten by family. Jack taught us the importance of freedom and how valuable it is. Whitey taught us how to have perspective and truly see people for the good that exists in us all.

TRIBUTE TO GRANDFATHER: LOREN HANCE BY PATRICIA BARNES

Loren Hance was born August 27, 1902, in Siloam Springs, Arkansas. He married Ruth Sherman and was living in Boise, Idaho in 1941. He was father to Shirley 5, Darlene 7, Jim 9, Betty12, Lorraine 17, Audrey 19, and granddaughter, Josephine three months. To support his family, he reluctantly left in September 1941 to work for the Morrison Knudsen Company on Wake Island. Ruth was concerned about the growing conflict with Japan and the danger of being on Wake. His response to her was that he would be there to help defend the island. That is exactly what he did.

He was recommended for the Medal of Freedom in May of 1946 for his service during the attack. Loren delivered water and supplies by truck during the battle to the Marines. Accounts from surviving POWs noted that he was one of the first to volunteer for military training by the Marines. After the island fell, he was taken to Camp 18, "Hell Camp" in Sasebo, Japan. He labored in the rock quarry for the construction of Soto Dam until he died of illness on April 25, 1943. His family had no information on what happened to him until after the war ended.

Loren is buried at the National Memorial Cemetery of the Pacific, Honolulu, Hawaii. Along with veteran status, he was awarded the Purple Heart. On December 7, 2013, a Wake Island Defender memorial was installed in Veterans Memorial Park, Boise, Idaho. The memorial, one of only two in the US, was dedicated in memory of Loren Hance. The memorial was an Eagle Scout project15-year-old Noah Barnes, Betty's grandson.

From Julie Wong – Family Of Civilian Kai Wong

During WWII, approximately 20,000 Chinese Americans served in various branches of the United States Armed Forces. Although Chinese Americans during this period continued to face discrimination and racial inequities, they persevered and served with dignity and honor. Kai Wong served our country only after two years of immigration into the United States. He was one of the 60+ Chinese Americans working as a civilian worker for Morrison Knudsen on Wake Island. Kai's service commenced in December 1941, but shortly after arrival on Wake Island, the island was attacked by Japanese forces. He was one of the few Chinese Americans who aided the Marines by loading 50-caliber ammunition into the belly of the F4F fighter planes. Sadly, by the end of December, the civilian workers and the US Armed Forces on Wake Island were captured and imprisoned for four years. In 1999, Kai was finally given Navy military status but reliving the unspoken war experiences were traumatic.

On December 20, 2018, the Chinese American WWII Veteran Congressional Gold Medal act was signed into law in recognition of their services. The Congressional Gold Medal is an award bestowed by the United States Congress and is Congress's highest expression of national appreciation for distinguished achievements and contributions by individuals or institutions. The medal was first awarded in 1776 by the Second Continental Congress to General George Washington. Finally, from July 3-5, 2021, 400 veterans and families of Chinese American WWII veterans were acknowledged and received the Congressional Gold Medal during the Northern California presentation in San Francisco. This is truly an honor and a special day for the family and friends of WWII veterans!

Tribute to Father Emil Schweizer, Jr. By Daughter Joan Schweizer Hoff

In his high school yearbook, our dad, Emil Schweizer Jr., was deemed "most likely to visit the Pacific Islands," so when Morrison Knudsen Construction Company offered civilians great pay and a 9-month contract to construct a military base on Wake Island, at age 24, he enthusiastically signed up. It was an opportunity to travel and get a leg up on his life. In Dec. 1941, with only weeks left on his contract, he, along with the civilian contractors and limited US military, found themselves defending the island in the Battle of Wake Island against Japan. Despite a valiant effort for 16 days, the island was captured, and he, military personnel, and civilian contractors became prisoners of war against the Japanese.

He spent nearly 4-years in captivity in Japan and China.

Emil was the first-generation son of immigrant parents. The oldest of 3 boys, he learned English in school and taught his parents and brothers the language. He was kind, helpful, and hardworking and would do anything to help others. He had a positive attitude about life and believed he could do anything he set his mind to. These traits were most likely helpful for his survival from the harsh treatment as a prisoner.

As was the case with many of the returning POWs, Dad did not talk about his experiences. We were told he was chosen to dish up the food because his fellow prisoners knew that he would treat everyone equally and not play favorites. He was well-liked and was a team player. He was distraught when one of his fellow prisoners died in the camp. His mom received only 9 letters from her son, many of the words were blacked out by the Japanese censors, but what remained were requests for letters from home, as he had received only 2, and the required statement that he was healthy and well treated. His handwriting changed when he wrote those final words on each card.

When Emil returned home after the war, he was eager to forge his new life. He purchased his first car. Because there was a shortage of vehicles for sale, he had to wait, but once in his possession, he loved his car and the sense of freedom and control it brought to his life. He drove to San Francisco to pick up his future wife, a family friend, who had been released from her Navy nurse post in San Diego. The car ride back to Boise cemented their relationship, and the wedding planning began.

Emil became active in the Survivors of Wake, Guam, and Cavite organization and as president of the Boise chapter, attended local meetings and national conventions. His family assumed it was there he shared his experiences and stories with those who were in the camps with him. Emil wanted civilians who stepped up to support and work alongside the US military during the battle on Wake Island to be recognized for their efforts and sacrifice. He worked tirelessly with others to gain veterans' benefits, which were finally granted 47 years after the war's end, just a year before he died.

Tribute To George Harris: Submitted By Granddaughter Annie Marroquin, Written By Bernice Harris, Daughter Of George Harris

My Father's name was George Harris. He was one of the Wake Island 98. My name is Bernice Harris DeCristoferi. By trade, my father was a general contractor. He built homes in Redwood City, CA, and surrounding areas. I was very young when one day he drove me to school, and he said that he was leaving for a while. He said that he would come home with enough money from working, and we were going to buy a ranch in Oregon. I cried and begged him not to go, but he was off to Wake Island as a civilian worker to help build a runway so planes could fly in. My mother, Frances, and my father communicated regularly thru the mail service. He sent her shells that he found on the beach there, which were turned into a necklace, and I now cherish this treasure.

When World War II began, my dad was taken prisoner by the Japanese. He was kept on Wake as he knew how to do many things. I remember two survivors came and talked to my mom at our house after the war ended. My mom was notified that my dad was one of the last ones to be killed. They informed my mom that he had been assigned to set equipment, so if American military ships came in range, they would be hit. He set the equipment off just a hair in case American ships came to regain the island they would not get struck. He was a hero, so they said, and I believe. He was in his 30's when he passed. His death remains painful still after all these years.

My Father is recognized on the mass grave memorial at the Punchbowl Cemetery in Honolulu, HI

Tribute To Father Joe Bayok: By Michael And Karlene Edwards

Our father, Joe Bayok, a civilian contractor, survived Japan. He told us he saw big strong men turn over, give up, and die, and he was just too ornery to do that. Ten years older than the others, he was called "Old Man" with great affection. This story is typical of Dad: When camp guards mocked the emaciated men's struggle to carry fifty-pound bags of salt, Dad and three other men lifted extra bags onto their own shoulders, two hundred pounds per man. They didn't carry the load to spite the guards. They carried it for each other to remind each other they were men.

During the Battle of Wake Island, Dad and other civilian warriors harnessed themselves to massive anti-aircraft guns, dragged them to new hiding places, then sandbagged and camouflaged them. Other nights they moved ammunition, sandbagged bridges, and built air raid shelters. Some manned gun emplacements or picked up rifles when Marines fell. With these few defenses, the Americans held off the Japanese Navy for fourteen days.

More important, I believe, though, is that Dad refused to let the war years embitter him. Instead, he filled our world with his wry humor, his big hugs, and his great-hearted warmth. He often told us he'd live to be a hundred — and we knew he intended to live each year with gladness.

To us, Dad was like the Idaho mountains he loved: enduring, steadfast, life-affirming. We are so grateful he was our father.

Barbara Bayok Davis, Karlene Bayok Edwards, Ronald James Bayok

From Brent Scott – Grandson of Allan Asbury O'Guinn

Allan Asbury O'Guinn, my maternal grandfather, had turned 46 years old April 28, 1941. He was born in 1897 in Arkansas. He signed up for the 9-month contract with CPNAB as a plumber, still trying to recover from the Depression. I do know he departed Los Angeles on the SS Lurline on May 16th, 1941 for Honolulu, then on to Wake. It took about 5 days to get to Hawaii and five more days to get to Wake. So, he probably got to Wake around June 1st. He was a father of five, though his oldest son was killed in 1939 at age of 18 in a tragic accident. He was orphaned at age 15 in Boyle Heights Los Angeles and lived at the YMCA run by a couple who took him under their wing. He met my grandmother, Susie Estella Snyder, riding his bike to go swimming in the Los Angeles River. She lived with her parents in a "section house" by the railroad tracks by the river. Her father was a "Section Chief, in charge of a section of the railroad track, and Allan had asked the family if he could park his bike in their fenced yard so it wouldn't be stolen. That's where he met Susie. Susie's father also played the fiddle at square dances and when her dad and mom left for a dance, a Hispanic man, one of his crew, sat on the porch with a machete on his lap as the guard. They married when he was 22, she was 18, in 1919 in Santa Ana California. His life and times were so extraordinary. In 1918 he created a bus business ferrying servicemen from Los Angeles to El Torro Marine Base. When the Influenza epidemic hit and they closed the base, he lost the business. While Allan was a prisoner of war, Susie worked at Douglass Aircraft as a fixture designer while taking care of her four remaining children. By 1945 her oldest daughter was in the coast guard, next daughter, Helen Marguerite O'Guinn, my mother, was in the Navy, stationed in Washington D.C., next youngest son was in the Navy on a ship. My youngest daughter was too young to join a service but worked at a ceramics manufacturer painting the color on plates and the like. The ceramics were called "apple ware". They had lost their home due to the lost income when Allan was captured and had moved into a shack on a piece of property they had purchased in El Monte California to grow berries as a cash crop. Friends had come and built other rooms on the shack to accommodate the family. This property is where I grew up and where Allan became my second father and taught me to wood carve and life lessons. He passed in 1974. Having known both of them gives me a moral compass to this day and the courage to carry on when the going gets tough.

When he got back to the States, he had to go to a sanatorium to recover from tuberculous. This is where he picked up whittling and later love of wood carving, which he taught me. Like men have dogs, he had me, his "boy" and grandson. He really became my dad. One of my jobs was to mow the lawn. He had a Sears riding mower that I loved to ride and do a good job on the lawn for he and Susie. He also lost his right eye due to malnutrition and had a tray of sample glass eyes he got from the prosthetic eye supplier. Probably talked him out of it. He was Irish, fun-loving, a kidder, and a deal maker. For a kid, a tray of glass eyes of all different tones and colors was a magical thing. When Allan had left for Wake, the property he and Susie had in El Monte to grow berries on was surrounded by many Japanese truck farms. He had had Japanese friends. When he came back, he helped some of his Japanese friends try and recover their property. After the war, he struggled with alcohol and overcame that. He was never able to overcome his smoking habit which was what actually killed him. After the war he and Susie created what I would later regard as Heaven on Earth. They had 30 different kinds of fruit trees, a large vegetable garden, including an asparagus patch, three different kinds of berries. Allan was in charge of the food production and the garden and orchard's care. Susie was in charge of planting bird attracting plants. She even grew giant sunflowers and when the huge flowers went to seed, laid them out on old tables for the birds. The only animals they really had to discourage were gophers, which were a constant battle in that soft loamy river soil. Next door was a rabbit farm where Allan would get manure for the trees and garden and would pick up bent nails at construction sites to put iron back in the soil around the fruit trees. He built Susie a "lath" house for shade loving plants and plumbed the overhead with sprinklers so you could make it "rain" inside. He carved tikis out of palm tree trunks that were around the deep residential lot. I was there many weekends and almost every summer and vacation. I saw Sputnik go over in 1957, or actually, it's booster stage that orbited with it as the actual satellite was too small to see from the ground.

Allan passed in 1974. Susie passed in 1994. I lived at that house in 1995. Several adults came to my door and wanted me to know how grateful they were to Susie. Apparently, she knew a lot of kids in the area, mostly Hispanic for teaching Catechism at the Catholic Church. Apparently, on their way home from school they would stop at Allan and Susie's house and Susie would help them with their homework. That's where I got the idea for "homework clubs" for neighborhoods. Imagine that, a safe place in the neighborhood to go after school and get help with your homework. No doubt they got fed too. In the Depression, in the '30s before WW2, Allan had a plumbing and appliance business. The local grocer admired his Hudson automobile. Allan traded his beautiful car for a year's worth of groceries. Many neighborhood kids ate at Allan's house during those tough years. At one time he had three pianos taken in as payment for plumbing work, as cash was scarce. Imagine a house full of kids and three pianos!

I carry Allan and Susie in my heart and mind today and it gives me strength and guidance to this very day. My mother, Helen Marguerite O'Guinn, Allan and Susie's second daughter wrote a book about her dad's life and times during WW2 and it's archived at the Hoover Institute at Stanford University under the Allan Asbury O'Guinn collection. Several books on Wake Island during the war referenced this work. The title of it is V.O. C. Here's the story of the title:

One the trip back from Japan after the war Allan was chosen to go to the ship's store and get things for the other returning civilian prisoners. After a while, he noticed that the military men were putting their rank after their names. Allan started putting V.O.C. after his name, just waiting for the clerk to ask him what that meant. Finally, he was asked. He stood up tall, pulled his shoulders back, and answered in an authoritative voice: "Victim Of Circumstance!" It got a big laugh and it illustrates his creativity and good humor. Irish, as I said. After the war, when he had a friend over, he would sit in his easy chair. On the mantel was a wooden snake he had carved. he had attached a wire to it so he could move it slightly and catch his guest's eye without being seen to pull the wire. He told my mom when she was writing the book, that in prison camp he would sometimes act a little crazy. Remember he was taller than most Americans and older too. He would act a little crazy and be able to get away with things, like sweeping the dust down the cracks in the floorboards, which was forbidden. The Japanese actually have empathy for the mentally ill. I guess every culture has its hardness and tenderness. I'm sure his creativity and racialism served him well in prison and helped him and others to survive. He related that at reunions of prisoners of Wake, Guam, and Cavette, men would tell him that he helped them to survive by being more mature and tough and keeping hope alive. Of course, he had a lot to live for. He said the men who didn't, didn't make it.

THE LAST LETTER SENT HOME TO HIS MOTHER BY RAY LEPINSKI (CIVILIAN) FROM GRANDSON – JIM GERCHY

Nov 27, 2941
Wake Island

Dear Mother,
How are you all—and I suppose it is getting a little chilly there. It is quite nice here now, not so hot in the day but the wind blows rather hard for the past month. Well it will soon be xmas again I suppose I will celebrate here on Wake. Bill Stone the chap that came here with me is leaving after the 15th of December for Honolulu then the mainland. I do not know how much longer I will stay after the 1st of the year as January and February in Honolulu is rather wet and the mainland is cold and wet so may stay on a while longer. Things are going quite well here. How is everybody in general. Had a letter from Uncle

Tony Ruhoff. He was up to see the Lightofields at Los Molinos. Well a Merry xmas and a Happy New Year to you all. Did you receive the shells I send you. You did not write and say you did or not.[1]
Love,
Ray

John O. ("J.O.") Young
WWII Japanese POW
Submitted by daughter Jorjette Young Bostrom

These events started in the fall of 1941 at the age of 19. I was six feet tall and weighed in at 119 pounds soaking wet. Pearl Ann Sparks and I were planning an October 1941 wedding.

After work that evening, I drove to Nampa and went out to the farm and picked up Pearl and started to town to see a movie. We got in the car, and she snuggled up to me as we started to talk. I informed her of my decision to go to Wake Island for nine months and be able to come home with $2000 cash. The announcement was not received with enthusiasm or cheering me on, but she scooted to the far side of the seat and remained there for most of the evening.

After four days in Honolulu, we sailed to Wake Island on a Navy transport called the USS Willie Ward Barrows. Was an interesting trip that took fourteen days.

---

[1] *The Bill Stone referred to in this letter was one of the Wake 98.*

We off-loaded onto the barge and went into the channel between Wilks Island and Wake Island. Then trucked to the barracks where the construction crews live. There were between 1150 to 1200 construction crews on the island. It was a navy base with Commander Winfield Cunningham in charge under the command of Major Devereaux.

Major Devereaux asked us civilians to come and train with them on the machine guns. This was about a month before the attack. As I recall I went a time or two. The powers that be know doubt knew that hostilities were eminent.

There was a ship in that had to be unloaded and for the next two nights, I drove the truck. The morning of December 8th the word came over the radio that Pearl Harbor had been attacked by the Japanese. We were across the International Date Line, so it was Monday of December 8th on Wake Island. Later in the morning I went down to the canteen where quite a group of the night shift workers were gathered talking about what was happening. I was drinking a milkshake when we heard the planes coming in. We assumed they were our planes. This was about 15 minutes to noon. We all ran outside looking toward the airstrip and then the strip started to explode, and the planes were flying right toward us. As they come close, above the roar of the engines we could hear a steady "tut-tut", and as dust started in little puffs realized that they were machine gunning us. I must have set some kind of record for the hundred-yard dash as I ran for the lagoon and ducked behind an outcropping of coral. That morning the China Clipper had taken off for Guam, but when the news of the attack on Pearl was received, they turned back, jettisoned their gas and landed. The Japanese bombers missed the plane but made a direct hit on the hotel burning it down.

After being captured we were taken in a camp in China. Camp life was an exercise in survival. Never enough food or the necessities of life. One thing that POW life did was separate the men from the boys. Most of the guards were quite civil toward us. Those who were most troublesome were those with little authority. If something went wrong the Japanese worked on the theory that "one man guilty, all men guilty". A number of times the whole camp would be brought into the yard and made to stand at attention for several hours and it would not matter if the weather was cold or hot.

The war prisoners were scheduled to be executed at the end of August, as the looked-for invasion would surely come. Had it happened, there would not have been thousands killed, but millions.

When it was finally over, we were taken to Yokohama. The prettiest sight we had seen was being greeted by the WAVES or WACS, whichever they were. We finally boarded the USS Ozark for our trip home.

At 19 when I went to the Island, I weighed 119 pounds. At age 24, even with the starvation diet I weighed 128 pounds. Most of the fellows were skin and bones and most had lost weight. My friend George Dinton for instance weighed 210 pounds when captured and 98 pounds when released.

We landed! As I was looking out over the crowd, I suddenly noticed a little blond in a red dress waving at someone. I suddenly dawned on me that was my girl Pearl, and beside her was my mother. When I finally was able to get off the ship it was a joyous reunion. I gave Pearl a big hug and kiss, and then my mother. Pearl was waiting to see who I would greet first. If it had been my mother, she would doubt what her rightful place was. Fortunately, my instinct was the right choice.

A month later we were married in the Salt Lake L.D.S. Temple for all time and all eternity. At this point in time, we have eight living children. One little girl aged 2 ½ died of polio in the 1952 epidemic. We are expecting our 36th grandchild in February and we have six great-grandchildren. In our 52nd year of marriage, things have turned out quite well for us.

IRENE KING READ: MOTHER OF FOREST READ

Tuesday, August 14: The happy news came that the Japs had surrendered. This time it was official. It sounded like the entire country had suddenly gone mad. For two days everyone celebrated. Every bell in town was ringing, whistles blowing, cars honking, shouting, and dancing. The war was over. Prison Camp was no more, and My Forrest was finally coming home!

After he was home awhile, I wrote these verses:

TO MY SON

For more than four years
For you I did fret,
Days dragged slowly by
Nights-my pillow was wet.
Constantly I prayed God
To watch over you
Keep you smiling and happy,
Brave and unharmed too
My prayers reached heaven

The months haven't been long
They now number seven,
And your healthy and strong.
Not harmed at all
Still jolly and sweet,
With a smile and glad hand
For each one you meet.
While the Japs held you prisoner,
Time slowly passed,
Now that your home again
The time passes too fast.
I am thankful and happy
You are back with us, Son
And I'll ever praise God
For what he has done.

The Man Behind The Glass
By Seth Randal
© 2021

Seth Randal is an Idaho-based writer, director and producer. He has spent ten years researching the stories of civilians captured on Wake Island for a documentary project currently titled "Workers of Wake." His projects have been featured in media including The New York Times, NPR, Boston Globe, The Advocate and Indiewire.

He's not related to anyone on Wake Island, although his father was a welder on the Trans-Alaska pipeline for Wake contractor Morrison-Knudsen, and his grandfather was involved in the construction of the Alcan Highway during

WWII. His mother was born in Munich, Germany, to Ukrainian parents detained by Nazis months before the end of the war. After living in a displaced persons camp for several years, her family emigrated to the United States in the early 1950s and she later became a naturalized citizen.

"There was just something soulful about his eyes. I had to have it."

Deanna Brown-Kane was searching an online auction for Civil War-era photos in 2016 when a small, nondescript portrait unexpectedly commanded her attention.

Looking back through the screen was a clean-shaven young man with wavy, dark chestnut hair and a strong nose, wearing a dark suit jacket and patterned tie. Circa 1930s or 1940s, seemingly hand colorized over sepia, illuminating a pair of warm, brown eyes. A slight smile curled impishly at the corners of his mouth, not unlike a male Mona Lisa. She won the auction, paying less than $15 with shipping.

"I collect photos from 1910 and before. Twentieth century photos just don't interest me. But for some reason this guy – he spoke to me. There was something about his smile in the picture, the rosy cheek, just something about it that drew me in. It lured me like a magnet."

The framed portrait finally arrived, and she unwrapped it, surging with enthusiasm and curiosity. Who was he? Would she ever know his story? She owns "Future's Past Boutique" in a Long Island, New York antique mall, selling treasures like artwork, vintage dolls, clocks, World War II, and military items. Her accent gives away her roots in Queens, where her grandmother instilled a love of collecting items from the past.

The worn, tarnished brass frame and dusty, dirty glass of the photo were holding something back. In hopes of cleaning the glass, Deanna delicately removed the cardboard easel back panel. “Lo and behold, it gave me a surprise… That's when everything came pouring, spilling out,” she said.

Her deep brown eyes widened in shock to discover a stack of items hidden inside the frame that would answer some of her questions. First one, then two, three —a total of five additional black and white photos showing cracks and heavy signs of wear. Several letters and a postcard, brittle and yellowed. The dried and discolored remains of a flower stem and leaf. A pocket calendar.

“My heart was racing a million miles a minute. What do I have here,” she thought? Then she gently peeled open one of the crisply folded letters. Through her innocent purchase of a simple framed photo, a remarkable and tragic Wake Island story started revealing itself to Deanna Brown-Kane.

“When I saw the Japanese braking sun, my heart sunk I knew I was seeing prisoner of war letters. I felt my heart sink to my knees. I felt this very sad feeling.”

The man behind the glass, whose pictures and letters were hidden within the frame, was Charles Austin Moe, a machine operator captured when Imperial Japan conquered Wake Island.

***

Charles Moe was born October 24, 1912, in Kooskia (Koos-kee), Idaho – a small mountain town of just 300 at the confluence of the middle and south forks of the Clearwater River, within the borders of the Nez Perce Indian Reservation. Kooskia is surrounded by millions of acres of national forest. In the town's early days, it was an outfitting station for miners, fur trappers, and loggers. With such a backdrop, it was no wonder Charles grew up with a love of fishing and hunting. What must he have thought of the town's landmark back then, the Kootenai Tramway, similar to a ski lift, carrying buckets of grain from a fertile plateau above town, a mile and a quarter through a rocky ravine to the mill near the town train station?

Charles was the baby of the family, the youngest of nine children born to Clarence Roswell Moe and Dora Mae Canfield, a family from Michigan who moved to Idaho before 1910. Charles was their only child to be born in Idaho. By October 1917, Clarence was working on a nearby ranch, according to a report in the Nez Perce Herald newspaper.

Clarence was the son of a Civil War hero. Sadly, tragedy seemed to follow his branch of the family.

Clarence and Dora May's baby girl Josey died in 1902. Their daughter Edith, Charles' sister, died in 1923 at the age of nineteen. Brother Melvin died in 1936 at age 27. The oldest sibling Harry, a WWI vet, died in 1946 at age fifty.

Before their passing, Clarence and Dora May would bury five of their nine children, including Charles Austin Moe.

***

In Long Island, New York, Deanna Brown-Kane was now looking at a different side to Charles Moe than originally caught her eye. She was holding a secret archive of long-forgotten photos, apparently taken during more carefree days before the war. In three of the pictures, possibly from a photo booth, Charles has a scruffy beard, with a scarf or jacket draped around his neck, looking somewhat evocative of a mountain man in a rustic toga or serape. He smirks mischievously in one, wearing a wide-brimmed hat with a large paper band reading "The Wild Spree." The fourth photo shows what may be Charles as a teenager, baby-faced.

Then there's the picture of a woman. Young, dark-haired, and elegant with high cheekbones and a graceful jaw. She wears a solid-colored, high-collared dress with asymmetrical, scalloped metal buttons. Was she in love with Charles? Or maybe a relative? Her name, and connection to Charles, remain unknown.

"Somebody lovingly hid that behind that frame to preserve it. It was placed in there so lovingly, that you can tell someone wanted to protect it. They loved him. Since the 1940s it could have been hidden behind that frame and not taken out. That's what makes it so mysterious. Who were these people? How did they live? How did they mourn for this poor man?"

***

Moe family ties date to Connecticut during the 1700s. In the decades since, they had slowly migrated west. Charles and his family continued to move throughout his life – with two common characteristics – being near the water and edging further westward.

In 1920, by the time Charles was seven, the family had moved to Lewiston, Idaho – a town fifty miles or so downstream from Kooskia, where the Clearwater and Snake rivers combine before their voyage to the Columbia and, eventually, the Pacific Ocean. Founded in 1860 as a gold rush supply center for miners working in the nearby mountains, Lewiston is Idaho's oldest incorporated town. The Moe family lived in the rear part of a home at 1904 Main Street, with the Clearwater River across the street, separated just by the road, a spur line of the Camas Prairie

Railroad. Charles was in school, and the census shows he was able to read and write. Clarence was employed doing "common labor."

When Charles was 17, in 1930, he lived with his parents at home on Maywood Avenue in Camas, Washington, a town of around 4,200 people along the Columbia River, about 20 miles from Portland, Oregon. Charles delivered groceries for a local market. His father Clarence and sister Ina – and most of the people in Camas – worked down the street at the massive Crown Zellerbach Mill, then the largest specialty paper mill in the world, according to the University of Washington. The Columbian newspaper reported that, during WWII, the mill would be refitted to produce rudders for Liberty ships.

Within a decade, much of the Moe family, Charles included, had moved to southwestern Oregon outside of Grants Pass. The 1940 census shows Charles living with his parents on a farm they owned in a tiny village along Slate Creek now called Wilderville. Overlooking the community, on pine-forested Marble Mountain, the Pacific Portland Cement Company's quarry dug up limestone for use in concrete.

In 1940 he had completed high school but not college. Twenty-seven-year-old Charles told the census taker he had made just $250 for the entire past year working as a firewood cutter. His Selective Service draft registration card filled out that year listed his employer as "Self."

***

On May 1, 1941, Charles Moe stood on the pier in San Francisco and prepared for his greatest westward adventure yet. Before him, the luxurious Matson liner S.S. Lurline, gleaming white superstructure with a smart, dark blue pin stripe running the length of the hull. The liner, 632 feet long with two funnels, already had a reputation for carrying the rich and famous – seven years earlier, it carried Amelia Earhart and her Lockheed Vega to Honolulu ahead of her record-breaking solo flight from Hawaii to Oakland.

From Honolulu – Moe and a group of other workers headed to remote Wake Island, a tiny tropical atoll more than 4,300 miles west of San Francisco. The government had hired a consortium of contractors to build a Naval Air Base. He would be operating an industrial vibrator, the kind used to tamp concrete and asphalt. Tiring work and long days, but at $145 a month, he could earn more in two months on Wake than he had the entire year previous. Not to mention the free room and board for the construction workers. It wouldn't last.

Wake Island came under attack just five hours after Pearl Harbor. Despite being dramatically outmanned and outgunned, the island withstood invasion until December 23, 1941 – more than two weeks – a feat compared to the Alamo.

***

Shanghai War-prisoners Camp

June 1, 1942

"Will write a few lines and let you know that I am feeling fine. I have been cutting wood for the kitchen and also building fires. That is my job here. It's a joke on me for I'm right back to the same job as when I left."

On January 12, 1942, after Wake Island fell to Imperial Japanese forces, Charles was one of some 1,200 civilians, and servicemen forced at gunpoint onto the Nitta Maru, a nearly brand-new NYK Line passenger ship transferred to military service. But instead of cabins, the men were forced down a ladder into a place humans were never intended to travel: the windowless cargo hold. Hardly enough room to even sit down. Buckets for toilets. A stifling lack of fresh air. Little to eat. Survivors would later remember it as a "Hell ship." Within two days of sailing, as Nitta Maru ventured further north, the frigid cold of winter became bitingly real for men dressed for sub-tropical weather. A handful of men were dropped off in Japan after a week at sea; Charles, and most of the other prisoners, had to stay on board a total of 16 days until their arrival at Shanghai, China, a coastal city then occupied by the Japanese. Charles' first stop: Shanghai camp barracks No. 5.

He sent several typewritten letters home to his parents in Oregon. The letters feature a stamp of Japanese censors in bright, red ink in the upper corner.

"Hoping this finds you well and worry-free… everything will be O.K. Love, Your Son, Chas. A. Moe."

The upbeat letters masked the grim reality of the brutal prisoner of war camps. Former Wake Island civilian POW Joe Goicoechea suffered from bronchitis so severe he couldn't move, as well as headaches, gangrene in one leg, a broken wrist and thumb – details left out of his own letters home. "You couldn't mention any of that," Goicoechea said. "If you did, it wouldn't go through. They'd (the military censors) black it out."

***

As Deanna Brown-Kane studied her unexpected discoveries from the picture frame, two other items stood out. She wondered about a wallet-sized 1938 calendar. Was that an important year in Charles' life? But more poignantly, leaves and a stem from a flower, mostly yellow and brown, but with some curious hints of green, perhaps preserved by the hiding place. Had it been a flower of love or loss?

Deanna became more introspective, remembering the seller of the photos online: Goodwill thrift stores.

"It was a Goodwill donation from somebody. Maybe the family was just getting rid of all the stuff in the house. He ended up in a Goodwill auction as if his life meant nothing. And that made me very sad. I just feel like he was forgotten."

***

The Moe family must have been delighted to receive a lengthy letter from Charles sometime after Easter 1943. A full page of single-spaced, typewritten greetings. He remained upbeat in it, with a wistful air of longing for his old life and home.

Shanghai War-prisoners Camp

April 27, 1943

"Dear Dad, Mother, and All:

Once again, thru the kind permission of the Japanese, we are allowed to write letters home again. Things are beautiful here now, but it doesn't take the place of home. I would give anything to be back with you all once again. I miss the hills and all that is home. But it won't be too [sic] much longer before I am back.

For Easter, we had a very nice dinner furnished by the Red Cross with the permission of the Japanese. We had boiled chicken, gravy and noodles, two eggs, two hot Cross buns and etc. We appreciated it very much.

I miss you all and wish I were back to go hunting and fishing with you all again, but I will be soon.

If it is at all possible, I would appreciate it very much if you could send me a package. Tobacco [sic], candy, a pair of shoes, clothes, and so forth. I would like some good old venison but will wait till I get back so I can kill my own."

***

Charles was not the first in his family to experience war. His grandfather Joshua Roswell Moe was a witness to a remarkable history. Born in Michigan in 1847, he enlisted as a private in Company A of the 4th Michigan Cavalry in January 1864. By that summer, he had fought in the Battles of Dallas, New Hope Church, Allatoona Hills, and Kennesaw Mountain during the Union's Atlanta Campaign push into Georgia. He likely witnessed hundreds of deaths. On May 10, 1865, Joshua and his regiment assisted in the capture of Jefferson Davis, the President of the Confederacy, in Irwin County, Georgia. He was one of the men selected to help escort Davis to Washington, D.C.

After the war, Joshua returned to Michigan, marrying Hannah Josephine Church the next year. They had seven children, including Clarence Roswell Moe, born in 1872. Joshua farmed the land, despite having an affliction with his lungs which he attributed to his Civil War service. Hannah died in 1891 when Clarence was 19.

Joshua Roswell Moe would remarry. When he died in 1937 at age 90, he was the last Civil War veteran to be buried in Grand Traverse County, Michigan.

***

A few weeks after his full-page letter, Charles sent a small postcard, the last correspondence found behind the glass of the picture frame. It reads in part:

May 17, 1943

"Dear Folks:

I hope the family are well and please, above all, do not worry about me, for I am O.K. and will be with you soon, I feel sure of that. It has begun to warm up here but I enjoy it very much. Well folks, I must close with all my love to you all, write and soon. Your Loving son, Chas. A. Moe

"He was trying to be so brave," Deanna said, reflecting on the letters and post cards she had read many times. "You could tell he was trying to be positive and upbeat for them. But you could tell this man was under duress when he was writing what he was writing. So, it made me feel really terrible for him."

***

In August of 1943, Moe and several hundred other POWs were transported to the Osaka camp in Japan. After so many years of moving westward, it would be his first move east.

Another U.S. prisoner of war captured on Wake Island, Naval Warrant Officer Walter John Cook, would later describe the Osaka experience in testimony before the War Department, "While at Osaka, we did all kinds of work, chiefly stevedoring (loading/unloading ships and trucks) … We were required to perform extremely strenuous labor and were poorly fed. Men were often forced to go out to work when they were actually weak and ill from malnutrition and fatigue. Due to this, and because there was little or no medical attention given us, approximately 100 men died during their imprisonment.

"The barracks were infested with rats, lice, fleas, and bedbugs, all of which caused us to have large sores on our bodies. We also had beri beri, pellagra, boils, scurvy, and various other skin infections. Some of the men also suffered from what we called 'electric foot' or 'hot foot,' a disease which causes the foot to swell enormously and turn black - then the foot or feet would fall off," Cook said.

Charles Austin Moe died within three months of arriving in Osaka. Accounts of his cause of death differ. A fellow Osaka POW, Army Major Warren A. Minton, kept records of deaths at the camp. He wrote that Charles died from cerebral malaria on November 20, 1943. His records, however, fail to enlighten on what Charles endured in his final days. As the parasite traveled through his bloodstream and entered his brain and body, Charles may have endured a high fever and chills, possibly severe anemia or hypoglycemia, brain swelling, organ failure, seizures, and finally, a coma.

A different report states Moe died of croup pneumonia, a condition the Mayo Clinic says frequently starts with a common cold, leading to a hoarse, barking cough. It would have become increasingly difficult to breathe as his lungs filled with infection and fluid.

He was thirty-one years old.

Coincidentally, while Charles Moe was held as a prisoner of Japan, the U.S. government would set up the Kooskia Internment Camp just thirty miles southeast of his birthplace, housing longtime U.S. residents of Japanese descent who were deemed "enemy aliens."

Nearly five years after his death, the remains of Charles Austin Moe eventually took one final trip home to the United

States. On Wednesday, November 10, 1948, his family gathered for a graveside service, officiated by Rev. John Phipps from St John's Presbyterian Church.

Clarence Moe, Charles' father, would bury five of his nine children, three of his four siblings, as well as several nieces. He died in 1959 at eighty-seven. Dora Mae remarried the following year, at age eighty-three, but passed away in October 1961. Clarence, Dora, and their son Charles are in adjacent plots without grave markers. Several other family members are buried in the same cemetery, mere blocks away from the Columbia River.

***

Shortly after her discovery of the photos, Deanna posted several videos online telling the story and looking for more information.

"I really didn't get too much feedback, then a few years later, I went on the antique message board. Everybody was intrigued by this man. That's when a bunch of people started doing research and found a relative." Deanna contacted the Moe family relative through social media.

"He's a history teacher in Alaska. He was just in shock. He was like, 'Wow!' I was willing to send him the stuff." But he didn't seem interested in the original pictures, so she kept them safe.

***

Since the discovery of the Moe photo collection, details about Deanna Brown-Kane's own family's WWII history have come into sharper focus. A DNA test connected her to a cousin and the tragic story of Deanna's great uncle Alexander J. Mercaldo.

Uncle Alexander was a first-generation American born to immigrants from Italy. Deanna learned he was so eager to join the Marines after Pearl Harbor that he endlessly pressured his mom Rose to sign papers allowing him to list at age seventeen.

As a Marine private, he ended up in the South Pacific aboard the U.S.S. McKean, a rickety old destroyer-built decades early. Early one morning, sailing near Bougainville in the Solomon Islands, an Imperial Japanese G4M "Betty" swooped down and launched a torpedo that speared the McKean's starboard side, exploding the ammo magazines and blasting a grizzly inferno of burning fuel oil onto the ship and into the sea.

"He was burned to death jumping overboard in a sea of boiling oil when the ship's boilers exploded," Deanna explained quietly.

She herself is a burn survivor, having nearly died from second and third-degree burns in 2008. She spent a month in intensive care and received very painful skin grafts. Still living with the scars, she empathizes deeply with the newly learned experience of her great uncle. "You feel the heat of like a thousand suns burning your skin," she said. "To think those were his last moments was so sad."

Alexander's military casualty card states it bluntly, "It is believed that this man was so badly burned in the resulting oil fire that the body could not be recovered." He was just 19. In all, an estimated 120 U.S. marines and sailors died in that attack, most from the waves of flaming fuel.

No one took Alexander's death harder than his mother Rose, who Deanna learned "never forgave herself. Every day she cried for him until the day she died. She never got over it. She blamed herself for giving him the permission to sign up." His name is engraved on a monument to the U.S.S. McKean at Manila American Cemetery and Memorial in the Philippines.

In a twist stranger than fiction, Deanna realized her Uncle Alexander died on November 17, 1943, just three days before Charles Moe, the man whose photo behind the glass gave her a new interest in WWII.

"It's really chilling," she said. "Could it be a coincidence, maybe? But sometimes things are too strange to be a coincidence."

***

2008 was just a few days old when Deanna was cooking a pot of spaghetti. She got too close to the stove, and the gas flame ignited her polyester shirt. It went up in seconds, melting plastic and burning away parts of her arm, shoulder, and torso. Doctors feared they would have to amputate her arm, but she still has it, stronger than ever. The experience, and long recovery, changed her life.

"I refused to let this beat me and never will," she said. "My accident has really changed my outlook on life. I am now interested in what really counts and am much more empathetic toward others. I'm no longer a victim of circumstances but a survivor. I will never let any of life's downs hinder my spiritual journey ever again."

Today, she continues her search for other unique antiques, saying it gives her passion for life. Sometimes she looks online, other times with a metal detector.

"I find each antique object has a story to tell, whether it's worth ten cents or ten thousand. Somebody held it and loved it. The stuff that was made years ago has a story to tell you of quality and how people lived back then. I'll always be a treasure hunter, I guess, looking for history. Before I found the letters, I didn't even know Wake Island existed."

She has instilled a love and curiosity for history in her own two daughters. One of them printed a picture of their great-great uncle Alexander J. Mercaldo, framed it, and put it on display in the Brown-Kane home. Similar, Deanna imagines how the picture of POW Charles Moe likely sat in a place of prominence for someone who loved him.

She hopes to one day find a place where the pictures of Charles can be put on public display, teaching people about Wake Island and the ordeal of the men who went there to work. Meanwhile, she quietly keeps alive the memory of a man she never met but to whom she still feels a deep connection.

"It's haunting. It gives me this haunting feeling. Like somebody put clues in there and wants us to find out. The intrigue is driving me crazy. It gives you that mysterious overtone like this ghost came back to tell his story.

She calls the story of the man behind the glass one of her "finds of the century."

"The picture could have been thrown in the garbage. It's like he's coming back from the grave to tell his story… and he wants to be remembered for what he endured and sacrificed for our country."

***

CHAPTER ELEVEN:
MY FINAL TRIBUTE

In my 72 years of life, I have been blessed to have been brought up in a loving, caring household. I heard early on the stories of Wake Island. It was always of great interest to me to hear them and to find meaning and integrate them into my daily life. I think first and foremost (my father's favorite) "Live by the golden rule, Be a fighter, don't give up. Tomorrow is another day." On Wake Island and in POW camps these very simple traits helped them survive. These lessons learned, to me, have been extremely valuable in my life. I owe them to my father. Writing this book has been a year-long endeavor. It has been a lifelong dream of mine to tell a personal story about them. It is and could be the story of many.

The Defenders of Wake Island survivor groups adopted a motto, "Destiny Forged Inextricable Bonds of Friendship"

I think it certainly now is a fitting eulogy. I had the distinct opportunity to personally get to know many of these gallant men, both marines and civilians. Now I am afforded an equal opportunity to get to know many of the families. We have a common bond. I would describe that bond as "Friendship" We learned much of what that word means from our survivor heroes. It is a lesson for all of us. We must, as families, also pass this on to future generations. It is our duty to do so.

Now I am going to ask that the memory of the Defenders of Wake Island never be forgotten.

To my Wake family – Tell the story of your father, your grandfather, your great grandfather, uncle, and cousins many times removed.

To the grandchildren:

Sam and Mary and great-grandchildren – Kamryn, Hazel, and Conner

Chris and Julie and great-grandchildren – Max, Jack, and Cole

Sarah and Bob and great-grandchildren – Maddy and Isaac

Amy and Peter and great-grandchildren – Greyson and Isla

Chelsea, Jacob, Cailey, and Chloe

And to all the other grandchildren - Catie, Phillip, and Tom

And to all future generations not yet born.

Remember Wake Island and your hero. Remember what they did for our country. Remember their heroism. Remember how they suffered and their perseverance to survive.

Now I leave you with a final picture. They are all gone now. We only have Pat Aki remaining (bless this man, bless all of them). However, we must still tell their story. It is how they will never be forgotten. Here Max Pearsall (son of my nephew Chris and wife Julie) stands by the grave of his Great-Grandfather.

In Memory of the Wake Island Defenders We Will Never Forget You!

Chapter Twelve:
Roosters of the Defenders of Wake Island

U.S. Marines Corps – 1st Defense Battalion:

USMC	LAST	FIRST	UNIT	Date of death	Location	POW Lib
SGT	Ackley	Edwin M.	MAG21			Rokorushi
PVT	Adams	Richard P.	1DB			Hak 2
PVT	Adams	E.O. Stephen	1DB			Rokorushi
SGT	Agar	Paul Raymond	1DB	11/29/1944	Kiangwan	N
TSGT	Allen	Jack V.	MAG21	12/8/1941	Wake	N
PFC	Andrews	Arthur Dale	1DB			OmoriTo1
SSGT	Arthur	Robert G.	MAG21			Tok3Omi
PhM2c	Atwood	Lawrence M.	Medical			Hak 3
PVT	Austin	Rufus B.	1DB			Hak 3
TSGT	Bailey	Vincent W.	MAG21	1/22/1942	NM exec	N
PFC	Baker	S. L.	1DB			Osaka
PVT	Bamford	Roger D.	1DB			Hak 2
PFC	Barger	Lester L.	1DB			Hak 2
CPL	Barnes	Earl Harry	1DB			Fuk 3
1LT	Barninger	Clarence A. Jr.	1DB			Hak 4
PFC	Bartelme	Herbert E.	1DB			Hak 2
PVT	Bastien	James S.	1DB			Hak 2
MAJ	Bayler	Walter L. J.				
PVT	Beaver	Darell Laverne	1DB	9/9/1945	Hak 2	N
PlSGT	Beck	William D.	1DB			Hak 2
PlSGT	Bedell	Henry A.	1DB	12/23/1941	Wake	N
PFC	Beese	Fred A.	1DB			Hak 2
PFC	Bendenski	Joseph B.	1DB			Osaka
PVT	Benedetto	Michael A.	1DB			Fuk 3
PFC	Benjamin	Armand E.	1DB			Fuk 3
PFC	Bennett	Arthur K.	1DB			Hak 2
PFC	Bentley	Joseph M.	1DB			Hak 3

PFC	Berkery	James M. Jr.	1DB			Hak 3
SGT	Bertels	Alton Jewell	1DB	3/23/1945	Kiangwan	N
SSGT	Blandy	John F.	MAG21			Sen7B
PFC	Bogdonovich	Edward M.	1DB			Ofuna?
PFC	Boley	Kenneth C.	1DB			Os5DKaw
PFC	Borchers	Orville N.	1DB			Tok 3
PFC	Borne	Joseph E.	1DB			Tok 5
Mgun	Borth	Harold C.	1DB			Zentsuji
PlSGT	Boscarino	James F.	1DB			Rokorushi
PFC	Bostick	William F.	1DB	9/6/2010	OR	
CPL	Bosher	Raymond R.	1DB			Hak 3
SGT	Bourquin	Robert E.	MAG21			Hak 3
SGT	Bowsher	Walter A. Jr.	1DB			Hak 3
SGT	Box	Robert S. Jr.	1DB			Hak 3
PVT	Boyd	Berdyne	1DB			Zentsuji
CPL	Boyle	Hugh L.	MAG21	12/23/1941	Wake	N
PVT	Bragg	Lorel J.	1DB			Hak 3
PFC	Breckenridge	Albert H.	1DB			Hak 3
PhM2c	Brewer	Artis T.	Medical			ShangJail
CPL	Brown	Gene E.	1DB			Hak 3
CPL	Brown	James R.	1DB			Hak 3
CPL	Brown	Robert M.	1DB			Hak 3
CPL	Brown	Robert L.	1DB			Os5DKaw
PFC	Brown	Buell S.	1DB			Hak 3
PFC	Brown	Kenneth L.	1DB			Hak 3
PFC	Browning	James S.	1DB			Hak 3
PVT	Broyles	Earl M. Jr.	1DB			Os5DKaw
PFC	Bryan	Pershing B.	1DB			Hak 3
PVY	Buckie	William B. Jr.	1DB			Os5DKaw
PFC	Buehler	William F.	1DB			Hak 3
PlSGT	Bumgarner	Alvin A.	1DB			Zentsuji
PFC	Burford	Philip L.	1DB			Hak 3
PFC	Busse	Wilbur J.	1DB			Hak 3
PFC	Byard	Lester C.	1DB			Osaka
PFC	Byer	Lawrence M.	1DB			Hak 3
PFC	Byrd	Harry J.	1DB			Hak 3
PFC	Byrne	Herbert R.	1DB			Osaka
SGT	Cain	Orville J.	1DB			Hak 2
PFC	Calanchini	Arthur J.	1DB			OmoriTo1
PFC	Caldwell	Richard R.	1DB			Osaka

CPL	Camp	Charles H.	1DB			Hak 2
MSGT	Carr	Gerald J.	1DB			Hak 2
TSGT	Cemeris	John	1DB			Os5DKaw
PFC	Cessna	Harry J.	1DB			Hak 2
PhM1c	Chambliss	Jesse R.	Medical			Hak 3
PFC	Chapman	Henry H. W.	1DB			Hak 3
PFC	Chew	Hoyle E.	1DB			Hak 3
PVT	Christensen	Alfred Bennett	1DB			Fuk 3
PVT	Chudzik	Joseph T.	1DB			Hak 3
PVT	Clark	Emery T.	1DB			Hak 3
PVT	Colby	Harold Gould	1DB			Fuk 3
PFC	Comfort	Floyd H.	1DB			Hak 3
SGT	Comin	Howard D.	MAG21	12/23/1941	Wake	N
CPL	Cominus	Gus J.	1DB			Osaka
PFC	Commers	Joseph Frederic	1DB	8/20/1942	ShangHos	N
2LT	Conderman	Robert J.	MAG21	12/8/1941	Wake	N
Ch-Ck	Condra	Charley H.	1DB			Hak 3
PFC	Conner	Warren D.	1DB			Zentsuji
PFC	Connor	Dennis Clifford	1DB			Fuk 3
SGT	Cook	Jack B.	1DB			Hak 3
CPL	Cook	Hal Jr.	MAG21	12/8/1941	Wake	N
PFC	Cooley	Delmar E.	1DB			Hak 3
CPL	Cooper	Clarence G. Jr.	1DB			Osaka
PFC	Cooper	Paul C.	1DB			Osaka
PFC	Cooper	Robert E.	1DB			Hak 3
PFC	Cornett	John	1DB			Os5DKaw
PFC	Couch	Claude C.	1DB			Hak 3
TSGT	Couch	Winslow	MAG21	12/8/1941	Wake	N
SGT	Coulson	Raymond L.	1DB			ShangJail
PVT	Covert	Phillip G.	1DB			Hak 3
PFC	Cox	Roy T.	1DB			Omori
PVT	Crouch	James A.	1DB			Hak 3
PFC	Culp	Joseph C.	1DB	5/5/1945	Os13BTsu	N
PVT	Cunningham	Kenneth E.	1DB			OmoriTo1
PFC	Curlee	Albert C.	1DB			Osaka
PFC	Curry	Robert E.	1DB			Hak 3
CPL	Dale	John R.	1DB			Hak 2
PFC	Dana	Max J.	1DB			Hak 2
2LT	Davidson	Carl R.	MAG21	12/22/1941	at sea	N
CPL	Davis	Eschol E.	1DB			Fuk 3

PFC	Davis	Jack E.	1DB			Hak 3
CPL	Davis	Floyd H.	1DB			Hak 2
PFC	Dawson	Harvey L.	1DB			Hak 3
CPL	Deeds	Robert Leon	1DB			Fuk 3
TSGT	DeHaan	Harmen	MAG21	1/11/1944	OS13BTsu	N
PVT	DeLoach	Emmett D.	1DB			Hak 3
PFC	Descamps	Clarence C.	1DB			Osaka
CPL	DeSparr	Marshall E.	MAG21	12/8/1941	Wake	N
MAJ	Devereux	James P. S.	1DB			Hak 3
PVT	Dimento	Frank	1DB			Hak 3
PFC	Dodge	Bernard A.	1DB			Fuk 3
CPL	Domingue	Alton J.	1DB			Hak 3
PVT	Dorman	Roger	1DB			Hak 3
CPL	Double	John F.	MAG21	12/14/1941	Wake	N
CPL	Drake	Elmer S. Jr.	1DB			Hak 3
PFC	Dunham	Estille F.	1DB			Hak 3
CPL	Durrwachter	Henry L.	1DB			Tok5DKaw
PFC	Eaton	Edward F.	1DB			Hak 3
CPL	Economou	Michael N.	1DB			Os5DKaw
SGT	Edwards	Robert P.	MAG21	12/8/1941	Wake	N
PVT	Elliott	Norman D.	1DB			Hak 3
CAPT	Elrod	Henry T.	MAG21	12/23/1941	Wake	N
PFC	Emerick	Billie Edward	1DB			Fuk 3
PVT	Enyart	Clinton H.	1DB			Os5DKaw
TSGT	Everist	Joseph L.	MAG21			Tok5BNii
SSGT	Farrar	Herbert D.	MAG21	12/8/1941	Wake	N
PFC	Fields	Marshall E.	1DB			Hak 2
PFC	Finley	Lloyd B.	1DB			Hak 2
CPL	Fish	Cyrus D.	1DB			Hak 2
PFC	Fitzpatrick	James Alburn	1DB			Fuk 3
PFC	Fleener	Gene A.	1DB			Hak 3
PVT	Fleming	Manton Leon	1DB	2/26/1944	Os13BTsu	N
SSGT	Fortuna	Stephen	1DB			Hak 3
PFC	Frandsen	Andrew J.	1DB			Hak 3
CAPT	Freuler	Herbert C.	MAG21			Hak 4
PFC	Frey	Robert L.	1DB			Hak 3
PFC	Frost	Lynn W.	1DB			Hak 3
PFC	Gardner	Douglas D.	1DB			Hak 2
SGT	Gardner	Glen G.	MAG21			Zentsuji
SGT	Garr	Robert F. Jr	MAG21	12/13/1941	Wake	N

PFC	Garrison	Everett	1DB			Os5DKaw
PFC	Gatewood	Martin A.	1DB			Fuk 3
CPL	George	Joseph E. Jr.	1DB			Hak 2
PFC	George	John F.	1DB			Hak 2
PVT	Giddens	George G.	1DB			Os5DKaw
PFC	Gilbert	Richard C.	1DB			Hak 2
PFC	Gilley	Ernest N. Jr.	1DB	12/23/1941	Wake	N
PlSGT	Gleichauf	William A.	1DB	12/23/1941	Wake	N
CAPT	Godbold	Bryghte D.	1DB			Hak 4
SSGT	Godwin	William F.	1DB			Os5DKaw
SGT	Gordon	William	1DB			Hak 3
SGT	Gragg	Raymon	1DB			Hak 3
PFC	Grant	Everard M.	1DB			Hak 3
1LT	Graves	George A.	MAG21	12/8/1941	Wake	N
CPL	Graves	Leon A.	1DB			Tok5DKaw
PFC	Gray	Robert L. J.	1DB			Os5DKaw
2LT	Greeley	Robert W.	1DB			Hak 4
PFC	Gregouire	Sylvester	1DB			Hak 3
CPL	Greska	Martin A.	1DB			Hak 3
CPL	Gross	Franklin D.	1DB			Rokorushi
PFC	Grubb	Glenn E.	1DB			Hak 3
CPL	Gruber	Walter J.	MAG21			Os5BTsu
PFC	Guilbeaux	Stanley P.	1DB			Hak 3
CPL	Guthrie	Frank A.	1DB	8/10/1944	Kiangwan	N
PFC	Haggard	Fred D.	1DB			Hak 2
SGT	Haggerty	Oliver P. Jr.	1DB			Hak 2
CPL	Haidinger	Robert F.	1DB			Tok5DKaw
PVT	Hair	Stephen Y.	1DB			Hak 2
SSGT	Haley	Gifford L.	MAG21	12/8/1941	Wake	N
SGT	Hall	James W.	1DB			Hak 2
CPL	Halstead	William C.	1DB	12/23/1941	Wake	N
Mgun	Hamas	John	1DB			Hak 3
PVT	Hamel	Fred M.	1DB			Hak 2
TSGT	Hamilton	William J.	MAG21			Tok3BOmi
2LT	Hanna	Robert M.	1DB			Hak 4
SGT	Hannah	Clyde W.	1DB			Hak 2
TSGT	Hannum	Earl R.	MAG21	1/22/1942	NM exec	Carl E?
PVT	Harper	Joel E.	1DB			Os5DKaw
PFC	Harringer	Ewald	1DB			Os5DKaw
PFC	Harrison	Charles L.	1DB			Hak 3

PFC	Hartung	Arvel N.	1DB			Rokorushi
TSGT	Hassig	Edwin F.	1DB			Hak 3
SGT	Haugen	Henry	1DB			Hak 3
PFC	Hearn	Jack D.	1DB			Hak 3
SSGT	Hemmelgarn	Paul F.	MAG21	6/5/1945	Kobe Hosp	N
PFC	Hendrickson	Russell W.	1DB			Hak 3
PVT	Herron	Merle L.	1DB			Hak 3
PFC	Hicks	Albert Jr.	1DB			Hak 3
PFC	Hill	Charles C.	1DB			Hak 3
PFC	Himelrick	John R.	1DB	4/26/1944	Fuk 3	N
1LT	Holden	Frank J.	MAG21	12/8/1941	Wake	N
SSGT	Holmes	Charles A.	1DB			Hak 3
CPL	Holewinski	Ralph J.	1DB			Zentsuji
PFC	Holt	Johnson P.	1DB			Os5DKaw
PFC	Hoskison	Lawrence O.	1DB			Hak 3
PFC	Houde	Woodrow A.	1DB	12/23/1941	Wake	N
PFC	Houschildt	Frank H.	1DB			Hak 3
PhM1c	Howard	John R.	Med			Hak 4
CPL	Hubley	George G.	1DB			Tok3Omi
PlSGT	Huffman	Forest	1DB			Hak 3
MessSGT	Hughes	A. R. Jr.	1DB			Hak 3
PFC	Hundley	Robert G.	1DB			Tok5BNii
SGT	Hunt	Quince A.	MAG21	12/9/1941	Wake	N
SSGT	Hyder	Luther E.	1DB			Hak 3
PFC	Hyzer	Morris F.	1DB			Hak 3
PFC	Jackson	Sammy C.	1DB			OmoriTo1
SGT	Jamerson	Joseph Paul	MAG21			Fuk 3
PVT	Jenkins	Haley B.	1DB			Hak 2
SSGT	Johnson	Ralph E.	1DB			Hak 3
CPL	Johnson	Thomas W.	1DB			Hak 3
CPL	Johnson	John S. Jr.	1DB			Hak 3
PFC	Johnson	George L.	1DB			Hak 3
PFC	Johnson	Solon L.	1DB			Hak 3
CPL	Johnson	Lillard L.	1DB			Tok12BMi
TSGT	Johnson	Ellis J.	MAG21			Nag10BFu
PFC	Johnson	Phillip W.	1DB			Fuk 3
PFC	Johnson	Harland R.	1DB			Osaka
PFC	Jones	Otis T.	1DB			Hak 3
PFC	Joyner	Paul C.	1DB			Osaka
TSGT	June	Randolph Marlin	1DB			Fuk 3

LTjg	Kahn	G. Mason	Medical			Hak 3
PVT	Katchak	John	1DB	12/8/1941	Wake	N
PFC	Kaz	Norman N.	1DB			Hak 2
CPL	Kelnhofer	Guy J. Jr.	1DB			Hak 3
SSGT	Kennedy	Walter Thomas	MAG21			Os7BTak
1LT	Kessler	Woodrow M.	1DB			Hak 4
PlSGT	Ketner	Bernard O.	1DB			Hak 3
PFC	Kidd	Walter	1DB			Os5DKaw
CPL	King	Kirby K.	1DB			Hak 3
MTSGT	King	Curtis P.	MAG21	12/8/1941	Wake	N
PFC	King	James Orlo	1DB			Fuk 3
2LT	Kinney	John F.	MAG21			esc 5/42
PFC	Kirk	John T.	1DB			Hak 3
PFC	Klein	Arthur A.	1DB			Osaka
MSGT	Kleponis	Vincent	1DB			Hak 3
2LT	Kliewer	David Donald	MAG21			Rokorushi
CPL	Kohlin	Alfred T.	1DB			Tok3Omi
CPL	Koontz	Benjamin D.	MAG21	12/8/1941	Wake	N
MSGT	Krawie	John W.	1DB			Hak 3
PFC	Krenistki	William	1DB			ShangHosp
PFC	Kroptavich	James S.	1DB			Tok4BNao
CPL	Kruczek	Walter J.	1DB			Os5DKaw
PFC	Lane	Lloyd G.	1DB	1/11/1944	ChikOs1	N
PFC	Langley	Edgar N.	1DB			Osaka
PhM1c	Lanning	John R.	MAG21?			Hak 3
PVT	LaPorte	Ewing E.	1DB			Hak 2
PFC	Larson	William C.	1DB			Os5DKaw
PFC	Latham	Joe T.	1DB			Osaka
CPL	Laursen	Norman J.	1DB			Fuk 3
CPL	Lee	Robert E.	1DB			ShangHosp
PVT	Lepore	Anthony	1DB			Fuk 3
1LT	Lewis	William W.	1DB			Hak 4
PFC	Lewis	Clifton H.	1DB			Hak 3
PVT	Lillard	George E.	1DB			Hak 3
PFC	Lindsay	Wilford J.	1DB			Hak 3
TSGT	Locklin	Eugene D.	MAG21	12/8/1941	Wake	N
PFC	Lorenz	Henry D.	1DB			Hak 3
PFC	Lutz	Eugene J.	1DB			Fuk 3
PVT	Madere	Joseph A.	1DB			Hak 2
SGT	Malleck	Donald R.	1DB			Osaka

PFC	Malone	Thomas J. Jr.	1DB			Hak 2
SGT	Manning	Bernard H.	1DB			Hak 2
PFC	Marlow	Clovis R.	1DB	12/23/1941	Wake	N
PFC	Marshall	Gordon L.	1DB	12/23/1941	Wake	N
PFC	Martin	Gerald J.	1DB			Hak 2
PFC	Martin	Virgil E.	1DB			Hak 2
CPL	Marvin	Kenneth L.	1DB			Tok4BNao
PFC	Mathis	Charles L.	1DB			Hak 2
2LT	McAlister	John A.	1DB			esc 5/45
CPL	McAmis	Terrence T.	1DB			Hak 2
CPL	McAnally	Winford J.	1DB			Hak 3
PFC	McBride	James E.	MAG21	12/8/1941	Wake	N
PFC	McCage	Harvey E.	1DB			Osaka
PFC	McCalla	Marvin P.	1DB			Hak 3
PVT	McCaulley	Wade B. Jr.	1DB			Hak 3
PFC	McClanahan	Wilbur C.	1DB			Osaka
PFC	McDaniel	George W.	1DB			Hak 3
PFC	McFall	William E.	1DB			Hak 3
PFC	McGee	Robert H.	1DB			Hak 3
Mgun	McKinstry	Clarence B.	1DB			Hak 3
CPL	McQuilling	Robert E.	1DB			Hak 3
CPL	McWiggins	James C.	1DB			Hak 3
PFC	Melton	Kenneth L.	1DB			Hak 3
PFC	Mercer	Harris L.	1DB			ShangHosp
PFC	Mergenthaler	John J.	1DB			Osaka
PFC	Mettscher	Leonard G.	1DB			Hak 3
PVT	Milbourn	Ival D.	1DB			Hak 3
CPL	Miller	Hershal L.	1DB			Hak 3
SGT	Miltwalski	Robert W.	MAG21	12/9/1941	Wake	N
PVT	Mitchell	James P.	1DB			Hak 3
PFC	Moore	John P.	1DB			Hak 3
PFC	Morgan	R. C.	1DB			Hak 3
PFC	Moritz	Lloyd G.	1DB			ShangHosp
PFC	Mosley	Harvey L.	1DB			Hak 3
PFC	Murphy	Leroy V.	1DB			OmoriTo1
PFC	Murphy	Robert B.	1DB			Hak 3
SGT	Nanninga	Henry D.	MAG21	12/8/1941	Wake	N
CPL	Nevenzel	Jay	1DB			Hak 3
PFC	Nowlin	Jesse E.	1DB			Hak 3
PVT	O'Connell	John J.	1DB			Hak 3

CPL	Oelberg	Christian Jr.	1DB			Hak 3
PFC	Olenowski	Michael	1DB			Hak 3
PFC	Oubre	Tony T.	1DB			Hak 3
PFC	Owens	Lester C.	1DB			Hak 3
CPL	Page	Robert E. L.	MAG21			Hak 2
CPL	Painter	John Scott	MAG21			Fuk 3
PFC	Parks	Laurence A.	1DB			Tok3Omi
MSGT	Paskiewicz	Andrew J.	MAG21			Os5BTsu
SGT	Patterson	Billy L.	1DB			Hak 2
PFC	Paul	Archie T.	1DB			Hak 2
CPL	Pearce	Herbert N.	1DB			Hak 3
PFC	Pearsall	John E.	1DB			Hak 3
CPL	Pechacek	Thomas J.	1DB			Hak 3
PFC	Pellegrini	Alfred F.	1DB			Hak 3
PFC	Percy	R. C.	1DB			Osaka
CPL	Petrick	Edward N.	1DB			Hak 3
PFC	Phipps	Ralph Edward	1DB	6/1/1944	Kiangwan	N
PFC	Pickett	Ralph H.	1DB	12/23/1941	Wake	N
PFC	Pippi	Louis	1DB			Hak 3
PFC	Pistole	Erwin D.	1DB			Tok3Omi
CAPT	Platt	Wesley M.	1DB			Hak 4
2LT	Poindexter	Arthur A.	1DB			Hak 4
TSGT	Polousky	Anthony	1DB			Os5DKaw
MAJ	Potter	George H. Jr.	1DB			Rokorushi
PFC	Pratt	Robert Merritt	1DB	4/17/1945	Os13BTsu	N
PFC	Prochaska	Albert J.	1DB			Osaka
SSGT	Puckett	Ray V.	MAG21	12/8/1941	Wake	N
SGT	Purvis	Gordon W.	MAG21	12/8/1941	Wake	N
MAJ	Putnam	Paul A.	MAG21			Rokorushi
PFC	Quinn	Fenton R.	1DB			Osaka
PFC	Rasor	Herman L.	1DB			Hak 2
CPL	Raymond	Samuel W.	1DB			Hak 2
PVT	Ray	Sanford K.	1DB			Hak 2
PFC	Reed	Clifford M.	1DB			Hak 3
PFC	Reed	Dick L.	1DB			Osaka
CPL	Reed	Alvey A.	1DB	12/23/1941	Wake	N
PFC	Reeg	Norman M.	1DB			Hak 3
PVT	Reeves	Joe M.	1DB			Hak 3
PVT	Reitzler	Junior H.	1DB			Hak 3
SGT	Renner	Francis J.	MAG21	12/8/1941	Wake	N

CPL	Richardson	Bernard E.	1DB	Hak 3
SGT	Richey	Lewis H.	1DB	Fuk 3
PFC	Richter	Eugene V.	1DB	Hak 3
CPL	Rickert	Albert P.	1DB	OmoriTo1
PFC	Robinson	George L.	1DB	Hak 3
PFC	Rogers	Charles G.	1DB	Hak 3
PFC	Roman	Oldrich B.	1DB	Hak 3
SGT	Rook	Edward Bakon	1DB	Fuk 3
CPL	Rozycki	Stanley J.	1DB	Osaka
PlSGT	Rush	Dave J.	1DB	Hak 3
PFC	Ryan	Eugene R.	1DB	Hak 3
CPL	Sado	John E.	1DB	Hak 2
PFC	Sanders	Clifton C.	1DB	Hak 2
PFC	Sanders	Jacob R.	1DB	Os5DKaw
PVT	Sapp	Charles W.	1DB	Hak 2
PFC	Schneider	Leroy N.	1DB	Tok4BNao
TSGT	Schulz	Glenn R.	1DB	Osaka
SGT	Schulze	Carl H.	1DB	Hak 2
PFC	Schumacher	William T.	1DB	Hak 2
SGT	Shellhorn	Melvin W.	1DB	Hak 2
PFC	Shelton	Clifford E.	1DB	Hak 3
PFC	Shores	Robert	1DB	Hak 3
SSGT	Short	Earnest Eugene	1DB	Hak 3
PlSGT	Shugart	Eugene W.	1DB	Hak 3
PFC	Shumard	Gene D.	1DB	Hak 3
PFC	Sickels	Percy H.	1DB	Hak 3
CPL	Sieger	Norman P.	1DB	Hak 3
PFC	Silverlieb	Irving B.	1DB	Hak 3
PFC	Simon	Adoph	1DB	Osaka
PFC	Skaggs	Jack R.	1DB	Tok5BNao
PVT	Slezak	Rudolph M.	1DB	Hak 3
PFC	Sloman	Wiley W.	1DB	Zentsuji
PFC	Smith	Robert N.	1DB	Hak 3
PVT	Smith	Dempsey	1DB	Hak 3
SSGT	Smith	Elwood M.	1DB	Tok5BNii
PVT	Smith	Gordon L.	1DB	Hak 3
PVT	Smith	John C.	1DB	Hak 3
CPL	Sorrell	Jesse D.	1DB	Hak 3
PFC	Stafford	Virgil D.	1DB	Hak 3
PFC	Stahl	Rudolph W. Jr.	1DB	Hak 3

PFC	Stegmaier	Carl E. Jr.	1DB			Hak 3
PFC	Stevens	Robert L.	1DB	12/23/1941	Wake	N
TSGT	Stewart	Jessie T.	MAG21			Os5BTsu
SGT	Stockton	Maurice E.	MAG21	12/8/1941	Wake	N
PFC	Stocks	Artie J.	1DB			Hak 3
PlSGT	Stowe	Joe M.	1DB			Hak 3
PFC	Stringfield	George W.	1DB			Hak 3
PVT	Sturgeon	Edward V.	1DB			Os5DKaw
PFC	Sutton	Mac P.	MAG21	12/8/1941	Wake	N
PFC	Swartz	Merle E.	1DB			Hak 3
PFC	Switzer	Raymond C.	1DB			Fuk 3
SGT	Tallentire	Gilson A.	1DB			Hak 2
PFC	Tate	Willis	1DB			Hak 2
PFC	Taylor	Rudolph J.	1DB			Hak 2
PFC	Taylor	Dale K.	MAG21	12/23/1941	Wake	N
PFC	Terfansky	Joseph E.	1DB			Hak 2
CPL	Terry	Arthur F.	1DB			Hak 2
SGT	Terry	Mabry A.	1DB			Osaka
PFC	Thaire	Grover E.	1DB			Hak 2
CAPT	Tharin	F. C.	MAG21			Hak 4
SGT	Tipton	Wiley E.	1DB			Osaka
PFC	Todd	Herman A.	1DB			Hak 3
CPL	Tokryman	Paul A.	1DB	12/8/1941	Wake	N
PFC	Tompkins	Raymond M.	1DB			Hak 3
PFC	Tramposh	Charles E.	1DB			Os5BTsu
CPL	Trego	Carroll E.	MAG21			Hak 3
PVT	Tuck	Erville R.	1DB			Hak 3
CPL	Tucker	William M.	MAG21	12/9/1941	Wake	N
CPL	Tusa	Joe N.	1DB			Tok5B
PhM3c	Unger	John I.	Medical			Hak 4
PhM3c	Vaale	Ernest C.	Medical			Hak 4
PFC	Vardell	Virgil P.	1DB			Hak 3
PFC	Vaughn	James	1DB			Hak 3
PFC	Venable	James C.	1DB			Hak 3
PFC	Venable	Alexander B. Jr.	1DB	1/7/1942	Wake	N
PFC	Verga	Vincent H.	1DB			Hak 3
SGT	Wade	Q. T.	1DB			Hak 2
PFC	Wallace	Verne L.	1DB			Hak 2
PFC	Waronker	Alvin J.	1DB			Osaka
PlSGT	Warren	Howard E.	1DB			Hak 2

SGT	Warsing	John W. Jr.	1DB			Os5DKaw
2LT	Webb	Henry Gorham	MAG21			Rokorushi
PFC	Webster	Guy P.	1DB			Hak 2
PFC	Weimer	Jacob G.	1DB			Hak 2
PFC	Wheeler	Mackie L.	1DB			Os5DKaw
PFC	Williams	Luther	1DB			Hak 2
PVT	Williams	Henry Jr.	1DB			Hak 2
PFC	Williamson	Jack R.	1DB			Tok4BNao
SGT	Wilsford	Clyde D.	MAG21	12/8/1941	Wake	N
PVT	Winslow	Robert E.	1DB	11/10/2008	OR	Osaka
PFC	Wiskochil	Robert I.	1DB	12/16/1942	Kiangwan	N
CPL	Woods	Chester J.	1DB			Hak 3
PFC	Woodward	Theodore H.	1DB			Hak 3
CPL	Woodward	David E.	MAG21	12/9/1941	Wake	N
PlSGT	Wright	Johnalson E.	1DB	12/21/1941	Wake	N
PFC	Wynne	Marion L.	1DB			Hak 3
PFC	Zarlenga	Joseph D.	1DB			Hak 3
PFC	Zellay	George P.	1DB			Hak 3
PFC	Zivko	Stephen M.	1DB			Hak 3
SGT	Zurchauer	Robert Jr.	MAG21	12/8/1941	Wake	N

U.S. Navy

USN	LAST	FIRST	DIED	DOD DET
RM3c	Anderson	John B. L.		
RM3c	Balhorn	Marvin C.		
Bx1c	Barnes	James E.	2/2/1944	Ichioka
RM3c	Besancon	Victor		
RM3c	Bird	Edwin A.	11/3/1944	Os13BTsu
S2c	Caldwell	Robert E.		
Aer1c	Cook	Walter John		
F1c	Cox	James H.		
CDR	Cunningham	Winfield S.		
S1c	Darden	James B.		
ENS	Davis	James J. Jr.		
S2c	Dixon	Floyd A.		
S2c	Doke	Cecil E.		
RM3c	Dreuger			
S2c	Franklin	Theodore Douglas	1/22/1942	NM exec
S2c	Fraser	Harry S.		

S2c	Fuller	Andrew A.		
RM3c	Gerberding	Oliver L.		
S2c	Gonzales	Roy J.	1/22/1942	NM exec
LTCDR	Greey	Elmer B.		
ENS	Henshaw	George H.		
AMM1c	Hesson	James Frank		
S2c	Hodgkins	Ray K.	8/15/1942	Woosung
XX	Holbrooks	Benjamin		
S1c	Horstman	Herbert J.		
S1c	Hotchkiss	Richard L.		
S2c	Jacobs	Richard W.	12/8/1941	Wake
S2c	Johnson	Edward E.		
CDR	Keene	Campbell		
F2c	Kibble	Dare K.		
RM3c	Kidd	Franklin B.	10/22/1944	Ofuna
EM3	Kilcoyne	Thomas P.	12/8/1941	Wake
RM3c	Krueger	Darius Cartier		
RM3c	LaFleur	Albert H.		
S1c	Lambert	John W.	1/22/1942	NM exec
ENS	Lauff	Benjamin J.		
S1c	Lechler	William R.		
S1c	Lewis	George H.		
BM2c	Ludwick	Kirby Jr.		
S2c	Mackie	Robert J.		
S1c	Manning	William H.		
Y3c	Mayhew	Richard C.		
F1c	McCall	James F.		
S2c	McCoy	William H.		
SK2c	McReynolds	Wendell W.		
Aer3c	Miller	Howard D.		
Senxx	Moore	Carl Jr.		
S2c	Mullen	James M. Jr.		
ENS	Olcott	Chester W.		
SK3c	Pickering	George F.		
F1c	Plate	William O.		
F2c	Plecker	McPherson		
COX	Roberson	Ted J. D.		
LTjg	Robinson	James B.		
S2c	Sandvold	Julian K.		
RM3c	Sargent	Charles Alfred		

SC2c	Skaggs	Victor V.		
S2c	Smith	Cassius E.		
CEM	Thompson	Harold Ray		
S1c	Thorsen	John Thomas		
Y3c	Tripp	Glenn Eugene		
S1c	Troney	Norris Henry		
ENS	Walish	Robert L.		
S1c	White	S. Clyde		
ENS	Williams	Belmont M.		
MM2c	Williams	Harold Raymond	2/2/1944	Os13BTsu
S1c	Wilson	Franklin M.		
S1c	Wolfe	Clarence E.		
COX	Wolney	George J.	12/8/1941	Wake
S1c	Wood	Ivan Sidney		

U.S. Army

USAAC	**LAST**	**FIRST**	**POW LIB**
SSGT	Rogers	Ernest J.	Zentsuji
SGT	Dilks	Carl William	Fuk 3
SSGT	Hotchkiss	Clifford E.	Tok4BNao
PFC	Futtrup	Paul F.	Tok5BKaw
CAPT	Wilson	Henry Stanley	Rokorushi
SGT	Rex	James B.	Hak 3

Civilians

LAST	**FIRST**	**HOME**	**DOB**	**DOD**	**ARR WAKE**	**POW lib**	**BOOK**
Aaron	Barney	ID Boise	9/28/1906	8/5/1986		Fuk-01-Main	32-21
Abbott	Cyrus W. Jr.	CA Oakland	5/25/1912	10/7/1943		n/a	38-57
Abraham	Theodore A. Jr.	CA LA	1/22/1919	5/7/2013	Bur 8/2/41	Sen-11-Kamikita	35-88
Ackland	Maurice F.	IA Laurens	8/10/1915	10/30/1984		Fuk-01-Main	32-36
Acorda	George J.	ID Boise	10/28/1918	11/13/1983		Tok-04B-Naoetsu	34-69
Acosta	Eleazar A.	CA SF	12/2/1898	11/1/1975	Reg 6/29/41	Tok area	34-27
Adams	Andrew F.	NE Morrill	1/9/1911	6/16/1969	Reg 5/23/41	Fuk-03-Yawata	34-07
Adams	Henry O.	TH HNL	10/8/1911	1977 Jan	Reg 9/30/41	Sen-07B-Hanaoka	N
Adams	James O.	CA Oakland	4/22/1910	4/14/1994	Reg 9/30/41	Tok-05B-Niigata	34-45
Adamson	Joseph W.	ID Twin Falls	1/14/1892	6/24/1975		Tok area	33-65

Adamson	Louis A.	ID Twin Falls	11/18/1914	12/9/1941		n/a	33-71
Ahlrich	Wayne H.	CA LA	10/11/1900	10/14/1946	Chau 2/1/41	Fuk-03-Yawata	34-20
Aikman	John H.	CA SF	8/22/1890	1965 Apr	Reg 6/29/41	Tok area	N
Aki	Patrick K.	TH HNL	2/20/1924	L	Bur 8/2/41	Fuk-06B-Mizumaki	N
Akin	Shirley	CA SF	2/28/1915	10/5/1986	Reg 9/30/41	Sen-07B-Hanaoka	N
Albertoni	Phillip H.	CA Oakland	2/18/1883	2/10/1960		Tok area	N
Alcorn	Richard A.	CA Berkeley	9/15/1910	10/4/1987		Fuk-03-Yawata	34-30
Aldous	Herbert S.	ID Boise	7/25/1909	8/31/2004		Fuk-04B-Moji	34-43
Allen	Horace L.	CA Sacramento	5/8/1913	10/7/1943	Bur 11/11/41	n/a	34-59
Allen	James A.	CA El Monte	8/14/1918	5/9/2012	Reg 9/30/41	Tok-05B-Niigata	32-37
Allen	John S.	CA Altadena	2/18/1920	7/31/1997		Tok-05B-Niigata	32-49
Allender	Harold S.	ID Boise	4/23/1916	10/15/2002		Tok-05B-Niigata	34-52
Anderson	Clyde	ID Burley	10/28/1920	8/24/2011		Sen-11-Kamikita	32-54
Anderson	Eric W.	CA Oakland	5/20/1913	1/2/1944		n/a	34-10
Anderson	Joseph A.	IA Odebolt	10/14/1889	9/14/1969	Curt10/22/41	Rokuroshi	32-04
Anderson	Norman A.	OR PDX	3/4/1920	10/7/1943	Reg 5/23/41	n/a	33-70
Anderson	Roy L.	CA Agnew	12/25/1891	3/1/1947	Bur 11/11/41	uk	N
Anderson	Warren G.	IN Martinsville	9/1/1922	8/25/1993	Reg 9/30/41	Tok-05B-Niigata	N
Andre	Roland A.	OR Pendelton	1/15/1899	10/7/1943		n/a	32-23
Andrus	Verdun L.	ID Firth	7/15/1919	10/21/1996	Bur 10/9/41	Tok area	34-70
Anhalt	Lawrence F.	AR New Blaine	9/16/1921	3/14/1995	Bur 10/9/41	Tok area	34-01
Anvick	Allen E.	CA Eureka	12/12/1901	10/7/1943	Bur 8/2/41	n/a	34-34
Arambarri	Frank I.	ID Gooding	10/17/1917	11/8/2001		Fuk-09B-Miyata	33-80
Archer	Ernest B.	CA Altadena	3/31/1886	6/15/1969		Tok-05B-Niigata	34-09
Armitage	Thomas B.	ID Nampa	6/20/1915	12/4/1959		Fuk-03-Yawata	33-67
Arterburn	Joseph H.	ID Boise	9/23/1903	9/19/1967		Tok area	34-29
Astad	Arne E.	CA Oakland	9/16/1893	6/16/1962	Bur 10/9/41	Tok area	N
Astarita	Joseph J.	ID Twin Falls	1/11/1919	6/28/2004	Reg 8/19/41	Tok-1-Omori	33-72
Atkins	Charles F.	CA Oakland	10/27/1909	9/29/1990		Fuk-03-Yawata	N
Ausland	William M.	CA Long Beach	8/13/1907	1974 Mar	Bur 9/5/41	Tok-05B-Niigata	34-35
Austin	Melvin A.	OR PDX	3/1/1899	9/4/1954	Reg 5/23/41	Tok area	33-76
Baasch	Carl A.	CA Oakland	5/28/1901	10/7/1943		n/a	N
Bailey	George E.	CA LA	8/28/1893	2/6/1943	Bur 3/16/41	n/a	34-13
Bainter	Raymond E.	WY Cheyenne	1/11/1914	2/27/1972	Bur 11/11/41	Fuk-03-Yawata	32-45
Baird	Kenneth C.	ID Nampa	8/5/1916	5/10/2002		Tok-04B-Naoetsu	32-32

Bakos	Peter P.	CA Van Nuys	7/5/1913	11/14/1992	Reg 9/30/41	Fuk-04B-Moji	N
Banks	Richard L.	CA Huntington Park	12/10/1918	4/19/1970	Reg 9/30/41	Fuk-03-Yawata	34-41
Barbour	Thomas J.	OR PDX	11/2/1919	9/4/1985	Reg 5/23/41	Fuk-01-Main	33-63
Bard	Melvin A.	CA SF	11/13/1919	7/15/1983	Bur 10/9/41	Tok area	34-44
Barden	Jay R.	IA Fairfield	1/2/1915	9/27/2007		Tok-04B-Naoetsu	34-36
Barger	Herbert M.	CA SF	5/31/1897	5/3/1961	Reg 9/30/41	Tok-05B-Niigata	N
Barnett	Ryland F.	ID Boise	1/16/1912	7/8/1991	Bur 8/2/41	Fuk-06B-Mizumaki	N
Barney	John F.	WI Abbottsford	4/16/1919	8/11/2001	Bur 3/16/41	Fuk-09B-Miyata	35-77
Barr	Frank R.	CA San Pedro	11/10/1897	4/4/1972		Fuk-01-Main	35-86
Barr	Fred S.	ID Melba	9/2/1911	10/18/1995	Bur 8/2/41	Tok area	34-28
Barr	William R.	ID Melba	12/26/1909	4/29/1985	Bur 8/2/41	Tok area	34-02
Bartlett	Harry E.	CA LA	11/24/1907	1955	Reg 9/30/41	Tok-05B-Niigata	N
Batscha	Alexander P.	OH Cincinnati	10/2/1920	6/6/1965	Reg 9/30/41	Tok area	N
Bauman	Arthur E.	ID Pocatello	3/25/1918	10/17/2000		Tok-05B-Niigata	32-51
Bayok	Joseph A.	ID McCall	1/14/1913	10/23/1992	Reg 5/23/41	Fuk-03-Yawata	38-14
Bechtold	John D.	CA SF	9/25/1900	1962	Bur 10/9/41	Tok area	N
Becker	Zane Q.	OR Riddle	8/15/1920	8/22/2015	Bur 8/2/41	Tok-05B-Niigata	3230-4617
Beebe	Leroy D.	WA Vancouver	3/18/1915	4/12/1974		Tok area	32-25
Beeman	Clarence E.	OR PDX	11/12/1886	1956		Tok area	N
Belknap	Fay E.	WA Valley	10/22/1916	5/12/1989		Tok-05B-Niigata	N
Bell	Eugene H.	ID Boise	9/3/1893	4/18/1963		Tok-05B-Niigata	N
Bellanger	George C.	CA SF	11/21/1905	10/7/1943		n/a	N
Bengston	Roy S.	CA SF	10/7/1919	9/3/2002	Bur 10/9/41	Tok area	34-15
Bentel	Guy C.	ID Pocatello	11/17/1900	7/10/1972		Tok area	N
Berger	Irving N.	NY Bedford Village	3/26/1917	12/25/1943	Bur 9/5/41	n/a	N
Bergman	Benjamin J.	CA LA	11/11/1910	2/13/1980	Bur 11/11/41	Tok-05B-Niigata	N
Berry	Orvel D.	ID Boise	4/6/1911	7/18/1950	Reg 5/23/41	Tok-05B-Niigata	34-31
Bethel	Jonathan B	CA Sausalito	1/22/1913	2/24/1985	Bur 8/2/41	Tok area	34-06
Betts	Jacob L.	WY Powell	4/25/1908	10/23/1992	Reg 6/29/41	Fuk-03-Yawata	32-07
Betts	Parlan M.	KS Smith Center	11/1/1917	11/15/1992		Tok area	34-37
Bigler	Harold D.	ID Boise	10/6/1912	9/6/1974		Tok-05B-Niigata	34-24

Binge	Glen R.	IL Galesburg	8/15/1894	1972 Jan	10/27/41	Fuk-09B-Miyata	32-58
Blake	Rayford B.	AR Sheridan	3/3/1922	11/6/1997	Reg 9/30/41	Tok-05B-Niigata	33-78
Bledsoe	Hollis E.	AR Bismarck	5/21/1919	12/10/2012	Reg 9/30/41	Tok area	N
Blessing	Frank L.	IA Sioux City	8/14/1903	2/23/1980	Bur 9/5/41	Tok area	32-03
Blessinger	Douglas L.	WA Dayton	5/29/1918	2/23/1991	Bur 3/16/41	Fuk-03-Yawata	32-01
Boesiger	Max A.	ID Nampa	4/30/1917	8/3/1999		Fuk-01-Main	34-38
Bolgiano	Fate O.	LA Leesville	9/3/1920	10/11/1970	Bur 8/2/41	uk	34-42
Bonat	George V.	OR PDX	11/23/1902	12/13/1956	Reg 5/23/41	Tok area	N
Bond	Gordon C.	CA N Hollywood	5/18/1898	12/8/1941	Bur 10/9/41	n/a	N
Bone	Richard O.	GA Atlanta	2/21/1920	10/21/2007	Reg 9/30/41	Sen-11-Kamikita	N
Booth	Gerald E.	CA LA	7/2/1918	1/7/2009	Bur 3/16/41	Tok-05B-Niigata	33-73
Boutell	Albert L.	CA LA	7/10/1910	9/4/1988	Bur 11/11/41	Sen-11-Kamikita	32-34
Bowcutt	Don R.	CA Oakland	2/14/1920	10/7/1943	Bur 10/9/41	n/a	32-12
Bowen	Ray E.	CA Berkeley	2/13/1912	7/20/1981	Reg 5/23/41	Fuk-01-Main	N
Bower	Jesse A.	CA Oakland	11/22/1912	4/22/1980	Reg 9/30/41	Tok area	36-12
Bowers	Frank B.	ID Weiser	2/24/1920	2/11/1944		n/a	32-24
Bowyer	Cecil R.	ID Moscow	8/28/1917	3/10/2009		Tok-05B-Niigata	36-39
Boyce	David M.	NE Hastings	9/10/1893	10/7/1943	Reg 5/23/41	n/a	N
Boyles	Joseph M.	AR Little Rock	8/24/1910	3/30/1977		Fuk-03-Yawata	34-11
Brandenburg	Loren G.	ID Boise	6/19/1905	1964 May		Fuk-01-Main	32-02
Brauer	Leslie D.	CA Hayward	9/11/1918	6/5/2002		Rokuroshi	35-78
Bray	Cleveland H.	ID Grimes	7/17/1917	1/29/1990	Reg 5/23/41	Rokuroshi	34-05
Brewer	Henry E.	NE Omaha	8/24/1899	2/11/1957	Reg 5/23/41	Tok-05B-Niigata	34-08
Brewster	Paul E.	IA Laurens	4/3/1908	7/9/1961		Fuk-03-Yawata	N
Bridges	Albert F.	MS Braxton	11/19/1915	12/28/1969		Fuk-06B-Mizumaki	32-47
Bridgman	Harold L.	AZ Tucson	3/25/1917	8/9/2007	Reg 5/23/41	Fuk-02B-Nagasaki	34-12
Briney	William M.	CA Concord	12/31/1915	5/22/1992	Reg 9/30/41	Sen-11-Kamikita	N
Brooks	Calvin B.	CA Yuba City	11/7/1906	3/29/1997	Reg 5/23/41	Fuk-01-Main	32-17
Brooks	Grover C.	CA Alameda	8/5/1907	12/21/1986	Bur 1/9/41	Fuk-01-Main	34-67
Brown	Delos B.	OR Grants Pass	4/8/1921	1/21/2007	Reg 5/23/41	Fuk-03-Yawata	N
Brown	Edward J.	CA San Pedro	8/2/1895	5/6/1943	Bur 8/2/41	n/a	34-21
Brown	Fred C.	CA LA	2/4/1907	7/3/1959	Reg 9/30/41	Fuk-03-Yawata	N
Brown	Herbert C.	TH HNL	6/22/1919	1/7/2014	Bur 3/16/41	Tok-04B-Naoetsu	N
Brown	Robert E.	ID Boise	6/22/1918	1/31/1999		Tok-05B-Niigata	32-26

Brown	Victor	WA Eatonville	9/3/1910	2/15/1984		Fuk-03-Yawata	N
Brown	John R.	ID Boise	8/28/1921	3/30/1996	Bur 8/2/41		32-18
Brownlee	James F.	CA San Pedro	7/28/1918	4/2/1984		Tok-05B-Niigata	32-46
Brueck	Albert L.	ID Boise	3/6/1912	1/2/1996	Reg 8/19/41	Tok-05B-Niigata	32-27
Bryan	Robert L.	CA San Pedro	5/25/1917	12/23/1941		n/a	34-48
Bucy	Eddie L.	ID Wilder	2/19/1915	12/8/1941		n/a	N
Budden	Clarence J.	IA Sioux City	1/13/1920	1971 Sep	Reg 6/29/41	Fuk-03-Yawata	32-50
Bukacek	Ludwick	NE Schuyler	12/15/1906	4/18/1945		n/a	N
Burge	Earl E.	ID Nampa	7/23/1903	1966 Aug		Tok area	34-04
Burke	Thomas W.	IA Sioux City	8/21/1900	7/26/1970	Reg 5/23/41	Fuk-01-Main	33-66
Burns	Edgar F.	WA Spokane	2/2/1914	9/14/2003		Fuk-01-Main	33-74
Burns	William J.	CA LA	6/31/1896	DK	Bur 11/11/41	Tok-05B-Niigata	48-39
Burroughs	John R.	CA LA	1/28/1902	11/7/1987		Sen-11-Kamikita	32-38
Burton	John H.	UT SLC	10/13/1913	3/13/2003	Cur 10/22/41	Fuk-03-Yawata	N
Butler	Don W.	IA Council Bluffs	11/13/1916	2/20/2008	Reg 5/23/41	Sen-05B-Kamaishi	32-31
Buttler	George A.	OR Grants Pass	1/22/1914	8/31/1989	Bur 8/2/41	Fuk-01-Main	32-40
Calkins	Clarence C.	NY Yonkers	10/4/1898	12/9/1941	Reg 9/30/41	n/a	34-49
Campbell	Claude L.	ID Caldwell	2/27/1909	3/11/1944	Bur 8/2/41	n/a	34-19
Campbell	Francis C.	OR Rogue River	4/9/1915	12/1/1994	Bur 8/2/41	Fuk-06B-Mizumaki	34-61
Cantry	Charles A.	NV Las Vegas	6/6/1903	10/7/1943	Reg 9/30/41	n/a	N
Capps	Arthur V.	TX Wellington	4/8/1915	1/8/1974		Tok area	34-14
Carden	Ivan R.	CO Bristol	2/22/1915	8/20/2005	Reg 5/23/41	Tok-05B-Niigata	33-81
Carlen	Delbert W.	WA Spokane	9/14/1899	9/5/1963		Fuk-03-Yawata	N
Carlsen	Carl H.	ID Pocatello	10/5/1899	1/18/1948	Reg 9/30/41	Fuk-01-Main	33-64
Carlson	Stanley A.	OR PDX	7/13/1893	10/7/1943	Col 6/6/41	n/a	N
Carney	Leslie J.	ID Wilder	4/19/1911	4/11/1985		Tok area	32-19
Carr	Louis	ID Boise	8/9/1918	10/31/1942	Reg 9/30/41	n/a	37-69
Carr	Reynold	ID Boise	4/23/1919	2/16/1947		Tok area	32-11
Carter	Wesley W.	OR Bonanza	10/25/1906	9/2/1980	Bur 8/2/41	Tok-05B-Niigata	32-43
Cash	William O.	ID Nampa	8/27/1903	8/28/1959	Reg 5/23/41	Fuk-03-Yawata	34-68
Castiglione	Carl J.	CA Bell	2/16/1912	11/2/1982	Reg 5/23/41	Tok-04B-Naoetsu	36-61
Catmull	Reed B.	ID Rupert	1/2/1901	7/15/1980	Bur 3/16/41	uk	N

Cavanagh	Allen A.	CA SF	2/22/1905	10/7/1943		n/a	34-40
Cerny	Frank J.	CA Chico	4/30/1888	12/9/1941	Reg 5/23/41	n/a	32-06
Cerny	Harry W.	ID Boise	12/10/1921	1/5/1954	Reg 5/23/41	Rokuroshi	32-08
Chambers	David S.	OR Grants Pass	6/5/1905	10/7/1943	Bur 8/2/41	n/a	32-55
Chambers	Edwin D.	NE York	10/26/1897	12/22/1945	Reg 6/29/41	Tok-04B-Naoetsu	33-68
Chambers	Percival H.	CA Huntington Park	4/18/1892	7/13/1976		Tok area	34-25
Chang	Kan Sung	TH HNL	12/5/1899	4/21/1989		Sen-11-Kamikita	N
Chard	Donley D.	WA Pomeroy	1/11/1907	10/7/1943		n/a	33-79
Charters	William L.	ID Emmett	10/14/1914	8/16/2006		Sen-11-Kamikita	N
Chartier	U. Sidney	ID Boise	6/15/1901	4/20/1961	Reg 8/19/41	Tok-05B-Niigata	34-32
Chenot	Harry E.	OK Hobart	11/25/1918	5/29/1980	Reg 9/30/41	Tok area	N
Chew	Bock T.	CA SF	12/12/1917	2/21/1991	Reg 9/30/41	Sen-11-Kamikita	N
Chin	Wing Fong	CA SF	6/15/1922	7/8/2011	Reg 9/30/41	Sen-11-Kamikita	N
Ching	Lawrence W.B.	TH HNL	5/31/1922	5/7/2012	Reg 9/30/41	Tok area	N
Chisholm	Ray V.	ID Boise	1/23/1916	9/7/1993		Fuk-01-Main	35-87
Choi	Alfred D.B.	TH HNL	7/9/1918	1981 Apr	Reg 9/30/41	Tok-05B-Niigata	N
Chow	Walter K.S.	TH HNL	11/4/1923	9/3/2013	Reg 9/30/41	Sen-11-Kamikita	N
Choy	Robert A.F.	TH HNL	2/1/1920	3/18/1996		Sen-11-Kamikita	N
Christensen	Earl V.	CA Oakland	6/16/1918	8/25/1999	Reg 5/23/41	Tok area	34-53
Christler	Elmer J.	WY Cody	10/9/1904	11/21/1979		Tok area	32-52
Christy	Arthur W.	ID Boise	10/12/1906	12/29/1943	Reg 9/30/41	n/a	33-75
Chuck	Kam C.	CA SF	11/14/1913	10/20/1995	Reg 9/30/41	Sen-11-Kamikita	N
Church	Carlton G.	CA Robles Del Rio	4/26/1903	10/7/1943		n/a	N
Clayville	Lawrence L.	ID Weiser	6/11/1917	11/24/2014	Bur 8/2/41	Fuk-09B-Miyata	32-10
Clelan	John L.	ID Meridian	9/20/1896	1/9/1945	Clip 6/7/41	n/a	N
Cleveland	Ernest B.	ID Boise	11/17/1922	12/28/1986	Bur 10/9/41	Tok area	32-09
Clift	Harold F.	WA Asotin	10/28/1909	3/30/1978		Tok area	32-13
Clubb	William F.	MO Fredericktown	7/10/1920	2/14/1981	Reg 9/30/41	Sen-07B-Hanaoka	32-05
Coates	George P.	CA LA	3/9/1906	7/20/1964		Tok area	N
Cochran	Thomas M.	MT Hamilton	3/26/1913	1965	Bur 10/9/41	Tok area	N

Coker	J. J.	TX Muleshoe	1/14/1919	6/26/2010		Tok-05B-Niigata	34-51
Collier	Robert G.	ID Boise	10/1/1916	4/22/1983		Sen-11-Kamikita	34-39
Collier	Rulen F.	ID Boise	12/2/1918	3/24/2005		Tok area	34-50
Collins	Charles F.	CA SF	12/30/1909	12/9/1978		Tok-05B-Niigata	32-28
Compton	Clair E.	CA LA	10/13/1901	7/5/1969	Reg 5/23/41	Tok-05B-Niigata	32-44
Comstock	Benjamin F Jr	IA Logan	8/2/1918	5/30/2006	Reg 5/23/41	Tok area	32-41
Comstock	Benjamin F Sr	IA Logan	6/27/1890	8/12/1959	Reg 5/23/41	Tok area	32-42
Condit	Gomer H.	ID Hagerman	1/25/1917	2/2/1997	Bur 9/5/41	Fuk-06B-Mizumaki	32-14
Congrove	Kenneth W.	ID Boise	3/6/1911	9/21/2000		Tok area	32-59
Conner	James E.	CA LA	12/19/1896	3/23/1967	Bur 11/11/41	Tok-05B-Niigata	N
Connors	Edward A.	CA LA	4/17/1897	5/18/1985	Reg 5/23/41	uk	34-03
Cook	Edward L.	CA Alameda	10/27/1910	2/11/1984	Reg 9/30/41	uk	34-16
Cook	Howard E.	FL Kissimee	5/15/1905	11/14/1956	Reg 8/19/41	uk	34-26
Cooper	Robert P.	WY Cody	8/11/1908	11/5/1944		n/a	32-56
Cope	H. T.	UT SLC	4/15/1922	1/7/1966	Reg 5/23/41	Tok-05B-Niigata	N
Cope	Joseph W.	UT SLC	2/25/1916	12/13/1998	Reg 5/23/41	Rokuroshi	N
Cope	Raymond	ID Homer	11/25/1910	7/4/1988	Reg 5/23/41	Fuk-01-Main	35-79
Cope	Thomas T.	ID Boise	11/11/1914	7/26/2006	Reg 5/23/41	Rokuroshi	N
Corak	John	ID Boise	11/28/1907	10/16/1944		n/a	33-77
Corbin	Sewel H.	CA LA	10/17/1896	8/31/1989	Bur 3/16/41	Tok-05B-Niigata	N
Cormier	Louis M.	DC Washington	1/12/1903	10/7/1943	Bur 3/16/41	n/a	N
Corn	Jess F.	ID Boise	1/3/1917	1/18/1973	Bur 8/2/41	Sen-07B-Hanaoka	34-17
Cornish	Frank M.	ID Boise	2/17/1906	8/9/1974		Fuk-06B-Mizumaki	32-20
Corten	Paul	CA SF	10/3/1894	12/9/1941	Reg 9/30/41	n/a	N
Couture	Carl J.	CA Temple City	3/11/1900	9/4/1980		Tok-05B-Niigata	34-23
Covalesk	John J.	MA Lawrence	6/7/1916	11/15/1950	Reg 9/30/41	Sen-07B-Hanaoka	N
Cox	Karl L.	WA Asotin	6/29/1899	10/7/1943		n/a	32-22
Cramer	Leroy G.	ID Boise	11/1/1892	11/27/1945	Reg 5/23/41	Fuk-01-Main	34-58
Crawford	Elmer L.	CA Chico	3/11/1917	9/23/2006	Bur 3/16/41	Tok-1-Omori	32-57
Crenshaw	Richard S.	OR Roseburg	12/18/1915	12/16/1985		Tok-05B-Niigata	33-61
Crom	John S.	NE Strange	9/22/1892	11/2/1954		uk	34-33
Crosby	Loyal E.	ID Wendell	7/29/1918	1/16/1974	Reg 9/30/41	Fuk-17-Omuta	32-53
Crow	Eldon A.	OR Kirby	9/3/1916	4/1/1988	Reg 5/23/41	Tok area	N
Crowe	Frank W.	ID Boise	7/2/1919	4/29/1987	Reg 8/19/41	Tok-05B-Niigata	32-29

Cummings	David E.	CA Santa Cruz	4/7/1919	10/7/1943		n/a	32-33
Cunha	James A.	CA SF	5/14/1893	10/7/1943		n/a	32-60
Curphey	Hugh A.	OR Grants Pass	5/3/1916	3/2/2011	Reg 5/23/41	Tok-05B-Niigata	33-62
Curphey	Robert E.	OR Grants Pass	1/22/1913	1/23/2005	Reg 5/23/41	Sen-11-Kamikita	32-48
Curtis	Myron L.	ID Pocatello	9/20/1917	10/11/2002	Reg 9/30/41	Tok area	32-15
Daly	Edward J. Jr.	CA San Gabriel	11/9/1897	10/20/1969	Bur 9/5/41	Tok-05B-Niigata	N
Danner	Melvin O. Jr	IL Paris	6/21/1920	2/16/2006	Bur 8/2/41	Tok area	34-47
Daudlin	Norman A.	CA Oakland	6/18/1919	7/12/1998		Tok area	N
Davidson	Melvin C.	OR Murphy	5/2/1919	1/24/2003	Bur 8/2/41	Tok-05B-Niigata	36-48
Davis	Charles R.	ID Boise	3/28/1894	4/7/1968	Bur 3/16/41	Fuk-06B-Mizumaki	33-69
Davis	Joseph R.	ID Mullen	5/4/1910	10/7/1943		n/a	32-35
Davis	Kenneth C.	CA Oakland	1/30/1906	10/9/1944		n/a	N
Davis	Lee R.	ID Boise	8/1/1910	4/21/1943	Bur 11/11/41	n/a	36-17
De la Cruz	Jack K.	TH HNL	4/19/1911	5/17/1995		Sen-11-Kamikita	40-36
Dean	George W.	ID Payette	1/28/1914	10/7/1943	Reg 5/23/41	n/a	35-90
Dean	Glen D.	OH Dayton	3/10/1922	8/28/2001	Reg 9/30/41	Tok-05B-Niigata	36-33
Deimler	Ward H.	OR Rogue River	5/18/1907	7/7/1993		Sen-11-Kamikita	N
Delap	Wesley F.	WI Rhinelander	6/28/1905	3/22/1973	Reg 9/30/41	Rokuroshi	37-82
Delay	Glen W.	ID Coeur d'Alene	2/8/1911	4/17/1997		Fuk-06B-Mizumaki	35-82
Delmore	Raymond F.	CA Alameda	6/11/1913	9/7/1973	Reg 6/29/41	Fuk-03-Yawata	N
Dennis	William M.	WA Pullman	5/17/1909	4/7/1998		Fuk-17-Omuta	36-43
Denten	George H.	ID Boise	12/17/1891	3/18/1958	Clip 6/7/41	Tok-05B-Niigata	35-83
Derbeck	Ray H.	ID Boise	4/25/1909	4/15/1983		Fuk-06B-Mizumaki	N
Dettra	Paul E.	CA LA	2/8/1897	6/15/1965	Reg 8/19/41	Tok-05B-Niigata	36-46
Dickey	Lee E.	MT Helena	3/26/1911	1/2/1996	Bur 8/2/41	Sen-11-Kamikita	37-74
Dillon	George O.	WA Metaline Falls	8/19/1902	12/23/1944		n/a	N
Dixon	Theron B.	MN Hendricks	1/4/1909	3/18/1943		n/a	37-80
Dobyns	Harold L.	CA Weaverville	4/20/1909	10/7/1943		n/a	36-44
Dodds	Darwin H.	ID Boise	5/2/1919	6/4/2008		Tok-1-Omori	41-96

Dogger	Martin H.	CA SF	11/9/1888	10/7/1943		n/a	N
Dolan	James A.	WA Metaline Falls	5/9/1919	7/31/2006		uk	37-84
Dolezal	John F.	NE Wahoo	4/6/1909	5/1/1958	Reg 6/29/41	Tok area	35-91
Dollar	Clyndon F.	CA Monrovia	2/28/1915	8/13/1995		Fuk-03-Yawata	36-06
Dominy	James W.	GA Dexter	7/27/1919	6/12/2007	Bur 8/2/41	Tok area	N
Donoho	Marshall M.	ID Boise	4/26/1913	6/14/1994	Reg 5/23/41	Rokuroshi	35-71
Donovan	Harry W.	CA Oakland	1/15/1893	7/24/1945	Bur 11/11/41	n/a	N
Donovan	Joseph P.	OR PDX	2/2/1878	7/1/1968		Fuk-01-Main	N
Dougal	James E.	ID Boise	6/22/1917	9/9/1979		Tok-05B-Niigata	36-42
Dowling	George W.	OR PDX	10/11/1886	1/4/1967	Col 6/6/41	Fuk-01-Main	N
Doyle	Edwin G.	ID Boise	6/28/1919	8/9/2013		Tok area	36-40
Doyle	Robert T.	ID Boise	11/11/1920	12/11/2000	Bur 8/2/41	Sen-11-Kamikita	36-41
Drake	Frank M.	ID Twin Falls	4/5/1919	10/9/1987	Bur 10/9/41	Fuk-06B-Mizumaki	36-49
Dressler	Leo A. Jr.	CA Crescent City	2/5/1921	10/4/1949	Bur 8/2/41	Tok-05B-Niigata	36-65
Dreyer	Henry M.	IA Aplington	2/4/1918	10/7/1943	Bur 8/2/41	n/a	37-81
Driscoll	Leo P.	CA LA	7/18/1898	5/20/1943	Reg 9/30/41	n/a	N
Dugas	Bert C.	CA SF	10/20/1895	4/14/1970	Reg 6/29/41	Tok area	N
Dunn	Edward L.	MI Gladwin	1/26/1913	3/1/1969	Bur 9/5/41	Sen-11-Kamikita	37-68
Dunn	Joseph M.	ID Boise	9/30/1905	10/7/1943	Reg 5/23/41	n/a	35-73
Dustman	John H.	ID Moscow	5/21/1908	4/18/1988	Reg 5/23/41	Tok-05B-Niigata	36-50
Dyer	Fredrick E.	CA San Fernando	2/17/1881	10/1/1943	Bur 11/11/41	n/a	N
Dyer	William W.	CA Cloverdale	4/30/1900	11/21/1948	Reg 9/30/41	Tok-05B-Niigata	36-14
Easter	George C.	OR PDX	1/8/1901	2/27/1944		n/a	37-87
Edwards	Clifton M.	ID Payette	5/1/1917	1972 Oct	Reg 5/23/41	Fuk-01-Main	36-07
Eiselstein	John E.	CA Berkeley	2/1/1888	11/11/1960		Tok area	36-53
Eliassen	John H.	WA SEA	12/18/1892	12/16/1944		n/a	N
Elliot	Elmer E.	IL Peoria	5/24/1914	1/8/1964	Bur 8/2/41	Tok-05B-Niigata	37-79
Elliott	Richard E., Sr.	CA Upland	2/10/1899	7/21/1980		Fuk-01-Main	N
Elliott	Thomas J.	NY Natural Bridge	12/28/1905	8/10/1971	Reg 8/19/41	Tok area	36-58
Enright	Merle B.	WA Metaline Falls	10/8/1918	10/30/1995		uk	36-19
Esmay	Wayne E.	WY Converse	2/14/1895	2/19/1943		n/a	34-22
Essaff	Thomas G.	CA SF	4/1/1910	11/18/2000	Reg 5/23/41	Tok area	N

Evans	Clifford A.	ID Mountain Home	9/25/1915	7/11/1996	Reg 9/30/41	Tok-05B-Niigata	38-44
Evans	David D.	CA Inglewood	12/7/1901	3/27/1974	Reg 5/23/41	Tok area	37-67
Ewing	James F.	CA Oakland	6/27/1907	7/10/1945	Bur 10/9/41	n/a	37-78
Fagerstrom	William B.	CA Oakland	3/1/1894	9/25/1980	Bur 10/9/41	Tok area	36-57
Fairey	William L.	CA SF	6/19/1915	6/16/1988	Bur 11/11/41+R9	Sen-05B-Kamaishi	36-28
Farmer	Louis B.	ID Boise	2/12/1900	9/28/1991		Tok-05B-Niigata	N
Farran	Louis L.	CA LA	2/18/1895	11/10/1976	Bur 1/9/41	Tok-05B-Niigata	41-90
Farstvedt	Knut	OR Clackamas	1/1/1893	3/27/1943		n/a	N
Faubion	Donald J.	ID Boise	10/13/1919	8/31/1996		Tok area	46-15
Fay	Lawrence J.	CA SF	4/7/1894	11/14/1948		Tok area	N
Fenex	Jack A.	WY Cody	3/6/1918	1943 July		n/a	36-05
Fenstermache	Henry M.	TH HNL	3/28/1923	1999 Apr		Tok area	37-85
Fenwick	Thomas L.	ID Pocatello	3/23/1906	4/6/1975	Reg 5/23/41	Tok area	38-60
Field	Harold G.	MN Minneapolis	6/11/1917	5/17/1984	Bur 3/16/41	Tok-05B-Niigata	N
Fink	Philo M.	CA Ft Richmond	12/26/1908	12/31/1980	Bur 10/9/41	Tok area	36-11
Fischer	Raymond W.	CA SF	2/21/1918	10/27/2004		Tok-1-Omori	N
Fisher	George W.	NE Chadron	7/23/1888	1967 May	Reg 6/29/41	Tok area	N
Fisher	Marvin C.	CA Venice	10/31/1913	6/19/1979	Reg 6/29/41	Fuk-03-Yawata	N
Fisher	Robert E.	NE Superior	8/5/1920	12/13/2007	Bur 9/5/41	Sen-11-Kamikita	38-55
Flagg	Walter B.	CA El Cerrito	2/15/1894	7/4/1981	Reg 9/30/41	Tok-05B-Niigata	N
Flanery	Frank K.	OR LaGrande	8/15/1920	7/30/1969		Fuk-01-Main	36-37
Fleming	Wallace L.	WA Spokane	9/25/1914	5/13/1976		Sen-07B-Hanaoka	36-52
Flint	Howard A.	ID Idaho Falls	7/28/1920	10/7/1943	Bur 8/2/41	n/a	35-76
Flores	Rudy F.	CA LA	11/5/1911	4/20/1999	Reg 6/29/41	Fuk-01-Main	36-20
Follett	Frank F.	OR Cloverdale	7/13/1892	3/23/1943	Col 6/6/41	n/a	36-60
Fong	Ginn Shew	CA SF	7/30/1920	2/14/1968	Reg 9/30/41	Sen-11-Kamikita	N
Fong	Yee Wo	CA SF	11/10/1915	DK		Sen-11-Kamikita	N
Fontes	Glenn B.	ID Boise	8/13/1922	10/7/1943	Bur 8/2/41	n/a	40-18
Ford	Jack E.	CA Santa Cruz	10/12/1919	5/17/1997	Bur 10/9/41	Tok-05B-Niigata	36-02
Forsberg	Floyd F.	CA Van Nuys	1/11/1906	10/7/1943	Bur 10/9/41	n/a	36-08

Forsberg	Harry J.	WA Clayton	11/7/1911	11/15/1998		Fuk-23-Keisen	N
Forsberg	Roy A.	WA Longview	1/22/1915	1/11/2001	Chau 2/1/41	Fuk-01-Main	N
Forster	William J.	CA LA	2/19/1901	4/9/1951	Reg 6/29/41	Fuk-23-Keisen	N
Forsythe	Raymond E.	ID Boise	12/18/1895	1/23/1965	Bur 8/2/41	Tok-05B-Niigata	N
Fortune	Robert C.	TX Post	10/25/1895	4/8/1979		Fuk-17-Omuta	36-03
Foss	Andrew H.	WA Tacoma	6/18/1919	9/14/2005	Bur 8/2/41	Fuk-06B-Mizumaki	38-27
Fraley	Leo E.	NE Wahoo	8/7/1892	1956	Reg 6/29/41	Tok area	36-56
Francis	Garland G.	CA Costa Mesa	3/7/1917	10/7/1943	Bur 8/2/41	n/a	N
Franklin	Mark B.	TH HNL	6/30/1896	1/12/1943		n/a	38-34
Fredrickson	Melvin C.	CA Oakland	8/12/1917	10/1/1977	Reg 9/30/41	Tok area	36-38
Freese	Albert S.	AZ Phoenix	8/7/1904	1/4/1991	Bur 11/11/41	Fuk-01-Main	N
Freestone	William F.	WY Cody	1/14/1908	10/14/1989		Fuk-01-Main	N
French	Albert P.	CA SF	10/24/1913	10/7/1943	Reg 9/30/41	n/a	38-68
Friberg	Carl V.	CA Bishop	7/23/1901	7/26/1969		Sen-11-Kamikita	36-36
Froberger	Lawrence G.	IL Alton	5/23/1896	10/7/1943	Chau 2/1/41	n/a	N
Fuller	Charles H.	CA Berkeley	6/10/1903	8/29/1980	Reg 9/30/41	Tok area	N
Fuller	Richard E.	MN N Robbinsdale	5/25/1911	2/2/1969	Reg 5/23/41	Tok-05B-Niigata	N
Fullmer	Emmett H.	CA Alameda	1/24/1905	9/15/1961	Reg 9/30/41	Tok area	36-01
Funk	Arthur J.	ND Richardson	8/19/1920	11/17/1985	Bur 8/2/41	Sen-07B-Hanaoka	36-59
Gabel	Walter L.	CA LA	5/12/1887	4/18/1950		Tok-05B-Niigata	N
Galloway	Joseph W.	ID Twin Springs	10/14/1912	7/21/1967		Sen-05B-Kamaishi	N
Gammans	John W.	CA Concord	1/14/1905	1/29/1944	Bur 10/9/41	n/a	35-89
Gans	George E.	WA Clarkston	12/4/1900	8/16/1962		Tok-05B-Niigata	N
Gans	Otto J.	WA Uniontown	4/14/1898	9/15/1958		Tok-05B-Niigata	N
Garrison	John R.	IL Enfield	11/14/1892	10/20/1943		n/a	35-92
Gates	Donald R.	TH HNL	7/3/1921	7/1/1994		Sen-07B-Hanaoka	N
Gates	George W.	MT Butte	1/11/1893	2/22/1965		Fuk-01-Main	37-76
Gates	William J.	ID Boise	4/9/1917	12/2/1984	Bur 8/2/41	Tok-05B-Niigata	38-63
Gay	Charles C.	CA Oakland	12/19/1914	9/25/1978	Reg 9/30/41	Tok-05B-Niigata	36-51
Gay	Paul J. Jr	TH HNL	2/13/1919	12/23/1941		n/a	46-12
Gebbie	John H. R.	CA LA	10/9/1907	7/20/1948	Reg 8/19/41	Fuk-01-Main	37-88
Gee	Yip G.	CA SF	6/12/1916	DK	Reg 8/19/41	Sen-11-Kamikita	N

Gehman	Ralph A.	ID Boise	12/13/1896	2/23/1944		n/a	35-72
Gell	Walter	IA Wadena	2/11/1889	2/1/1975		Fuk-23-Keisen	37-75
Gentile	Walter	CA Hollywood	1/18/1912	1/23/1982	Bur 9/5/41	Tok-05B-Niigata	36-64
Geoghegan	Edward W.	CA Oakland	1/10/1903	8/25/1969	Reg 6/29/41	Tok area	N
Gerard	Morris K.	ID Shoshone	6/25/1916	9/5/1974	Reg 9/30/41	Tok area	34-63
Gerdin	William P.	NY Little Falls	2/1/1916	10/7/1943	Bur 1/9/41	n/a	36-31
Gerhart	Walter W.	CA Oroville	1/10/1918	5/23/1947		Tok area	37-71
Gibbons	Fred S.	CA Redding	6/13/1891	12/30/1960		Tok-05B-Niigata	36-32
Gibbons	George F.	CA Redding	5/31/1915	12/23/1941	Bur 10/9/41	n/a	36-45
Gibbs	Charles A.	CA LA	10/23/1896	10/7/1943	Chau 2/1/41	n/a	36-27
Gibson	George E.	CA LA	9/3/1901	1979 Feb		Fuk-03-Yawata	36-18
Gilbertson	Nurbert H.	ID Moscow	3/10/1897	9/20/1960		Tok area	36-63
Gillen	Thomas A.	OR PDX	4/25/1888	3/5/1966	Col 6/6/41	Fuk-01-Main	N
Gillespie	Robert P.	ID Boise	11/2/1921	4/9/1998	Bur 8/2/41	Sen-11-Kamikita	35-75
Gillis	Lawrence C.	WA Tacoma	11/9/1908	3/13/1998		Fuk-06B-Mizumaki	35-80
Gilmore	Leo R.	ID Boise	6/20/1913	6/9/1980		Tok-05B-Niigata	34-56
Girgal	Charles	TH HNL	3/15/1888	5/13/1964		Tok-05B-Niigata	N
Glaze	Miles	CA LA	8/25/1894	1967 Nov	Clip 6/7/41	Tok-05B-Niigata	36-62
Glazier	Milton A.	WA Chewelah	9/7/1916	11/4/1988		Tok-1-Omori	35-81
Glenamen	Frances D.	OH Glouster	7/26/1922	7/15/1998	Reg 9/30/41	Sen-07B-Hanaoka	36-23
Glenning	John A.	CA LA	1/16/1903	2/10/1971	Reg 5/23/41	Tok-05B-Niigata	36-29
Go	Benjamin S.W.	TH HNL	1/25/1923	4/14/2001		Sen-11-Kamikita	40-67
Gochnour	Harold E.	ID Nampa	5/6/1914	2/2/1951	Bur 8/2/41	Tok-05B-Niigata	N
Goembel	Clarence R.	CA LA	2/8/1910	10/7/1943	Reg 9/30/41	n/a	N
Goicoechea	Joe	ID Boise	7/31/1921	12/31/2016	Bur 8/2/41	Tok-1-Omori	N
Gomes	Fred H.	IL N Springfield	2/17/1893	8/6/1951	Bur 11/11/41	Tok area	N
Gooding	William B.	ID Gooding	8/2/1919	10/5/2003		Sen-11-Kamikita	34-57
Goodpasture	Dexter D.	CA Burbank	11/17/1897	12/11/1944	Bur 10/9/41	n/a	N
Goodpasture	John I.	CA Daly City	3/13/1895	9/13/1979	Bur 10/9/41	Fuk-03-Yawata	N
Goodwin	Ralph H.	AZ Phoenix	4/29/1894	12/26/1944		n/a	36-35
Gordon	Ellis	MD Belto	12/12/1898	12/12/1964	Bur 9/5/41	Sen-07B-Hanaoka	N
Gordon	Lloyd W.	MO Jefferson	3/18/1910	1980 Sep		Tok-05B-Niigata	36-15

		City					
Gorman	James V.	MI Pontiac	1/20/1902	9/10/1986	Bur 11/11/41	Tok area	N
Gossman	Paul A.	OH Crooksville	1/12/1922	12/9/1941		n/a	36-04
Gottlieb	Henry	CA Venice	10/12/1895	1/13/1945	Reg 8/19/41	n/a	N
Gough	Bernard M.	ID Boise	8/16/1918	2/15/1990		Sen-11-Kamikita	34-65
Gough	William W.	ID Boise	8/29/1916	8/8/1991	Reg 9/30/41	Fuk-01-Main	34-66
Goulding	Alonzo L.	ID Boise	10/14/1918	7/15/1999		Fuk-01-Main	37-72
Graham	Ellsworth M.	WA Spokane	7/10/1914	3/7/2002		Tok-05B-Niigata	36-16
Graham	Lyle E.	WY Sundance	7/21/1907	1961 May	Bur 10/9/41	Fuk-01-Main	36-10
Graham	Milo S.	WI Viroqua	10/16/1915	12/9/1941		n/a	N
Grancich	John A.	CA SF	6/12/1916	11/12/1993		Fuk-23-Keisen	N
Grandy	George	CA Chatsworth	6/26/1896	8/10/1980	Bur 9/5/41	Tok-05B-Niigata	N
Granstedt	Theodore Jr	TH HNL	1/17/1909	2/20/1985	Bur 11/11/41	Fuk-01-Main	35-93
Grant	Laurence V.	ID Emmett	11/1/1914	9/23/1972	Bur 8/2/41	Fuk-01-Main	N
Graves	Winfield V.	MT Fairfield	6/2/1911	6/5/1986		Fuk-03-Yawata	38-46
Green	Arnold R.	OH Cincinnati	9/7/1923	3/26/2009		Fuk-09B-Miyata	N
Green	Claude G.	OR Grants Pass	12/1/1912	10/13/2011	Reg 5/23/41	uk	3783-4428
Gregory	Bert D.	ID Boise	2/10/1917	6/24/2009	Reg 9/30/41	Tok-05B-Niigata	36-21
Gregory	Jesse J.	ID Boise	6/14/1897	4/15/1962	Reg 5/23/41	Tok area	37-73
Gress	Howard A.	ID Grandview	12/6/1918	7/11/1976		Tok-05B-Niigata	34-64
Greve	Louis	AZ Flagstaff	6/26/1898	3/15/1943	Bur 8/2/41	n/a	N
Griffith	Arthur W.	ID Boise	4/12/1918	12/7/1989		Tok-05B-Niigata	N
Grim	William B.	NH Portsmouth	4/17/1921	3/10/1943		n/a	N
Groshart	Jay A.	WY Worland	11/3/1896	2/20/1971	Bur 11/11/41	Tok area	36-55
Gross	Marvin E.	ID Boise	8/22/1908	1/30/1982		Fuk-01-Main	34-62
Groth	Ernest	MN Worthington	5/3/1901	1977 Sep		Tok area	47-65
Gushwa	Frank L.	ID Firth	2/19/1920	2/21/1990	Reg 9/30/41	Fuk-03-Yawata	38-56
Gustafson	Naad R.	CA SF	4/2/1907	3/7/1969	Reg 9/30/41	Tok area	36-13
Haakonstad	Clinton H.	WA Vancouver	10/18/1913	3/23/1994		Tok area	39-79

Hadley	Thomas W.	ID Swan Lake	3/6/1914	7/16/1995		Tok area	35-74
Hadsel	Floyd E.	CA Hayward	12/25/1905	2/17/1988	Bur 8/2/41	Fuk-06B-Mizumaki	35-85
Hahn	Charles B.	CA El Cerrito	2/21/1918	7/28/1999		Fuk-01-Main	N
Hahne	Henry J.	CA Richmond	8/27/1911	7/30/2003		uk	37-70
Haight	Ralph E.	IA Winfield	12/23/1907	10/7/1943		n/a	35-94
Haines	William H.	ID Boise	11/20/1917	10/7/1943		n/a	37-86
Hall	Daniel C.	ID Boise	3/9/1892	1976 Mar	Reg 5/23/41	uk	36-66
Hall	Frederick G.	OR Grants Pass	5/2/1907	3/28/1990	Bur 8/2/41	Tok-05B-Niigata	N
Hall	John E.	CA Belvedere Gardens	11/13/1898	12/8/1941	Bur 11/11/41	n/a	N
Hall	Kenneth B.	NV Reno	2/26/1909	11/29/1985	Bur 11/11/41	Fuk-01-Main	N
Hall	Lester E.	CA SF	8/20/1907	1/10/1986		Tok area	N
Halloway	Roger G.	IA Churden	3/8/1898	6/14/1976		Fuk-03-Yawata	36-09
Hamilton	John K.	OR Grants Pass	9/15/1890	8/21/1977	Bur 8/2/41	Tok-05B-Niigata	N
Hammond	Willard D. Jr	NJ Maplewood	8/25/1916	3/22/1994	Bur 1/9/41	Fuk-06B-Mizumaki	36-25
Hance	Loren H.	ID Boise	8/27/1901	4/25/1943	Bur 10/9/41	n/a	34-54
Hancock	Jack M.	OR Gold Hill	5/27/1918	6/7/1966	Reg 5/23/41	Fuk-06B-Mizumaki	35-84
Hansen	Peter W.	CA Inglewood	3/5/1901	3/21/1945	Cuy 3/24/41	n/a	36-26
Hansen	Vernon L.	NE Wahoo	6/2/1921	10/7/1943		n/a	37-77
Hansen	Villy M.	CA Oakland	9/27/1898	7/22/1974		Tok area	N
Hanson	Ernest T.	ND Oberon	6/20/1916	3/9/1990	Bur 11/11/41	Sen-07B-Hanaoka	38-73
Hanson	Fred A.	CA Oakland	11/1/1893	4/1/1944		n/a	36-34
Hanson	Ray F.	CA Oakland	8/21/1906	11/28/1983	Reg 5/23/41	Tok area	36-24
Hanson	William A.	WI Dallas	4/3/1914	7/17/1992		Fuk-01-Main	36-22
Harbeck	Lester W.	OR Grants Pass	11/3/1911	10/14/1979	Bur 8/2/41	Tok-05B-Niigata	N
Hardisty	Herbert A.	OR John Day	5/4/1910	7/4/1943		n/a	3647-4603
Hardt	Henry S.	CA Oakland	1/11/1920	1/16/2003	Reg 5/23/41	uk	N
Hardy	Robert J.	CA Rio Oso	3/17/1896	3/2/1980	Bur 10/9/41	Tok-05B-Niigata	36-54
Hargis	Eldon F.	OR Roseburg	1/29/1905	2/3/1983	Reg 5/23/41	Sen-11-Kamikita	N
Hargis	Eugene D.	OR Roseburg	9/5/1919	6/24/2011	Reg 5/23/41	Tok-05B-Niigata	N
Harper	William C.	WI Lancaster	2/24/1917	5/21/2009		uk	40-65
Harrell	Henry C.	GA Hilton	8/27/1918	12/16/1983	Reg 9/30/41	Tok-05B-Niigata	39-78

Harris	George	CA Redwood City	5/10/1904	10/7/1943	Bur 10/9/41	n/a	N +1
Harris	Oliver J.	MI Detroit	7/13/1907	6/14/1989	Bur 11/11/41	Sen-11-Kamikita	N
Harris	Theron J.	OR Roseburg	5/10/1898	3/12/1966	Reg 5/23/41	Tok area	38-41
Harrison	Robert H.	CA Wheatland	3/10/1917	11/25/1992		Fuk-23-Keisen	38-53
Hart	Irving W. III	ID Boise	12/7/1922	3/18/1943	Bur 8/2/41	n/a	38-69
Harvey	Burdette	OR Oakland	9/16/1919	5/6/1987	Reg 5/23/41	Tok area	N
Harvey	Wilbur C.	NH Portsmouth	9/29/1892	10/7/1943		n/a	N
Hastie	Frank	WV Charlston	12/2/1916	10/7/1943	Reg 9/30/41	n/a	40-39
Hastriter	John H.	ID Nampa	4/17/1884	1/9/1958	Bur 1/9/41	Fuk-01-Main	39-91
Hauner	John F.	CA LA	2/8/1910	2/13/1997		Sen-11-Kamikita	38-37
Hayes	Ortis B.	ID McCall	6/17/1915	6/6/1974		Tok area	42-73
Head	Robert P.	OR Tygh Valley	12/31/1921	8/5/1992	Reg 9/30/41	Sen-11-Kamikita	38-04
Heidle	Ralph E.	CA Nevada City	6/13/1911	11/2/1977	Reg 5/23/41	Tok-05B-Niigata	38-71
Helander	Charles O.	IL Lake Forest	10/3/1908	11/13/1942		n/a	N
Helgemo	George S.	CA LA	2/22/1911	11/19/1986	Bur 9/5/41	Tok area	N
Hellyer	James B.	IA Hillerton	1/2/1913	8/15/2002		Fuk-03-Yawata	N
Henderson	Gene L.	UT Logan	9/20/1918	5/15/2009	Bur 8/2/41	Sen-11-Kamikita	40-42
Henderson	Wilson P.	ID Boise	11/19/1918	9/23/2001	Reg 5/23/41	Sen-07B-Hanaoka	39-96
Hendricks	John B.	TX San Antonio	11/9/1913	1/25/1969	Bur 3/16/41	Sen-07B-Hanaoka	40-62
Henriksen	Gerald H.	ID Weiser	7/31/1919	9/29/2017		Tok area	38-42
Hensel	James H.	WA Burbank	8/20/1913	5/27/1997	Bur 1/9/41	Fuk-01-Main	N
Hensel	Theodore F.Sr	WA Burbank	8/10/1881	5/1/1943	Bur 1/9/41	n/a	N
Hepa	Abraham	TH Kauai	1/5/1923	7/31/1985		Tok area	N
Hernandez	William J.	CA LA	4/30/1920	8/31/2003		uk	N
Herndon	Howard W.	WY Fox Park	3/27/1903	1946		uk	40-53
Hesseltine	Claude R.	IA Knoxville	3/27/1900	6/24/1964		Tok-05B-Niigata	38-08
Hession	Francis I.	CA Lone Pine	12/15/1915	11/20/1981	Reg 5/23/41	Fuk-01-Main	39-76
Hettick	Howard L.	CA San Bernardino	7/30/1913	10/7/1943	Clip 6/7/41	n/a	N
Hewitt	Spencer E.	CA San Diego	11/17/1912	10/21/1987		Sen-05B-Kamaishi	41-99
Hewson	Albert A.	NY Rome	9/4/1917	1/11/1943	Bur 1/9/41	n/a	40-61

Hickenbottom	John	WA SEA	9/1/1893	4/23/1963	Bur 3/16/41	Sen-11-Kamikita	N
Higdon	Ralph N.	TH HNL	8/14/1902	12/23/1941	Reg 8/19/41	n/a	N
Higgins	Lorne H.	OR Grants Pass	1/8/1917	11/6/1994	Reg 5/23/41	Tok area	39-84
High	Lennie L.	CA LA	2/17/1895	11/16/1975		Tok-04B-Naoetsu	38-24
Hill	Norman L.	WA Clarkston	8/15/1894	6/4/1943	Reg 6/29/41	n/a	40-75
Hizer	Joseph	CA LA	11/21/1899	4/24/1970		Tok-05B-Niigata	N
Ho	Moon	TH HNL	2/1/1921	11/23/1991		Tok area	N
Hochstein	Ernest A.	OR Newburg	7/17/1913	10/7/1943	Bur 8/2/41	n/a	38-65
Hodgson	Harry W.	NE Scottsbluff	7/13/1895	6/8/1975	Reg 5/23/41	Tok-05B-Niigata	38-49
Hoffman	Kenneth	CA Maywood	2/9/1899	9/28/1970		Tok area	38-15
Hofmeister	Julius M.	CA SF	2/7/1906	5/10/1942	Reg 9/30/41	n/a	N
Hofschulte	Peter B.	CO Ft Collins	1/23/1897	11/4/1959	Bur 11/11/41	Tok area	38-18
Hogan	William F.	OR PDX	10/7/1913	4/2/1964		Fuk-01-Main	38-01
Hokanson	Walter N.	CA LA	9/15/1908	12/24/2007	Bur 3/16/41	Fuk-01-Main	40-74
Hong	Bing Tong	CA SF	3/11/1913	3/21/1982	Reg 8/19/41	Sen-11-Kamikita	N
Hopkins	Kenneth H.	OR Canyonville	2/26/1909	12/22/1987	Bur 8/2/41	Tok area	N
Hornyak	John M.	OR PDX	6/25/1909	3/16/1945		n/a	N
Hoskin	Chester D.	ID Lewiston	6/9/1903	12/9/1941		n/a	40-51
Hoskins	John R.	WA Okanogan	6/9/1919	1/22/2005	Jun	Tok area	38-74
Howard	Donald W.	CA Oakland	2/27/1918	3/20/1992		Sen-07B-Hanaoka	38-12
Howard	Ray L.	CA Rosemead	11/13/1913	10/10/1943	Bur 10/9/41	n/a	40-38
Howes	Claude D.	OR PDX	12/4/1893	4/28/1966	Col 6/6/41	Fuk-23-Keisen	N
Hubbard	Harvey T.	ID Boise	5/13/1917	12/15/1993		Fuk-01-Main	39-94
Huber	Charles H.	MO Boonville	5/28/1895	6/20/1962	Bur 11/11/41	Sen-11-Kamikita	39-99
Huddleston	Walter L.	MO Joplin	7/17/1923	1/18/2001	Reg 9/30/41	Tok area	40-71
Hudson	Glen R.	CA LA	9/10/1906	3/27/1989	Bur 9/5/41	Sen-11-Kamikita	N
Huntley	John W.	ID Boise	10/6/1911	3/1/1943		n/a	N
Hurst	Curtis L.	TX Beaumont	12/1/1897	8/2/1952	Bur 8/2/41	Sen-11-Kamikita	N
Huskisson	Tompie G.	KY Owensboro	1/31/1910	8/21/1986		Fuk-06B-Mizumaki	39-83
Ingham	Ralph P.	ID Boise	7/28/1920	11/15/2000		Tok area	38-61
Irons	Edwin H.	ID Boise	4/29/1918	11/14/1986		Tok area	40-47
Jackson	Melvin F.	CA LA	12/7/1900	12/6/1972	Reg 6/29/41	Tok area	40-70

Jaffe	Herbert E.	CA SF	9/24/1915	7/6/1983	Reg 9/30/41	Sen-07B-Hanaoka	N
Jakobsen	Oscar D.	CA Pasadena	11/29/1910	8/12/1975	Reg 9/30/41	Fuk-03-Yawata	39-86
Jee	Nee Pon	CA SF	8/15/1915	3/2/1961	Reg 9/30/41	Sen-11-Kamikita	40-08
Jensen	George A.	CA Parlier	9/9/1908	10/7/1943	Bur 1/9/41	n/a	40-31
Jernberg	Andrew A.	WY Cody	10/12/1890	12/5/1963		Tok-05B-Niigata	39-97
Jew	Hong Nay	CA SF	8/26/1913	DK		Sen-11-Kamikita	N
Jimison	Harold E.	CA La Jolla	8/7/1915	12/9/1942		n/a	38-26
John	Richard C.	OR PDX	8/12/1909	6/8/1998	Bur 8/2/41	Sen-11-Kamikita	N
Johnson	Arthur S.	WA Spokane	1/11/1909	9/14/1968		Tok area	38-25
Johnson	Axel R.	WY Manderson	10/10/1909	7/5/1985		Tok area	39-88
Johnson	Conrad I.	OR Grants Pass	5/23/1914	2/23/1997	Reg 5/23/41	Tok-1-Omori	48-37
Johnson	Edwin W.	CA Monterey	2/14/1896	3/30/1943		n/a	41-95
Johnson	Harold L.	ID Boise	5/29/1893	9/6/1944	Reg 5/23/41	n/a	42-04
Johnson	Kenneth A.	ID McCall	11/4/1912	5/9/2006	Reg 5/23/41	Tok-05B-Niigata	34-60
Johnson	Lee Jr.	WY Jackson	3/31/1918	1981 Nov	Bur 9/5/41	Tok area	N
Johnson	Lyman O.	ID Boise	8/18/1917	5/7/1995		Tok-05B-Niigata	39-89
Johnson	Malcom D.	WA Rice	2/14/1921	6/20/2016		Tok-05B-Niigata	38-28
Johnson	Nelson L.	IL Alton	9/15/1918	8/24/2002	Reg 6/29/41	Fuk-06B-Mizumaki	40-37
Johnson	Oreal J.	ID Boise	10/14/1907	3/24/1984		Fuk-01-Main	38-11
Johnston	Leon S.	IA Atlantic	11/24/1894	7/31/1946	Reg 9/30/41	Tok area	40-33
Jones	Alfred A.	CA San Bernardino	10/31/1908	10/7/1943		n/a	38-67
Jones	Charles	ID Boise	11/14/1914	10/30/1998		Fuk-01-Main	N
Jones	Chester J.	WA Spanaway	2/28/1914	10/28/1994		Fuk-06B-Mizumaki	N
Jones	Herbert	ID Boise	4/7/1917	4/5/1993		Tok-05B-Niigata	N
Jones	Humphrey A.	CA Stockton	8/21/1908	3/30/1983	Bur 11/11/41	Fuk-03-Yawata	N
Jones	Jesse C.	CA Millville	5/24/1897	11/23/1976		Tok area	38-50
Jones	Rex Dean	CA LA	10/15/1913	12/23/1941	Bur 11/11/41	n/a	N
Judd	Clayton F.	CA LA	5/16/1902	2/25/1945	Bur 8/2/41	n/a	N
Kahinu	Ah Chang	TH HNL	4/29/1901	1970 Jul	Bur 11/11/41	Fuk-17-Omuta	N
Kahm	Clarence J.	CA Oakland	10/15/1905	11/18/1974	Bur 11/11/41	Tok-05B-Niigata	38-13
Kahn	Albert T.F.	TH N Kahala	2/13/1923	5/13/2007		Sen-11-Kamikita	N
Kapaole	Adam	TH HNL	12/30/1918	8/21/1993	Bur 3/16/41	Fuk-06B-Mizumaki	N
Kapihe	Robert	TH HNL	8/31/1908	2/26/1945	Reg 5/23/41	n/a	N
Kapinos	George F.	MT	10/29/1914	1/23/1995	Reg 5/23/41	Sen-11-Kamikita	38-72

		Townsend					
Kay	Logan S.	CA SF	6/15/1891	7/19/1975		Fuk-23-Keisen	N
Keech	Evan J.	ID Caldwell	4/3/1908	1/13/1973		Fuk-06B-Mizumaki	38-45
Keech	Leo M.	ID Homedale	6/17/1913	2/22/1953	Bur 10/9/41	Tok-04B-Naoetsu	N
Keeler	Ora K.	IA Waterloo	10/17/1911	10/7/1943		n/a	N
Kelley	Sidney D.	WA Rosalia	7/24/1909	2/12/1945		n/a	38-02
Kelly	Frederick W.	WA Electric City	6/7/1904	3/9/1943	Reg 6/29/41	n/a	N
Kelly	George	CA Lomita	1/5/1895	9/20/1969	Bur 8/2/41	Tok area	N
Kelly	Jay Joe	CA Richmond	1/16/1915	1/7/1948		Fuk-06B-Mizumaki	38-54
Kelly	Martin T.	OR Roseburg	3/26/1906	10/7/1943	Bur 8/2/41	n/a	40-59
Kelly	Samuel D.	WA Electric City	4/27/1901	10/26/1943	Bur 3/16/41	n/a	N
Kelly	Thomas F.	CA Lomita	8/15/1908	1/26/1965	Reg 8/19/41	Tok-1-Omori	N
Kelso	Orval A.	ID Emmett	4/4/1904	4/8/1943	Bur 8/2/41	n/a	39-87
Kennedy	Buren C.	OR Rogue River	6/7/1902	10/31/1994	Bur 8/2/41	Tok-05B-Niigata	40-28
Kennedy	Thomas F.	CA SF	6/22/1915	10/7/1943	Reg 9/30/41	n/a	38-10
Kent	Lloyd R.	CA LA	11/7/1896	2/29/1944		n/a	38-75
Kephart	Rodney P.	ID Boise	7/3/1917	2/5/2003	Bur 11/11/41	Fuk-06B-Mizumaki	41-98
Kerr	Samuel R.	CO Sterling	1/15/1916	8/29/1983		Fuk-04B-Moji	41-84
Keyes	Walter A.	WA Pasco	8/17/1891	4/20/1984	Bur 3/16/41	Fuk-01-Main	38-58
Keyser	George E.	ID Boise	9/16/1913	12/10/1944		n/a	41-88
Kidd	Murray A.	ID Boise	8/6/1922	6/15/2002	Bur 8/2/41	Fuk-01-Main	38-52
Kidwell	Charles A.	IL Alton	3/18/1920	10/7/1943	Reg 9/30/41	n/a	39-98
Kim	Robert S. H.	TH HNL	3/18/1923	8/24/1991	Reg 9/30/41	Sen-11-Kamikita	N
Kimball	Patrick C.	CA LA	6/15/1912	9/27/1994	Reg 8/19/41	Fuk-09B-Miyata	N
Kimes	Realto E.	ID Twin Falls	3/29/1914	10/18/1989		Fuk-01-Main	38-05
King	Fred M.	OR LaGrande	1/17/1895	4/21/1962	Bur 3/16/41	Fuk-02B-Nagasaki	38-36
King	Lloyd M.	IL Brunside	4/2/1916	11/5/2005	Bur 8/2/41	Sen-11-Kamikita	40-32
King	Raymond L.	CA Pasadina	7/6/1920	6/10/2003	Bur 8/2/41	Tok area	40-56
Kinney	Jesse G.	CA Ventura	1/14/1886	4/8/1957		Tok-05B-Niigata	N
Kinney	Maurice L.	ID Boise	3/7/1917	2/26/1990	Reg 5/23/41	Tok-05B-Niigata	39-90
Kirk	John E.	OR Sitkum	6/6/1915	11/29/1971	Bur 8/2/41	Fuk-06B-Mizumaki	39-77
Kiser	Hugh M.	ID Melba	11/11/1911	11/21/1974	Reg 6/29/41	Fuk-03-Yawata	38-66
Kmiec	Alfred P.	WA SEA	4/30/1913	DK		uk	40-01

Knight	Frederick A.	KS Blue Rapids	4/15/1900	4/14/1985		Tok-05B-Niigata	38-06
Knowles	Iran H.	ID Meridian	11/22/1917	2/9/2003		Tok area	38-70
Knox	Elbert H.	WI Cuba City	12/30/1900	1/14/1944		n/a	38-31
Kon	Sing Wong	TH Kahala	2/10/1923	2/15/2001	Bur 8/2/41	Sen-11-Kamikita	N
Kong	Henry H. C.	TH HNL	4/10/1924	DK	Bur 8/2/41	Sen-11-Kamikita	N
Koski	Edwin P.	CA SF	6/11/1919	8/11/1999	Reg 9/30/41	Tok-05B-Niigata	38-47
Kraus	Oral	ID Boise	7/14/1912	12/14/1983		Tok-05B-Niigata	38-21
Kroeger	Woodrow W.	ID Nampa	1/30/1914	10/7/1943		n/a	38-43
Krohnert	Albert E.	CA Mt Shasta	12/28/1910	7/10/1985	Bur 11/11/41	Tok-05B-Niigata	N
Krueger	Reinhard W.	NE Kenesaw	9/8/1897	12/9/1941		n/a	N
Krysan	Gordon J.	IA Calmar	1/17/1916	2/22/1989	Bur 3/16/41	Fuk-01-Main	38-29
Kulick	Thomas	ID Boise	12/12/1902	6/18/1952		Fuk-06B-Mizumaki	40-46
Kurt	Nicholas D.	WA Spokane	11/21/1913	11/30/2009		Fuk-09B-Miyata	40-02
Lambirth	George L.	OR Umatilla	9/23/1920	1/28/1978	Bur 8/2/41	Tok area	N
Lancaster	Robert H.	ID Mountain Home	2/3/1908	6/14/1995	Bur 8/2/41	Fuk-01-Main	N +1
Landreth	Thomas C.	CA Whittier	2/19/1919	12/5/2008	Bur 3/16/41	Tok area	38-35
Lane	James H. Jr.	ID Boise	8/12/1914	1976 Jul	Bur 8/2/41	Tok area	38-59
Lane	Victor D.	OK OKC	5/3/1905	7/9/1979	Bur 10/9/41	Tok-05B-Niigata	40-11
Lange	John W.	CA LA	7/18/1914	7/14/2013	Bur 8/2/41	Sen-11-Kamikita	38-22
Lanning	Frank L.	CA Alhambra	11/23/1894	4/21/1960		Fuk-01-Main	39-85
Lapay	John	OR Seaside	7/11/1908	3/5/1983		Fuk-01-Main	40-35
Larsen	Andrew	NE Omaha	12/8/1887	1968 Apr		Tok area	N
Larson	Julius L.	CA Glendale	3/7/1905	2/17/1943		n/a	N
Laubach	George S.	NE Omaha	6/6/1885	10/8/1974		Tok-05B-Niigata	38-19
Lawrence	Clyde F.	ID Boise	1/1/1912	3/12/1966		Tok area	N
Lawson	William S.	ID Idaho City	4/5/1920	1/28/1945	Bur 8/2/41	n/a	38-16
Lawyer	Luther E.	NE N Platte	7/20/1900	2/7/1982		Fuk-06B-Mizumaki	N
Leahey	Larry M.	CA Hollywood	3/8/1908	4/11/1944		n/a	N
Lee	Ben Yin	CA SF	11/10/1905	DK	Reg 9/30/41	Sen-11-Kamikita	N
Lee	Clement	TH HNL	8/25/1920	11/30/1989	Reg 6/29/41	Sen-11-Kamikita	N
Lee	Edwin M. S.	TH HNL	8/24/1918	2/28/2001	Bur 3/16/41	Tok-1-Omori	40-57
Lee	Gee Kow	CA SF	2/10/1910	DK		Sen-11-Kamikita	N

Lee	Gim Y.	CA SF	10/9/1905	3/21/1979		Sen-11-Kamikita	N
Lee	Joseph H. C.	TH HNL	6/8/1923	6/24/2001	Reg 9/30/41	Sen-11-Kamikita	N
Lee	Koon Wah	TH HNL	9/14/1918	1/4/2014		Sen-11-Kamikita	N
Lee	Lenzie J.	NC Roanoke Rapids	5/14/1911	8/12/1988		Tok area	40-72
Lee	Sucy	CA SF	10/18/1914	2/19/2018	Reg 8/19/41	Sen-11-Kamikita	N
Lee	T. Bailey Jr.	ID Burley	3/14/1910	10/30/1982		Sen-07B-Hanaoka	38-40
Lee	Quong Bing	CA SF	2/6/1903	4/15/1981	Reg 8/19/41	Sen-11-Kamikita	N
Lehtola	Eric H.	MI Detroit	4/3/1916	1947		Fuk-03-Yawata	38-07
Lemke	Myron A.	WI Wausau	2/18/1899	12/9/1941		n/a	42-52
Lemken	Frank H.	CA LA	5/16/1902	11/15/1987	Reg 9/30/41	Tok area	N
Lemmon	Ralph P.	CA Pasadina	7/13/1906	11/1/1988	Reg 6/29/41	Fuk-03-Yawata	38-32
Lendewig	Lloyd T.	CA SF	2/14/1916	2/3/1945		n/a	N
Leng	Shee Sun	CA SF	11/2/1912	5/2/1988	Bur 9/5/41	Sen-11-Kamikita	N
Lent	Oscar C.	OR PDX	11/26/1914	7/18/1982	Col 6/6/41	Fuk-06B-Mizumaki	38-17
Leong	Kam Choy	TH HNL	12/19/1920	11/16/2013	Reg 6/29/41	Sen-11-Kamikita	N
Leong	Sit F.	CA SF	9/21/1908	DK	Reg 8/19/41	Sen-11-Kamikita	N
Leong	Thomas Y.C.	TH HNL	2/2/1914	12/31/2005		Fuk-23-Keisen	N
Lepinski	Ray H.	MN St Cloud	1/5/1901	5/20/1957	Bur 3/16/41	Tok-05B-Niigata	N
L'Esperance	James P.	CA Inglewood	12/8/1913	4/20/2002	Bur 9/5/41	Sen-11-Kamikita	39-92
Letcher	Ardell	CA Huntington Park	3/4/1902	3/22/1962		Fuk-23-Keisen	41-89
Levon	Harry	CA LA	9/30/1897	2/22/1984		Fuk-23-Keisen	38-38
Lew	Sing Mee	CA SF	1/1/1908	6/1/1946	Bur 9/5/41	Sen-11-Kamikita	N
Lewis	Seigel T.	CA Fresno	7/28/1898	7/1/1948	Bur 3/16/41	Tok-05B-Niigata	N
Lewis	Walter L.	OR PDX	3/24/1903	1/13/1975		Fuk-06B-Mizumaki	39-80
Light	Rolland E.	ID Boise	10/14/1913	10/7/1943		n/a	N
Lile	Woodrow F.	KS Corbin	8/31/1916	4/13/1952		Sen-11-Kamikita	41-97
Lilinoe	George K.	TH HNL	12/17/1922	11/11/1990		Sen-11-Kamikita	N
Lilly	David E.	CA Richmond	5/26/1911	12/23/1941	Bur 11/11/41	n/a	N
Lim	Hong	CA SF	5/7/1905	1981 Apr		Sen-11-Kamikita	N
Lim	Wing Gim	CA SF	8/29/1916	DK	Reg 8/19/41	Sen-11-Kamikita	N

Linder	John A.	ID Wilder	6/10/1920	4/18/1957		Fuk-01-Main	38-64
Lindquist	William O.	WI Hayward	3/31/1899	2/22/1943		n/a	N
Ling	Henry C.	TH HNL	8/9/1912	10/7/1943	Bur 1/9/41	n/a	N
Lippy	William H.	ID Boise	1/22/1913	6/20/1994		Sen-11-Kamikita	39-81
Lockridge	Harold E.	CA Monterey Park	3/22/1898	1974 Mar		Tok area	40-40
Look	Hang Chew	CA SF	2/18/1906	DK		Sen-11-Kamikita	N
Loosli	Merlin H.	ID Rupert	9/16/1914	3/17/1999		Tok area	40-49
Loveland	Chalas	ID Boise	3/6/1920	2/5/2013	Reg 8/19/41	Sen-11-Kamikita	38-62
Loveless	Phillip V.	ID Twin Falls	5/7/1894	12/19/1944		n/a	N
Lowman	Joseph Jr.	CA Oakland	10/30/1922	2/9/1992	Reg 9/30/41	Tok area	38-23
Ludington	Don W.	WA SEA	7/23/1916	1/29/2006	Bur 8/2/41	Tok-05B-Niigata	38-51
Luleich	Otto H.	WA Metaline Falls	12/19/1914	5/7/1949		Fuk-01-Main	44-46
Lum	Ambrose C.S.	TH HNL	7/7/1912	1951		Sen-11-Kamikita	N
Lyall	Thomas	CA Alameda	10/23/1904	11/27/1976		uk	N
Lyle	Harry J.	MT Billings	9/25/1908	6/6/1956		Fuk-01-Main	38-48
Lythgoe	Eugene	WA Selah	2/13/1918	10/7/1943	Reg 9/30/41	n/a	38-03
Mace	Frank R.	WA Medical Lake	5/27/1917	4/12/2011		Tok area	39-82
Mackie	Elmer E.	OR PDX	5/13/1912	1942 May		n/a	38-39
MacLean	Hector H.	TH HNL	9/16/1906	8/13/1986	Bur 1/9/41	Tok area	N
MacPherson	William W.	CA SF	2/15/1905	10/31/1965	Reg 6/29/41	Tok-05B-Niigata	N
Madarieta	Angel	ID Boise	4/9/1921	6/19/2009	Bur 8/2/41	Tok area	39-93
Mahler	Oscar H.	CA Eureka	3/13/1899	7/2/1968		Sen-11-Kamikita	40-10
Maiden	George W.	OR Coquille	4/4/1900	5/25/1947		Tok area	38-33
Malanya	Clifford E.	ID Rathdrum	12/15/1904	10/13/1992		Fuk-17-Omuta	38-30
Mallery	Ray F.	CO Denver	4/30/1893	10/14/1958	Reg 9/30/41	Tok area	N
Mallo	Franklin E.	CA Reseda	7/31/1907	9/5/1983	Bur 9/5/41	Sen-11-Kamikita	N
Manson	William R.	CA S Pasadena	12/2/1917	3/22/1945	Bur 3/16/41	n/a	38-09
Mansur	Elbert D.	OR Vale	12/10/1914	7/19/1969		Sen-11-Kamikita	40-45
Maple	Robert C.	CA Altadena	12/24/1916	5/24/2003	Bur 1/9/41	Fuk-06B-Mizumaki	38-20
Marable	John W.	AR Traskwood	3/27/1920	10/16/1990	Bur 8/2/41	Fuk-01-Main	42-49
Marcotte	Clayton J.	LA Morrow	8/7/1921	8/1/1980		Tok area	43-76
Marcoux	John J.	NH Manchester	1/12/1889	DK		Tok-05B-Niigata	42-23
Marsh	Benjamin	CA Compton	5/1/1903	1/10/1976	Reg 9/30/41	Fuk-01-Main	42-37

	J.						
Marsh	John H.	CA LA	11/15/1904	1/4/1986	Reg 9/30/41	Fuk-03-Yawata	N
Marshall	Irving E.	NY Lowville	6/22/1913	10/7/1943		n/a	43-93
Marshall	Lawrence A.	AR Harrison	5/10/1905	7/22/2001	Bur 11/11/41	Tok area	43-89
Martin	Jack S.	ID Boise	2/29/1888	4/23/1983		Tok-05B-Niigata	42-07
Martin	John W.	KY Covington	8/15/1917	3/18/1982		Sen-11-Kamikita	42-12
Martin	Ralph T.	OH Marietta	2/3/1920	7/31/2003	Bur 8/2/41	Tok-05B-Niigata	42-70
Martin	Robert	CA LA	10/2/1891	10/28/1960		Sen-11-Kamikita	N
Martin	John	WA Pomeroy	7/11/1903	10/7/1943		n/a	41-81
Martin	Robert G.	CA SF	2/12/1908	1968 Jul	Bur 10/9/41	Sen-11-Kamikita	N
Martineau	Marcel J.	MA Lawrence	9/25/1911	4/9/1998	Chau 2/1/41	Fuk-01-Main	N
Marz	Joseph V.	ID Boise	10/6/1918	2/22/2000		Tok-05B-Niigata	41-79
Masoner	Wilbur M.	ID Rupert	8/4/1907	1/6/1987	Bur 3/16/41	Tok-05B-Niigata	41-94
Massey	Garlin T.	AR Hoxia	1/15/1921	5/17/1992	Reg 9/30/41	Tok area	42-72
Mathson	Lloyd H.	NE Mitchell	6/20/1911	1/29/1982		Fuk-03-Yawata	43-92
May	Homer P.	WA Vancouver	4/13/1898	3/25/1971	Nov	Tok area	N
May	Paul E.	PA York	10/19/1914	12/29/2011	Bur 8/2/41	Sen-11-Kamikita	40-52
Mayberry	Charles R.	UT Ogden	10/30/1907	2/27/1979	Bur 3/16/41	Tok-05B-Niigata	40-23
Mayer	Herman J.	WA Colton	6/1/1911	11/19/1995		Tok area	40-22
McCay	William A.	ID Jerome	1/30/1900	7/7/1947		Tok area	43-77
McClure	Manfred C.	CO Boulder	5/26/1912	7/10/1999	Bur 3/16/41	Sen-11-Kamikita	42-08
McCullah	Howard W.	OR Riddle	2/20/1919	11/15/1996		Tok-05B-Niigata	34-55
McCulley	Charles E.	TH HNL	4/1/1912	1/22/1944	Bur 10/9/41	n/a	N
McCurry	Lauchlin S.	ID Boise	10/5/1917	8/5/1991	Reg 8/19/41	Sen-11-Kamikita	42-54
McDaniel	James B.	CA LA	11/9/1903	10/7/1943		n/a	42-32
McDonald	Harry L.	ID Boise	3/2/1919	4/3/1982		Tok area	40-05
McDonald	Joseph F. Jr.	NV Reno	9/8/1916	12/23/1984	Reg 6/29/41	Tok-05B-Niigata	40-66
McDonald	Joseph T.	WY Cody	8/4/1906	12/9/1941		n/a	42-57
McEvers	Ralph	OR PDX	3/10/1911	3/22/1943		n/a	N
McGallister	William	OR PDX	1899 Mar	12/17/1941	Reg 5/23/41	n/a	N
McGee	Guy C. Jr.	ID Moscow	8/1/1917	1/12/2003		Sen-05B-Kamaishi	42-02
McGill	Warren O.	ID Meridian	5/3/1907	7/10/1950	Bur 8/2/41	Fuk-17-Omuta	42-68
McGinnis	Robert S.	MO Richmond	3/11/1911	7/4/1949		uk	42-27

McInnes	Thomas L.	WA Tacoma	8/7/1893	10/7/1943	Justine Foss	n/a	N
McIntosh	Robert	KY Winchester	1/28/1920	6/28/1998	Reg 9/30/41	Sen-11-Kamikita	42-22
McKay	Alvin E.	WA Spokane	2/24/1909	9/8/1975		Tok area	42-47
McKee	Gerald E. Jr.	OR Corvallis	11/13/1915	5/9/2000		Fuk-03-Yawata	45-92
McKee	William C.	IA Boone	11/26/1893	DK		Tok area	42-56
McKeehan	Lloyd S.	CA SF	6/25/1908	2/25/1943		n/a	4251-4815
McKinley	Jack F.	CO Branson	2/13/1911	12/23/1941	Bur 10/9/41	n/a	40-60
McKinney	Richard A.	CA SF	7/24/1917	12/3/2012	Bur 8/2/41	Sen-11-Kamikita	42-28
McLeod	John F.	ID Boise	3/29/1919	12/22/1983		Tok area	40-06
McMurren	Virgil L.	CA LA	3/16/1896	6/13/1964	Reg 8/19/41	Tok-05B-Niigata	N
McNichols	Joseph L.	CA Venice	6/21/1910	4/23/1994		Fuk-03-Yawata	N
McPherran	George W.	OR Azalea	1/5/1905	1/12/1962	Bur 8/2/41	Tok-05B-Niigata	42-59
McQuitty	Frank L.	KS Grinnel	4/21/1920	5/25/1999		Tok-05B-Niigata	41-91
McTee	John R.	WY Rock Springs	1/1/1920	8/26/2000		Sen-07B-Hanaoka	42-10
Mead	Arthur R.	ID Pocatello	11/15/1912	11/5/1989		Fuk-01-Main	43-81
Mead	Ernest C.	ID Pocatello	8/12/1916	1/11/2002		Tok-05B-Niigata	42-60
Meek	John E.	OR Cornelius	2/21/1912	4/22/1988	Bur 11/11/41	Tok area	40-27
Meiners	Darwin L.	OR Seaside	4/16/1912	5/15/1956		Tok area	40-34
Mellor	Charles B.	ID Idaho City	8/18/1919	2/13/2002	Bur 8/2/41	Tok-05B-Niigata	43-79
Mendiola	Joseph L.	ID Twin Falls	6/16/1917	10/22/1993	Reg 9/30/41	Sen-11-Kamikita	N
Menezes	Arthur W.	TH HNL	4/5/1917	2/15/2011		Tok-05B-Niigata	N
Menique	Ramon	ID Boise	2/22/1901	5/13/1982		Tok area	41-83
Mercer	Raymond E.	MO Hayti	9/15/1924	4/23/2009	Reg 9/30/41	Tok area	N
Meyer	Lester T.	CA SF	9/18/1912	4/29/1943	Reg 9/30/41	n/a	N
Migacz	Frank	WI West Allis	2/14/1904	10/7/1943	Bur 3/16/41	n/a	42-53
Migacz	Melvin	WI West Allis	12/13/1915	10/7/1943	Reg 9/30/41	n/a	N
Miles	John M.	ID Donnelly	10/22/1907	12/26/1976		Fuk-17-Omuta	N
Miles	William J.	CA SF	8/5/1888	7/15/1942	Reg 5/23/41	n/a	N +1
Miller	Benjamin F.	WA Yakima	4/9/1905	1969 May		Tok-05B-Niigata	43-87
Miller	Charles M.	IL Enfield	9/16/1879	2/14/1943		n/a	42-21
Miller	Darwin W.	AR England	9/16/1920	6/18/2004	Reg 9/30/41	Tok-05B-Niigata	N
Miller	Don K.	OR Cove	3/28/1921	12/23/1941		n/a	40-20
Miller	Donald G.	CA Oakland	4/23/1921	12/16/1948		uk	42-42
Miller	Frank B.	CA San	11/12/1913	4/27/1943	Nov	n/a	42-64

	Jr.	Mateo					
Miller	Irvin E.	ND Price	4/4/1921	10/7/1943		n/a	43-88
Miller	Jack L.	TH HNL	10/23/1921	11/6/1994	Bur 10/9/41	Tok-05B-Niigata	N
Miller	Joe E.	ID Boise	9/30/1917	2/21/2009	Reg 5/23/41	Fuk-03-Yawata	42-14
Miller	Silas W.	ID Nampa	2/10/1900	3/21/1943	Reg 5/23/41	n/a	N
Milliken	Charles R.	NV Wells	9/15/1917	12/22/1982	Reg 8/19/41	Sen-11-Kamikita	42-15
Minkler	John D.	ID Boise	7/4/1912	5/20/1996		Tok area	40-21
Mitchell	Elmer G.	ID Homedale	2/10/1911	3/19/1982	Reg 5/23/41	Rokuroshi	40-30
Mitchell	Howard H.	UT Duchesne	3/16/1918	10/7/1943	Reg 6/29/41	n/a	N
Mitchell	Wayne E.	UT Duchesne	6/24/1920	10/7/1943	Bur 11/11/41	n/a	N
Mittendorf	Joseph F.	AZ Mayer	1/13/1919	10/7/1943	Reg 5/23/41	n/a	42-24
Moe	Charles A.	OR Grants Pass	10/24/1912	11/20/1943		n/a	43-83
Moening	Charles B.	OH Lima	10/22/1922	9/19/2017	Bur 8/2/41	Tok area	43-94
Mongrain	Stanley A.	MT Townsend	9/13/1916	7/12/1983		Tok area	39-95
Montagriff	Raymond E.	NY Yonkers	10/22/1906	2/2/1999	Bur 11/11/41	Fuk-01-Main	42-44
Moody	Barnard N.	CA Monrovia	12/3/1903	10/12/1975		Fuk-03-Yawata	42-38
Moon	Clarence L.	ID Lewiston	6/12/1902	3/21/1944		n/a	N
Moore	George	CA LA	10/15/1897	DK	Bur 11/11/41	Os-09B-Notogawa	N
Moore	Harry	CA Roscoe	9/6/1890	DK	Reg 6/29/41	Tok area	N
Morris	Cleo E.	ID Meridian	2/9/1919	5/19/1988	Reg 9/30/41	Fuk-01-Main	N
Morris	Matthew	MT Augusta	1/23/1913	1/23/2009		Tok area	40-69
Moser	Walter L.	ID Twin Falls	7/29/1916	8/8/1990		Tok-05B-Niigata	N
Mueller	Carl W.	NY Long Island	7/28/1900	10/7/1943		n/a	N
Muir	William D.	CA Willits	5/13/1902	1/23/1973	Reg 5/23/41	Sen-05B-Kamaishi	N
Murdock	William I.	NV Elko	12/26/1920	5/27/1945	Bur 8/2/41	n/a	43-90
Murphy	Gerald L.	WY Cody	5/12/1914	12/23/1984		Tok-1-Omori	42-55
Mussman	John A.	ID Idaho Falls	12/28/1919	10/30/1980		Tok area	40-41
Myers	Charles L.	CA Chico	5/5/1920	4/12/2020	Reg 5/23/41	Fuk-01-Main	43-82
Myers	Charles W.	CA Chico	6/11/1896	7/4/1970	Bur 3/16/41	Fuk-01-Main	42-05
Myers	Ivan D.	CA Hopland	3/11/1904	9/4/1987		Tok area	42-19
Myers	Richard B.	WA Clarkston	12/2/1910	10/7/1943		n/a	42-09
Nagele	Raymond O.	NY St Johnsville	9/12/1914	3/22/1997	Bur 1/9/41	Tok area	43-98
Nault	Norman P.	ID Boise	6/10/1915	1/29/2003	Reg 6/29/41	Sen-07B-Hanaoka	42-34
Nead	Ralph E.	IA Gilman	7/16/1917	8/1/1945	Reg 9/30/41	n/a	42-06

Neblett	Norman H.	CA Eagle Rock	10/11/1899	12/24/1981	Reg 9/30/41	Tok area	42-69
Nelles	Carl	NY Brooklyn	7/24/1903	7/11/1993		Fuk-03-Yawata	N
Nelson	Bert A.	ID Wendell	4/26/1908	4/8/2004	Reg 9/30/41	Tok-05B-Niigata	42-58
Nelson	Edward A.	WY Wheatland	5/2/1893	10/5/1942	Bur 1/9/41	n/a	42-11
Nelson	John A.	NE Omaha	1/26/1886	11/15/1964	Reg 5/23/41	Rokuroshi	44-61
Nelson	Lloyd O.	OR Roseburg	5/1/1918	12/1/2011	Reg 5/23/41	Tok-1-Omori	42-01
Nelson	Willard A.	ID Emmett	1/20/1914	6/30/1964		Tok area	40-26
Newell	Emmett L.	ID Ola	12/9/1919	1/27/1987	Reg 9/30/41	Sen-11-Kamikita	42-71
Newell	Glenn L.	ID Ola	10/20/1921	12/18/2014	Reg 9/30/41	Sen-11-Kamikita	42-40
Newhart	Dencil M.	OH Ewington	7/16/1921	4/24/1996	Reg 9/30/41	Sen-07B-Hanaoka	42-13
Newhoff	Benjamin H.	CA SF	11/7/1892	3/14/1944	Reg 9/30/41	n/a	42-33
Neylan	Robert F.	CA Oakland	10/26/1912	4/15/1981	Bur 11/11/41	Fuk-01-Main	42-17
Ng	Shew Shung	CA SF	12/4/1908	DK		Sen-11-Kamikita	N
Nichols	Harry R.	WI DeForest	11/18/1913	3/18/2004	Reg 9/30/41	Tok area	42-66
Nichols	Oral C. Jr.	NM Carlsbad	3/26/1921	L	Bur 8/2/41	Sen-11-Kamikita	42-41
Nicks	Quinton D. IV	AR Pine Bluff	2/23/1919	4/4/1943	Bur 8/2/41	n/a	42-36
Niklaus	J. Florian	PA North East	7/30/1880	1/26/1943		n/a	N
Nokes	Charles H.	ID Pocatello	3/10/1921	7/6/2005	Reg 9/30/41	Tok area	40-14
Nonn	Leo L.	IL Granite City	5/21/1918	11/28/2011		Tok-05B-Niigata	N
Norbury	Harry S.	OR Grants Pass	2/13/1920	11/14/1969	Reg 5/23/41	Tok-05B-Niigata	4063-4429
Nutley	Joseph H.	CA Marysville	11/13/1914	6/26/1999		Tok area	N
Nye	Edwin D.	DC Washington	5/3/1917	8/23/1997	Reg 8/19/41	Sen-11-Kamikita	43-80
Nygard	Andrew	CA SF	7/26/1892	3/15/1943		n/a	N
Oakes	Raymond J.	CA SF	4/22/1907	7/21/1961	Reg 9/30/41	Tok area	N
Ockel	William R.	CA LA	8/14/1917	4/15/1990	Reg 9/30/41	Sen-07B-Hanaoka	N
O'Guinn	Allan A.	CA Montebello	4/28/1897	11/21/1974	Sir 6/1/1941	OS-03B-Oeyama	43-86
O'Hearn	Richard E. Jr	MT Townsend	4/3/1910	6/9/1976	Bur 8/2/41	Tok-05B-Niigata	41-82
Olmstead	Clifford A.	CA Millville	6/16/1906	10/7/1943	Reg 5/23/41	n/a	N
Olsen	Lawrence C.	OR Ashland	11/25/1894	3/17/1977		Fuk-01-Main	46-16

Olson	Haftor H.	NE Columbus	2/3/1893	6/30/1988	Reg 5/23/41	Fuk-01-Main	N
Olson	Lawrence O.	MT Fairfield	8/21/1907	12/20/1961		Fuk-06B-Mizumaki	40-03
Olson	Theodore B.	OR PDX	6/19/1919	1/14/1994	Reg 6/29/41	Fuk-03-Yawata	34-46
O'Neal	John H.	CA Glendale	4/8/1900	2/27/1943	Reg 9/30/41	n/a	43-84
O'Neill	Joseph C.	CA Bakersfield	9/10/1902	1/26/1944	Reg 5/23/41	n/a	40-13
Oolman	George E.	MN Worthington	6/7/1916	4/1/2007	Bur 8/2/41	Tok area	42-62
Oriva	Edward H.	CA LA	5/14/1910	3/11/1975		Fuk-01-Main	N
Ortendahl	Leonard L.	CA Bell-Aire	8/6/1910	9/16/1995	Reg 9/30/41	Fuk-03-Yawata	N
Osborn	David E.	OR Medford	7/2/1913	4/7/1953		Fuk-01-Main	40-44
Ow	Yu Yen	CA SF	7/25/1922	12/29/1991		Sen-11-Kamikita	40-58
Pace	John R.	AZ Casa Grande	1/13/1912	1976 Feb	Bur 8/2/41	Tok-05B-Niigata	42-25
Packard	Forrest L.	ID Meridian	7/26/1893	1/7/1963	Reg 5/23/41	Tok-05B-Niigata	44-73
Pagoaga	Richard J.	ID Boise	10/11/1922	11/27/2015	Bur 8/2/41	Tok area	43-91
Papock	Herbert	CA LA	8/23/1917	2/9/2004	Bur 3/16/41	Sen-11-Kamikita	40-55
Park	Hio Whoon	TH HNL	2/16/1923	11/6/2010		uk	42-61
Parks	Robert P.	CA Vallejo	1/9/1906	10/27/1964	Reg 9/30/41	Fuk-03-Yawata	40-04
Parrott	William W.	CA Willmington	3/22/1917	3/1/2010	Bur 8/2/41	Fuk-06B-Mizumaki	42-18
Patterson	Howard C.	WY Cody	9/4/1902	DK		Tok area	42-50
Pawlofske	Richard P.	OR PDX	10/5/1890	2/17/1943		n/a	42-48
Pay	Alexander E.	CA Ocean Park	3/3/1912	3/9/1973	Bur 3/16/41	Sen-11-Kamikita	40-48
Payne	Chester H.	MO Morehouse	8/2/1920	6/15/1992	Reg 9/30/41	uk	40-54
Payne	Herman E.	MO McGee	6/5/1922	4/20/2009		Tok area	N
Pease	Gordon H.	WY Midwest	12/15/1909	10/7/1943		n/a	40-16
Peepe	William G.	CA Crescent City	8/11/1916	8/9/2009	Bur 8/2/41	Sen-07B-Hanaoka	41-92
Penner	Omer A.	OK Farris	8/4/1914	5/27/2000	Reg 9/30/41	Tok area	N
Pennington	William G.	AL Nauvoo	2/5/1918	9/17/1998	Bur 3/16/41	Tok-05B-Niigata	N
Pepple	Lloyd F.	OR Bonanza	6/24/1907	10/19/1989	Bur 8/2/41	Fuk-06B-Mizumaki	42-16
Percy	Richard G.	CA Chico	3/22/1917	9/6/2013	Clip 6/7/41	Fuk-01-Main	N
Peres	Edgar A.	CA SF	1/26/1892	8/15/1964	Bur 10/9/41	Tok area	N
Perrine	Ronald K.	CA Oakland	8/17/1915	3/11/1989	Reg 6/29/41	Rokuroshi	N
Peterson	Charles R.	CA Watsonville	5/17/1916	8/21/1984		Fuk-04B-Moji	41-78
Peterson	Elmer C.	ND Allendale	6/21/1897	9/21/1967		Tok-05B-Niigata	42-03
Peterson	Hjalmar M.	ID Boise	5/31/1879	11/2/1942	Reg 5/23/41	n/a	N
Peterson	Hurschel L.	TH Oahu	9/23/1915	12/23/1941		n/a	N
Peterson	Oscar R. Jr.	ID Jerome	5/8/1918	6/6/2005	Bur 11/11/41	Fuk-17-Omuta	43-96
Peterson	Robert M.	ID Sterling	9/17/1915	12/11/2003		Fuk-03-Yawata	40-17

Peterson	Roland W.	CA South Gate	1/26/1909	7/25/1981		Fuk-03-Yawata	42-30
Pfost	Orlie E.	ID Gooding	3/10/1910	9/6/1943	Bur 10/9/41	n/a	41-76
Pinkney	Harold R.	CA LA	1/1/1898	8/20/1977		Tok area	N
Pitcher	Henry J.	CA Burbank	5/25/1908	1/29/1992	Reg 9/30/41	Fuk-03-Yawata	N
Pitochelli	Edward	CA Glendale	6/4/1897	1/11/1990	Reg 6/29/41	Fuk-23-Keisen	40-25
Planansky	Oscar L.	ID Boise	2/15/1912	5/13/1995	Reg 9/30/41	Tok-05B-Niigata	40-09
Pohl	Herbert F.O.	NJ PerthAmboy	4/1/1900	3/24/1980	Bur 3/16/41	Fuk-09B-Miyata	42-63
Polak	John V.	MT Townsend	2/14/1905	2/9/1994	Bur 1/9/41	Tok area	40-07
Polinsky	Alex E.	OH Niles	9/1/1923	2/27/2008	Reg 9/30/41	Tok area	41-87
Poon	Harry B.	CA SF	12/12/1908	DK		Sen-11-Kamikita	N
Popson	John	PA Swoyerville	6/22/1912	9/22/1993	Reg 9/30/41	Tok area	42-31
Porter	Theodore H.	CA San Pedro	4/3/1903	3/29/1975		Sen-07B-Hanaoka	34-18
Pratt	Archie H.	CA SF	8/18/1902	10/7/1943	Reg 5/23/41	n/a	42-20
Preston	William D.	ID Lewiston	1/26/1906	10/7/1943		n/a	41-93
Price	Arthur G.	CA SF	11/6/1902	1/26/1973	Reg 5/23/41	Fuk-01-Main	40-43
Price	Edward J.	MT Bozeman	6/22/1920	3/26/1972		Tok area	41-86
Priebe	Gustaf A.	OR Creswell	12/10/1916	9/27/2016		Tok area	40-19
Proteau	George F.	OR PDX	4/4/1885	3/30/1943	Reg 5/23/41	n/a	43-75
Proteau	Lawrence H.	OR PDX	11/27/1920	3/23/1943	Reg 5/23/41	n/a	43-85
Pryor	Lindley H.	CA LA	2/4/1893	2/29/1968	Bur 3/16/41	Tok-05B-Niigata	42-43
Puccetti	Elmer	CA Sacramento	7/24/1906	3/12/1943	Reg 5/23/41	n/a	40-50
Purcell	Delbert F.	WA Ione	5/23/1919	1970 May		Tok area	40-15
Quigley	James E.	OR Roseburg	2/5/1904	1/2/1973	Reg 5/23/41	Sen-11-Kamikita	N
Quille	Lawrence W.	CA Fullerton	5/12/1912	4/3/1992	Reg 6/29/41	Tok-1-Omori	40-12
Quinn	Raymond G	ID Boise	8/31/1899	2/22/1975		Tok area	42-74
Ralston	Doris L.	OH Barden	10/12/1922	4/21/1984	Reg 9/30/41	Tok-05B-Niigata	N
Ramsey	Alfred B.	OR Riddle	3/27/1910	11/22/1986	Reg 5/23/41	Tok-05B-Niigata	N
Rankin	Morton B.	ID Caldwell	5/27/1914	10/7/1943		n/a	40-68
Raspe	Herman H.	CA LA	6/25/1886	12/20/1969	Nov	Tok area	42-29
Ratekin	Chester M.	ID Nampa	10/13/1912	9/6/1986		Tok area	42-45
Ray	Clyde W.	WA Republic	8/18/1899	12/17/1941		n/a	42-46
Ray	Oscar Jr.	ID Boise	3/31/1921	12/29/1994		Sen-11-Kamikita	40-24
Ray	William H.Jr.	IL Downers Grove	10/29/1907	10/7/1943	Reg 5/23/41	n/a	43-78
Read	Forrest D.	ID Boise	1/22/1918	8/5/1998		Tok-04B-Naoetsu	41-80
Reed	Harry E.	CA SF	4/4/1900	4/3/1945	Reg 5/23/41	n/a	Reed
Reed	Warren V.	CA LA	5/21/1896	8/11/1974		Fuk-23-Keisen	Reed
Reese	Ivan S.	CA SF	6/17/1921	12/16/1988	Bur 10/9/41	Tok-05B-Niigata	Reese
Reeves	Forrest W. Jr.	CA Palo Alto	2/25/1920	12/22/1941	Reg 8/19/41	n/a	Reeves
Reid	Raymond S.	PA Kane	3/26/1913	DK	Reg 9/30/41	Tok area	Reid
Reid	Russell	AZ Phoenix	8/14/1896	8/16/1943	Bur 3/16/41	n/a	Reid

Reiger	Gregory C.	TX Dallas	1/27/1897	12/23/1941	Reg 9/30/41	n/a	Reiger
Reilman	Theodore T.	OH Cincinnati	1/11/1920	7/2/2007		Tok area	Reilman
Rensberg	Harold O.	CA SF	9/3/1891	11/23/1943	Bur 11/11/41	n/a	Rensberg
Revell	James D.	UT Price	3/24/1898	8/29/1966	Reg 5/23/41	Sen-11-Kamikita	Revell
Reynolds	Henry W.	ID Nampa	4/23/1920	7/2/1978	Bur 8/2/41	Tok area	Reynolds
Reynolds	John W.	NE Guide Rock	9/20/1904	10/10/1974	Bur 9/5/41	Sen-11-Kamikita	Reynolds
Reynolds	William H.	OR Brightwood	11/28/1906	10/7/1943	Chau 2/1/41	n/a	Reynolds
Rice	James C.	CA San Bernardino	4/28/1900	1/11/1956		Tok-05B-Niigata	Rice
Rice	William H.	OR Grants Pass	8/12/1895	2/29/1984	Bur 8/2/41	Sen-11-Kamikita	Rice
Richardson	Louis W.	ID Nampa	10/26/1921	2/25/1999	Reg 5/23/41	Fuk-23-Keisen	Richardson
Riddle	Lonnie B.	CA Yuba City	4/17/1915	6/18/1942		n/a	Riddle
Riddle	Pearson	NC Pensacola	10/15/1921	L	Bur 8/2/41	Sen-07B-Hanaoka	Riddle
Riebel	Chester A.	OR Grants Pass	2/22/1894	7/15/1973	Reg 5/23/41	Fuk-01-Main	Riebel
Riendeau	William J.	CA Oakland	5/10/1891	12/25/1975		Tok area	Riendeau
Rienks	Donald H.	CA Port Chicago	11/11/1911	3/20/1945		n/a	Rienks
Riffel	John H.	CA Azusa	2/22/1900	12/20/1942	Reg 9/30/41	n/a	Riffel
Ritter	Commodore P.,	ID Banks	2/26/1912	12/11/1941		n/a	Ritter
Rivers	Albert S.	ID Boise	6/5/1916	7/26/2003		Tok-04B-Naoetsu	Rivers
Robbins	Paul J.	ID Boise	1/18/1909	3/25/1943	Clip 6/7/41	n/a	Robbins
Robbins	Sheldon G.	CA LA	5/29/1906	10/7/1943		n/a	Robbins
Roberts	Alvin B. Jr	ID Grass Valley	1/18/1922	2/20/1976		Sen-11-Kamikita	Roberts
Roberts	Raymond W.	CA Coronado	9/22/1917	1978 Jul	Bur 8/2/41	Sen-11-Kamikita	Roberts
Robertson	Arnold A.	UT SLC	9/20/1914	9/15/1996		Tok area	Robertson
Robertson	Charles B.	WY Manderson	5/28/1898	9/12/1943	Bur 11/11/41	n/a	Robertson
Robertson	Dale O.	UT SLC	5/12/1916	2/19/1945		n/a	Robertson
Robertson	Harley E.	UT SLC	5/26/1912	11/30/1966		Tok area	Robertson
Robnett	Elmo E.	OR LaGrande	7/11/1902	7/2/1975		Tok-05B-Niigata	Robnett
Rogde	Gerhart S.	ID Boise	10/5/1916	1/21/2012		Fuk-09B-Miyata	Rogde
Rogers	Jerold K.	SD Isabel	1/26/1921	9/26/1991		Fuk-01-Main	Rogers
Rogge	John D.	ID Weiser	7/14/1920	12/4/2002	Bur 8/2/41	Sen-11-Kamikita	Rogge
Rogge	Warren O.	CA Watsonville	11/17/1916	11/16/1984		Fuk-09B-Miyata	Rogge
Rohan	Joseph D.	OR LaGrande	10/20/1904	10/29/1955	Bur 3/16/41	Fuk-01-Main	Rohan
Romine	James B.	WA Spokane	11/8/1914	12/1/1956		Tok area	Romine
Rosandick	George D.	ID Boise	11/1/1921	10/14/2005	Bur 8/2/41	Tok-05B-Niigata	Rosandick
Rose	Benjamin	CA Inglewood	2/4/1895	DK		Sen-11-Kamikita	Rose

Roth	Fred P.	ID Nampa	7/10/1907	2/17/2006	Reg 9/30/41	Tok area	N
Rout	Richard C.	CA Watsonville	4/14/1907	7/19/1985		Fuk-03-Yawata	44-08
Row	Earl R.	IN Greensburg	1/16/1908	11/18/1993	Reg 8/19/41	Sen-11-Kamikita	45-81
Rucker	Raleigh K.	OH Lucasville	6/15/1923	2/16/2002	Reg 9/30/41	Sen-11-Kamikita	44-34
Rudolph	Robert W.	CA Gilroy	9/18/1898	5/1/1950	Bur 8/2/41	Fuk-01-Main	N
Rumpel	Fred R.	ID Parma	2/11/1900	1/24/1995	Reg 5/23/41	Tok area	44-01
Russell	Leal H.	OR LaGrande	11/12/1899	7/20/1957	Bur 1/9/41	Sen-05B-Kamaishi	46-29
Rutledge	Raymond R.	OH Cambridge	2/25/1895	10/7/1952		uk	44-50
Ryan	William F.	OR PDX	9/17/1906	11/11/1959		Fuk-23-Keisen	N
Sager	James T.	ID Cottonwood	4/17/1910	9/19/1996	Reg 6/29/41	Fuk-03-Yawata	44-37
Samms	George E.	WA Metaline Falls	4/21/1920	10/28/1971		Tok area	N
Sanders	Harry R.	IN Terre Haute	3/10/1922	1986 Aug	Reg 9/30/41	Tok area	N
Sanford	Thomas W.	OR Williams	7/20/1917	8/27/1972	Bur 8/2/41	Tok area	44-51
Santos	Elvyn J.	TH HNL	5/2/1922	2/12/1988	Bur 10/9/41	Tok-05B-Niigata	N
Sappington	Clinton	CA Inglewood	10/14/1901	1/20/2000	Reg 9/30/41	Fuk-03-Yawata	N
Sardone	Michael A.	WA Uniontown	1/23/1911	4/8/2000		Tok area	44-12
Sater	Harry E.	CA Inglewood	2/8/1900	8/6/1972	Reg 6/29/41	Fuk-03-Yawata	44-68
Savitz	Harvey E.	WA Tekoa	8/20/1921	6/19/2009	Cur 10/20/41	Tok-05B-Niigata	45-82
Schafer	Fred H.	ID Nampa	6/26/1919	12/20/2002	Reg 9/30/41	Tok area	45-97
Schemel	Charles M.	WA Uniontown	5/27/1913	10/7/1943		n/a	45-83
Schieferstein	John A.	OR Grants Pass	6/6/1891	5/11/1964	Bur 8/2/41	Tok area	N
Schmaljohn	George W.	ID McCall	3/10/1919	9/6/2006		Fuk-01-Main	45-79
Schmidt	Henry J.	WY Lowell	5/13/1911	8/11/2002	Bur 11/11/41	Tok area	46-02
Schmidt	Julius E.	OH Columbus	12/15/1923	L	Reg 9/30/41	Tok-05B-Niigata	44-52
Schoeningh	Herman H.	CA Petaluma	3/24/1904	8/12/1965	Reg 9/30/41	Tok area	44-49
Schottler	Herman	CA SF	5/4/1904	10/7/1943	Reg 9/30/41	n/a	44-53
Schrader	Herman A.	UT SLC	5/20/1882	5/6/1958		Tok-05B-Niigata	44-54
Schultz	John E.	ID Boise	1/5/1916	5/18/2003		Sen-07B-Hanaoka	N
Schweizer	Emil J. Jr.	ID Boise	2/24/1917	7/25/1982		Tok-05B-Niigata	43-95
Schwenke	Ralph E.	IL Centralia	7/1/1915	3/23/1989	Reg 5/23/41	Tok area	N
Scott	Chester A.	CA Sacramento	6/3/1891	8/21/1980	Bur 11/11/41	Fuk-06B-Mizumaki	45-98
Scott	Lawrence L.	WY Sheridan	4/6/1898	8/30/1992		Tok-05B-Niigata	45-76
Scott	Robert R.	CA LA	12/4/1916	DK	Bur 9/5/41	Fuk-03-Yawata	47-51
Seastrom	Hilmar A.	IA Jefferson	6/9/1913	9/5/1979		Tok area	46-08
Seelke	Fred	CA Encino	1/6/1905	Sep-76	Reg 8/19/41	Sen-11-Kamikita	44-17
Selleseth	Oscar A.	CA Alameda	10/9/1902	5/6/1944		n/a	N
Serdar	Anthony Z.	WA Metaline Falls	6/4/1921	3/19/2017		Tok area	44-44

Serven	Martin L.	NY NYC	9/29/1899	8/24/1982		Tok area	N
Shamel	Lewis W.	OR Grants Pass	6/10/1920	1/24/2005		Tok-1-Omori	N
Shank	Lawton E.	IN Angola	4/29/1907	10/7/1943		n/a	N +2
Shattles	Stephen H.	CA LA	4/14/1915	6/4/1992	Bur 9/5/41	Tok-1-Omori	44-69
Shenkman	David S.	CA LA	2/22/1916	8/9/1949		Tok-05B-Niigata	N
Shepherd	Orbin R.	OR PDX	9/8/1910	10/7/1943		n/a	44-11
Sherard	Elza J.	MO Maysville	8/1/1895	11/22/1977	Bur 9/5/41	Sen-11-Kamikita	44-66
Sherman	Glenwood H	CA San Jose	3/10/1902	10/7/1943		n/a	N
Sherwood	Gerald G.	ID American Falls	8/11/1900	3/12/1966		Fuk-09B-Miyata	N
Shields	Hugh J.	IA Council Bluffs	4/5/1895	6/14/1983	Reg 9/30/41	Sen-07B-Hanaoka	48-07
Shim	Adam S.K.	TH Kohala	9/28/1912	1/22/1981	Reg 6/29/41	Sen-11-Kamikita	N
Shim	Edward Y.S.	TH Kohala	6/26/1922	10/23/2013		Sen-11-Kamikita	N
Shott	Van R.	OR Rickreall	11/19/1905	3/26/1956		Tok-05B-Niigata	44-40
Shriner	Gould H.	IA Sioux City	6/24/1901	10/7/1943	Bur 10/9/41	n/a	44-31
Shumaker	John C.	WA Valley	6/5/1906	1/27/1968		Fuk-23-Keisen	44-33
Sigman	Russell J.	ID Idaho Falls	11/11/1913	10/7/1943		n/a	N
Silverman	Samuel N.	CA SF	12/2/1913	1/18/2008	Reg 9/30/41	Tok-04B-Naoetsu	N
Simeona	John K.	TH Kailua	2/24/1911	1962	Bur 11/11/41	Sen-11-Kamikita	N
Simmons	Stanley J.	CA Long Beach	9/15/1912	1/7/1998		Fuk-09B-Miyata	N
Simmons	Sterling C.	AR Augusta	8/14/1917	4/7/1976	Reg 9/30/41	Fuk-06B-Mizumaki	44-41
Simpers	William T.	WY Wapiti	3/22/1915	10/7/1943		n/a	44-36
Simpson	Lawrence A.	CA Gilroy	2/11/1895	5/17/1968	Reg 9/30/41	Sen-11-Kamikita	N
Six	Daniel M.	UT SLC	12/6/1913	10/17/1996		Tok-05B-Niigata	N
Skirvin	Olin G.	CA LA	6/14/1898	3/27/1964		Tok area	N
Slafer	Edward W.	NY NYC	4/11/1920	12/9/1941	Bur 8/2/41	n/a	44-20
Slagle	Jack	CA SF	11/7/1903	4/30/1971	Reg 9/30/41	Fuk-03-Yawata	44-13
Smalley	Roger H.	CA Oakland	2/4/1921	10/27/1996		Tok-05B-Niigata	N
Smith	Abner J.	ID Boise	9/25/1920	9/15/1944	Bur 10/9/41	n/a	N
Smith	Charles E.	FL Grant	1/5/1916	10/7/1943	Reg 6/29/41	n/a	44-48
Smith	Charles R.	MT Townsend	3/21/1919	7/28/1996		Sen-11-Kamikita	44-04
Smith	Eugene	CA LA	5/19/1915	6/21/2004	Reg 9/30/41	Fuk-03-Yawata	N
Smith	George	PA Philadephia	7/16/1911	DK		Sen-07B-Hanaoka	45-88
Smith	Harold E.	OR Roseburg	12/25/1911	5/28/1970	Bur 8/2/41	Sen-11-Kamikita	N
Smith	Harold H.	ND Cleveland	6/1/1908	12/31/1979		Tok area	44-59
Smith	Joseph D.	ID Emmett	4/23/1915	9/19/1992		Sen-11-Kamikita	44-25
Smith	Joseph E.	CA Oakland	2/22/1908	4/7/1979	Reg 9/30/41	Sen-07B-Hanaoka	N
Smith	Kenneth M.	CA Oakland	3/29/1896	DK		Sen-11-Kamikita	48-11
Smith	Lewis H.	OR Rogue River	9/19/1919	7/6/1986	Reg 5/23/41	Sen-11-Kamikita	44-30
Smith	Wayne D.	NE Beatrice	8/1/1912	1/21/1970	Reg 9/30/41	Fuk-04B-Moji	44-56

Smith	William A., Jr.	AR Gould	5/11/1922	10/2/1958	Bur 8/2/41	Tok area	N
Smith	William C.	CA Pomona	1/6/1914	4/25/1975	Bur 8/2/41	Tok-05B-Niigata	N
Smyth	Edwin F.	ID Nampa	8/20/1912	3/27/1999		Fuk-01-Main	44-43
Snipes	John O.	CA Altadena	12/14/1914	5/17/1990	Bur 8/2/41	Tok area	45-96
Snyder	Floyd A.	NE Wahoo	2/7/1920	6/28/1966	Bur 8/2/41	Sen-11-Kamikita	44-19
Sorensen	John P.	CA SF	2/17/1902	12/23/1941		n/a	N
Spang	Mathias	ID Nampa	5/13/1913	1/7/1965		Tok area	45-90
Sporer	Robert D.	OR Roseburg	12/9/1919	2/20/1989	Reg 5/23/41	Tok-05B-Niigata	N
Sprague	Steven W.	OR Redmond	8/10/1911	10/26/2001	Bur 8/2/41	Tok area	N
Spurlin	William D.	IN Shelbyville	7/30/1921	10/31/1951	Reg 9/30/41	Sen-11-Kamikita	44-10
St. John	Francis C.	IL Liberty	8/17/1905	10/7/1943		n/a	44-55
Starnes	Elik R.	CA South Gate	12/28/1904	2/19/1978	Reg 9/30/41	Fuk-03-Yawata	N
Staten	Mark E.	CA LA	5/21/1914	2/16/1942		n/a	N
Steffes	Albert P.	MN St Cloud	1/12/1907	12/18/1976	Reg 9/30/41	Tok-1-Omori	48-18
Stennis	James H.	MS Dekalb	3/20/1915	1/19/2006	Bur 11/11/41	Tok area	N
Stephens	Roy V.	TX Tahoka	4/19/1915	5/1/2000		Tok-05B-Niigata	46-27
Stevens	Clifford F.	ID Twin Falls	3/24/1921	9/28/1988		uk	N
Stevens	Fredrick J.	IA Sioux City	5/15/1896	11/10/1965	Reg 6/29/41	Fuk-01-Main	N
Stevens	Paul B.	CA Bell	6/27/1904	3/10/1976		Sen-11-Kamikita	N
Stevenson	Clinton L.	CA LA	7/17/1906	12/23/1941	Bur 8/2/41	n/a	N
Stewart	James E.	ID Nampa	5/29/1921	6/26/2002		Sen-11-Kamikita	45-89
Stewart	Victor L.	CA Alhamora	12/8/1895	2/2/1969	Bur 9/5/41	Tok-05B-Niigata	47-60
Sthole	Carl A. M.	CA LA	1/17/1893	2/27/1960		Tok-05B-Niigata	N
Stites	Howard M.	NE Grand Island	2/16/1890	1/14/1949		Sen-11-Kamikita	44-57
Stoddard	Ira E.	ID Boise	10/14/1910	11/18/1989		Fuk-03-Yawata	45-86
Stofle	Thomas L.	CA Fresno	6/15/1919	4/9/1998	Bur 10/9/41	Fuk-23-Keisen	44-21
Stone	Clinton M.	OR PDX	3/9/1908	3/20/1943		n/a	44-39
Stone	James M.	CA LA	10/7/1913	DK		Fuk-01-Main	44-45
Stone	Willis C.	TH HNL	1/10/1914	10/7/1943	Bur 3/16/41	n/a	Stone
Streblow	Alvin L.	WI Wisconsin Rapids	3/21/1905	10/7/1943		n/a	Streblow
Streeter	Mark L.	ID Lewiston	5/11/1898	3/24/1986		Tok-1-Omori	Streeter
Strickland	Cecil H.	CA Williams	7/26/1919	1/11/1999	Reg 5/23/41	Tok area	Strickland
Stringer	Wesley W.	OR Grants Pass	8/30/1918	10/7/1943	Reg 5/23/41	n/a	Stringer
Sturdevant	Marshall G.	WA Dayton	7/18/1916	11/10/2008	Bur 3/16/41	Fuk-06B-Mizumaki	Sturdevant
Sullivan	Donald L.	WA Longview	4/11/1917	1942 May		n/a	Sullivan
Susee	Arthur J.	OR Hillsboro	3/20/1917	10/7/1943		n/a	Susee
Sutherland	Hudson C.	OR PDX	10/25/1885	7/6/1977	Bur 11/11/41	Tok area	Sutherland
Swanson	Norman J.	WA Osborne	11/8/1920	3/15/2016	Reg 9/30/41	Tok-04B-Naoetsu	Swanson
Sweet	Harry V.	CA LA	3/10/1894	2/17/1943	Reg 5/23/41	n/a	Sweet
Sweiberg	James J.	WA Vancouver	8/13/1916	3/15/2009	Bur 8/2/41	Tok-04B-Naoetsu	Sweiberg

Swift	Samuel P.	WA LaConner	6/2/1903	1/31/1994	Reg 5/23/41	Fuk-06B-Mizumaki	Swift
Swobe	Elmer D.	CA SF	11/11/1907	3/14/1954		Fuk-03-Yawata	Swobe
Talbot	Marshall E.	WA Metaline Falls	2/3/1911	10/14/1997		Tok area	Talbot
Tallmon	David W.	OR PDX	8/29/1905	1/27/2000		Fuk-01-Main	Tallmon
Tart	Lacy F.	NC Raleigh	6/8/1918	10/7/1943	Reg 9/30/41	n/a	Tart
Taylor	Allen F.	TN Brownsville	3/15/1919	1/29/1999	Reg 9/30/41	Fuk-17-Omuta	Taylor
Taylor	Donald C.	WA Vancouver	12/6/1914	5/20/2005		Sen-05B-Kamaishi	Taylor
Taylor	Harold S.	CA Long Beach	9/27/1906	3/1/1961		Fuk-03-Yawata	Taylor
Taylor	John D.	CA LA	9/8/1910	8/5/1996		Tok area	Taylor
Taylor	William L.	CA LA	5/18/1917	5/25/2011	Reg 8/19/41	Escaped	Taylor
Tellier	Clair W.	CA Hayward	7/29/1886	1/14/1966	Reg 9/30/41	Tok-05B-Niigata	Tellier
Teters	Nathan D.	WA SEA	9/25/1900	7/25/1960	Bur 1/9/41	Tok area	Teters
Thatcher	Frank M. Jr.	CA Oakland	8/14/1912	8/8/2009		Tok-05B-Niigata	Thatcher
Thayer	Frank D.	NE N Platte	6/10/1904	5/17/1976	Bur 1/9/41	Fuk-23-Keisen	Thayer
Thomas	Owen G.	OR PDX	7/18/1872	4/30/1943	Reg 5/23/41	n/a	Thomas
Thomas	Russell A.	CA Oakland	5/4/1918	10/1/2013		Tok area	Thomas
Thompson	Glenn H.	OH Cadiz	3/7/1921	10/7/1943	Reg 9/30/41	n/a	Thompson
Thompson	Walter T.	ID Boise	10/14/1893	5/27/1985		Fuk-01-Main	Thompson
Tice	Henry J.	TX Arlington	3/15/1915	5/17/1985		Tok area	Tice
Tom	Yen Tick	CA SF	1/8/1907	DK	Reg 8/19/41	Sen-11-Kamikita	Tom
Tomko	Aloysius A.	WA Spokane	6/25/1915	1/31/2000		Tok area	Tomko
Toohey	Richard J.	CA Berkeley	11/1/1912	4/15/1982	Bur 11/11/41	Tok area	Toohey
Topham	Elgin H.	WI Fernwood	1/2/1909	3/8/1992	Reg 8/19/41	Tok area	Topham
Toy	Art H.	CA SF	1/13/1919	DK	Reg 8/19/41	Sen-11-Kamikita	Toy
Trammell	J. Clarence	CA Sacramento	8/23/1896	5/8/1959		Sen-11-Kamikita	Trammell
Troxell	Roy L.	OK Ringling	12/17/1905	12/5/1981		Fuk-03-Yawata	Troxell
Truy	Joseph D.	Cuba Havana	9/5/1903	8/29/1945	Reg 9/30/41	n/a	Truy
Tucker	Earl E.	OR Gold Hill	2/27/1893	10/7/1943	Bur 8/2/41	n/a	Tucker
Tumelson	Obie R.	ID Coeur d'Alene	9/26/1904	8/1/2001		Tok-05B-Niigata	Tumelson
Tunnicliffe	John E.	IL Moline	2/2/1915	3/5/2002	Bur 9/5/41	Tok-1-Omori	Tunnicliffe
Turner	Floyd H.	CA Pittsburg	10/16/1912	10/3/1979	Reg 9/30/41	Tok area	Turner
Turner	Lester L.	OR Ontario	7/30/1908	10/16/1979	Bur 8/2/41	Tok area	Turner
Tuttle	Virgil	KY Witt Springs	2/18/1918	11/8/1958	Reg 8/19/41	Tok-05B-Niigata	Tuttle
Unger	Lewis O.	WY Casper	2/11/1913	1/13/1982	Bur 11/11/41	Fuk-01-Main	Unger
Valov	John M.	CA Bell	1/9/1904	9/20/1953	Reg 9/30/41	Tok-05B-Niigata	Valov
Vance	Walter G.	OK Skedee	7/8/1918	9/16/1984	Bur 3/16/41	Fuk-03-Yawata	Vance
Vancil	Vernon	CO Snyder	1/20/1914	10/7/1943		n/a	Vancil
Vanderwilt	Dick J.	ID Boise	5/3/1904	11/11/1958		Tok area	Vanderwilt
VanValkenbur	Ralph W.	CA Oakland	7/28/1906	10/7/1943	Justine Foss	n/a	VanValkenbur

Varney	Charles B.	NE Culbertson	11/19/1916	1/31/2008	Bur 3/16/41	Tok area	Varney
Vasquez	Albert F.	CA LA	2/19/1918	2/23/1984	Reg 8/19/41	Fuk-01-Main	Vasquez
Vent	William G.	CA Modesto	8/12/1918	10/7/1943	Reg 5/23/41	n/a	Vent
Villa	Edward E.	OR PDX	8/19/1908	3/20/1943		n/a	Villa
Villines	Charles M.	ID Boise	3/31/1918	10/7/1943	Bur 8/2/41	n/a	Villines
Vincent	Ernest D.	CA LA	9/3/1899	10/27/1994	Reg 6/29/41	Fuk-03-Yawata	Vincent
Vlist	Denis	WA Bremerton	9/14/1896	11/19/1952	Bur 3/16/41	Tok area	Vlist
Wade	Edwin E.	ID Boise	6/17/1919	6/6/1997	Reg 5/23/41	Tok area	Wade
Walden	Clayton P.	CA Fresno	11/15/1918	7/12/1999	Reg 6/29/41	Fuk-06B-Mizumaki	Walden
Walden	Glen W.	AR Carlisle	12/18/1921	9/11/2008	Reg 9/30/41	Tok area	Walden
Walker	George M.	OR John Day	12/26/1914	5/4/1943	Reg 5/23/41	n/a	Walker
Wallace	Anthony G.	CA LA	2/14/1917	9/13/1988	Bur 10/9/41	Sen-11-Kamikita	Wallace
Wallin	John E.	OR PDX	4/2/1902	11/22/1977		Fuk-09B-Miyata	Wallin
Walters	Joseph H.	MO St Louis	4/24/1907	9/23/1984	Bur 11/11/41	uk	Walters
Walters	Larry R.	OR PDX	6/8/1908	3/1/1968		Fuk-23-Keisen	Walters
Ward	Jack E.	ID Meridian	9/23/1921	1/23/1981		Tok-04B-Naoetsu	Ward
Ward	Leonard R.	TX El Paso	8/21/1903	2/15/1985	Bur 11/11/41	Fuk-01-Main	Ward
Ward	William C.	ID Boise	9/8/1919	10/3/2001	Reg 9/30/41	Fuk-01-Main	Ward
Wardle	Isaac J.	ID Boise	11/4/1910	11/7/1992	Bur 3/16/41	Fuk-01-Main	Wardle
Wardle	Miles R.	ID Emmett	12/30/1919	1/25/1990	Bur 8/2/41	Fuk-01-Main	Wardle
Wardle	Porter R.	ID Boise	6/25/1918	12/15/1987	Bur 8/2/41	Fuk-01-Main	Wardle
Wattles	Gurdon H.	CA Glendale	5/24/1910	1/22/1985		Tok-05B-Niigata	Wattles
Weatherbee	Jacob B.	WA SEA	3/19/1895	12/14/1976	Bur 9/5/41	Sen-11-Kamikita	Weatherbee
Weaver	Oliver R.	CA Bell	10/24/1896	1/17/1979	Bur 3/16/41	Tok-05B-Niigata	Weaver
Wedin	Lawrence E.	CA Anaheim	1/13/1911	9/6/1984		Fuk-01-Main	Wedin
Weible	Charles D.	ID Nampa	9/30/1907	12/8/1974		Fuk-03-Yawata	Weible
Weldon	William H.	WA Snohomish	12/10/1901	3/18/1976	Reg 9/30/41	Tok area	Weldon
Wells	Thomas W.	CA LA	8/27/1908	8/5/1983	Chau 2/1/41	Sen-07B-Hanaoka	Wells
West	Edward D.	MI Hancock	3/25/1921	11/24/2001		Fuk-01-Main	West
Westby	Graydon K.	ID Boise	1/24/1918	1/29/1996		Sen-11-Kamikita	Westby
Wester	William G.	WA Metaline Falls	7/24/1914	11/12/1963		Tok area	Wester
Wheeler	Raymond H.	CA Arrowhead	4/5/1909	5/19/1994		uk	Wheeler
White	Amos J.	NJ Rahway	3/17/1910	9/11/1947	Bur 10/9/41	uk	White
White	J. Edward	SC Gaffney	4/22/1916	11/26/1971	Bur 8/2/41	Fuk-01-Main	White
White	Raymond J.	IN Terre Haute	7/14/1923	11/9/1996	Reg 9/30/41	Tok-05B-Niigata	White
Whitehouse	Sherman A.	CA SF	2/11/1908	8/1/1964	Reg 9/30/41	Tok area	Whitehouse
Whitney	Hans W.	CA West Point	3/31/1911	7/19/1973	Bur 10/9/41	Tok area	Whitney
Whittenburg	Woodrow W.	OR Roseburg	8/11/1917	1/1/2010		Sen-11-Kamikita	Whittenburg
Whittom	Dorman	ID McCall	3/15/1916	8/17/1992	Bur 10/9/41	Sen-07B-Hanaoka	Whitto

	W.						m
Wiedenmayer	Albert O.	NY Johnsville	4/23/1908	8/27/1979	Bur 1/9/41	Tok area	Wiedenmayer
Wieler	Paul E.	CA Hollywood	11/22/1910	6/17/1991	Reg 9/30/41	Fuk-03-Yawata	Wieler
Wiggenhorn	John G.	CA LA	12/28/1916	1/13/1998	Bur 3/16/41	Tok-05B-Niigata	Wiggenhorn
Wilcox	George B.	OR Dallas	10/8/1901	7/27/1957	Reg 5/23/41	Fuk-06B-Mizumaki	Wilcox
Wilcox	Lee W.	CA Santa Monica	2/14/1898	2/28/1947	Bur 3/16/41	Fuk-01-Main	Wilcox
Wilder	Howard C.	CA San Jose	7/9/1923	5/8/2000		Tok area	Wilder
Wilderson	William A.	NE Kennard	3/15/1898	1972 Oct	Reg 6/29/41	Fuk-01-Main	Wilderson
Wildman	Ora M., Jr.	ID Boise	5/13/1918	1/22/2013		Tok-05B-Niigata	Wildman
Wilkerson	Earl C.	TX San Antonio	4/10/1914	6/23/1997		Sen-11-Kamikita	Wilkerson
Wilkin	Robert S.	CA Berkeley	8/30/1913	8/24/1945	Reg 5/23/41	n/a	Wilkin
Williams	Donald M.	CA Oakland	5/14/1921	3/9/1943	Reg 9/30/41	n/a	Williams
Williams	Joseph V.	CA Tunjunga	3/28/1900	3/9/1943	Chau 2/1/41	n/a	Williams
Williams	Kenneth D.	TH HNL	2/24/1906	4/4/1983	Bur 3/16/41	Tok area	Williams
Williams	Lloyd H.	OH Beaver	10/24/1921	11/3/1997	Reg 9/30/41	Sen-07B-Hanaoka	Williams
Williams	Vinson V.	CA LA	7/31/1902	2/25/1960		Fuk-06B-Mizumaki	N
Williamson	Frank E.	CA Alameda	7/31/1902	10/7/1943	Reg 5/23/41	n/a	47-62
Williamson	James O.	CA LA	9/25/1905	3/31/1963	Bur 3/16/41	Fuk-01-Main	N
Williamson	Richard T.	GA Savannah	2/14/1921	7/25/2005	Bur 8/2/41	Tok-04B-Naoetsu	46-38
Wilper	Redmond J.	ID Boise	5/19/1916	10/7/1943	Reg 5/23/41	n/a	45-84
Wilson	Earl J.	OR PDX	6/17/1905	1979 Oct	Reg 5/23/41	uk	46-10
Wilson	John B.	NJ N Arlington	1/11/1910	DK	Reg 9/30/41	Tok-05B-Niigata	N
Wilson	John B.	OR Grants Pass	2/27/1923	DK	Bur 8/2/41	Fuk-01-Main	32-39
Winegarden	Lester W.	CA Hemet	8/28/1904	12/9/1941		n/a	N
Wing	Walter H.	CA Long Beach	1/24/1918	DK	Reg 8/19/41	Fuk-06B-Mizumaki	48-24
Wise	Franklin R.	CA Oakland	4/6/1903	2/1/1955		Fuk-01-Main	46-36
Wojtysiak	Edward	MI Flint	9/21/1913	7/1/1983	Reg 9/30/41	Tok-05B-Niigata	46-31
Wolf	Jack M.	ID Emmett	3/26/1911	1960		Fuk-01-Main	46-26
Wong	Bing Sing	CA SF	10/6/1911	1/2/1996	Reg 9/30/41	Sen-11-Kamikita	N
Wong	Bing You	CA SF	1/1/1901	12/24/1948	Bur 9/5/41	Sen-11-Kamikita	N
Wong	Chin Chew	CA SF	5/11/1914	6/3/1987	Reg 9/30/41	Sen-11-Kamikita	N
Wong	Fook Hing	CA SF	12/29/1905	8/9/1989	Reg 8/19/41	Sen-11-Kamikita	N
Wong	Gan Woo	CA SF	1/3/1914	2003 Aug		Sen-11-Kamikita	N
Wong	Guey Suey	CA SF	9/1/1915	DK	Reg 8/19/41	Sen-11-Kamikita	N
Wong	Guey Yick	CA SF	11/29/1916	9/10/2001		Sen-11-Kamikita	N

Wong	Hing Shuck	CA SF	10/30/1921	2/12/2001		Sen-11-Kamikita	46-32
Wong	Hong	CA SF	6/30/1910	12/11/1977		Sen-11-Kamikita	N
Wong	Jung	CA SF	3/4/1915	DK		Sen-11-Kamikita	N
Wong	Kai	CA SF	10/30/1920	3/26/2020	Oct	Sen-11-Kamikita	N
Wong	Kay Ming	CA SF	2/29/1915?	DK	Reg 8/19/41	Sen-11-Kamikita	N
Wong	Kwok Hoy	MT Helena	9/9/1914	8/7/1988	Reg 9/30/41	Sen-11-Kamikita	N
Wong	Kwong Yee	CA SF	1/6/1916	1/29/1985	Reg 8/19/41	Sen-11-Kamikita	N
Wong	Robert G.	TH HNL	7/12/1922	1/23/1989		Sen-11-Kamikita	N
Wong	Sam What	CA SF	12/3/1903	9/9/1981		Sen-11-Kamikita	N
Wong	Thyn Wah	CA SF	11/29/1909	4/2/1982	Reg 9/30/41	Sen-11-Kamikita	46-30
Wong	Wah Jing	CA SF	11/29/1917	5/5/1999		Sen-11-Kamikita	N
Wong	Wing Nguay	CA SF	5/30/1912	1981 Mar		Sen-11-Kamikita	N
Woods	Charles	OH Lockland	9/14/1902	10/7/1943	Reg 9/30/41	n/a	44-74
Woodward	George L.	NM Albuquerque	8/1/1919	12/9/1941	Reg 8/19/41	n/a	44-75
Wooley	Raymond C.	OH Akron	2/14/1921	3/14/1966	Reg 9/30/41	Fuk-06B-Mizumaki	44-14
Worley	William J.	CA National City	8/24/1893	2/27/1945	Bur 11/11/41	n/a	N
Wung	Clarence A.K.	TH HNL	8/30/1921	9/27/1996	Reg 6/29/41	Sen-11-Kamikita	N
Yarina	Michael	OH Cleveland	5/15/1921	7/7/1989		Sen-11-Kamikita	44-62
Yeager	Harry H.	CA LA	4/4/1891	12/23/1941		n/a	47-67
Yeamans	Arthur W.	ID Mountain Home	5/10/1901	2/20/1967	Bur 11/11/41	Fuk-06B-Mizumaki	44-15
Yee	Foon Lee	CA SF	9/14/1914	5/21/1979	Bur 9/5/41	Sen-11-Kamikita	N
Yeramian	Vahran J.	CA SF	9/16/1895	1/5/1944		n/a	N
Young	Edmund H.	OR Grants Pass	8/5/1892	3/30/1963	Bur 8/2/41	Fuk-01-Main	N
Young	Edwin J.	ID Rathdrum	6/18/1913	10/1/1975		Fuk-01-Main	44-72
Young	John O.	ID Boise	5/18/1922	1/28/2016	Bur 10/9/41	Tok-04B-Naoetsu	44-60
Young	Reland E.	ID Rathdrum	5/19/1892	10/10/1953		Tok area	44-63
Yriberry	Robert L.	ID Boise	10/24/1914	12/9/1941	Bur 1/9/41	n/a	N
Yuan	Quock Jing	CA SF	3/17/1917	6/3/1998	Reg 9/30/41	Sen-11-Kamikita	46-09
Yuen	Harry T.K.	TH HNL	9/16/1920	10/7/1943		n/a	N
Zeh	Frederick	CA SF	9/7/1904	2/28/1944	Bur 11/11/41	n/a	47-58
Zimmerman	Edward J.	OR Astoria	2/20/1917	8/12/1986	Reg 5/23/41	Fuk-06B-Mizumaki	46-42
Zivic	John S.	ID Boise	7/21/1918	8/3/1999		Sen-07B-Hanaoka	48-10
Zivic	Thomas J.	ID Boise	11/28/1914	4/21/2001	Sen-07B-Hanaoka	Zivic	Thomas J.

Pan American Airways

EMP	**LAST**	**FIRST**	**Middle**	**DIED**
PAA	Aguiningoc	Antonio	Taitano	
PAA	Aguon	Pedro	Flores	9/24/2003
PAA	Baleto	Jesus	Concepcion	

PAA	Blanco	Francisco	Manibusan	D WAKE
PAA	Blas	Jose	Perez	D WAKE
PAA	Blas	Emeterio	Ogo	
PAA	Cabrera	Juan	Muna	D WAKE
PAA	Camacho	Jesus	Perez	D POW
PAA	Camacho	Alfonso	Meno	
PAA	Carbullido	Francisco	Chaco	
Lib Mutual	Clancy	Edward		
PAA	Concepcion	Jose	Mendiola	
PAA	Cruz	Felix	Rojas	
PAA	Flores	Joseph	Cruz	
PAA	Garcia	Jesus	Atoigue	
PAA	Garrido	Enrique	Santos	
PAA	Garrido	Vincente	Aguon	
PAA	Guerrero	Manuel	Calvo	
US Govt	Hevenor	Herman		
PAA	Ignacio	Felipe	Cruz	D WAKE
PAA	Iriarte	Tomas	Duenas	
PAA	James	William	Flores	D WAKE
PAA	Leon Guerrero	Balvino	Duenas	
PAA	Lizama	Jose	Quitugua	
PAA	Mafnas	Jose	Santos	D WAKE
PAA	Manalisay	Francisco	Tedpahago	D WAKE
PAA	Manibusan	Vincente	Chargualaf	D WAKE
PAA	Marion	Edward	Benavente	
PAA	Mendiola	Pedro	Perez	
PAA	Mendiola	Sergio	Maanao	
PAA	Mesa	Vincente	Castro	
PAA	Namauleg	Antonio	Espinosa	
PAA	Naputi	Jesus	Benavente	
PAA	Pablo	Serafin	Aguon	
PAA	Peredo	Antonio	Mendiola	
PAA	Quan	Gregorio	Concepcion	D WAKE
PAA	Quidachay	Juan	Babauta	
PAA	Quinata	Francisco	Babauta	
US PAA	Raugust	Waldo		
PAA	Reyes	Ignacio	Cruz	
PAA	Rivera	Juan	Unpingco	
PAA	Sablan	Silvestre	Arriola	D WAKE

PAA	Salas	Joaquin	Cruz	
PAA	San Nicholas	Jose	Torres	
PAA	Santos	Roque	Tenorio	
PAA	Taijeron	Vincente	Lujan	
PAA	Taijeron	Geronimo	Soriano	D POW
PAA	Villagomez	Francisco	Perez	

Made in the USA
Columbia, SC
14 August 2022